MEETINGS WITH
MOUNTAINS

"It is not the mountain we conquer but ourselves.**"**

Edmund Hillary

MEETINGS WITH
MOUNTAINS

Stephen Venables

Foreword by Sir Chris Bonington

CASSELL
ILLUSTRATED

First published in Great Britain in 2006 by
Cassell Illustrated,
a division of Octopus Publishing Group Limited
2-4 Heron Quays, London E14 4JP

A CIP catalogue record for this book is available from the British Library.

Project Editors: Karen Dolan and Robin Douglas-Withers
Managing Editor: Anna Cheifetz
Designer: Tony Cohen
Picture Researcher: Vickie Walters
Art Director: Auberon Hedgecoe

ISBN-13: 978-1-844034-49-9
ISBN-10: 1-844034-49-6

10 9 8 7 6 5 4 3 2 1

Printed in China

Contents

Foreword

It is a real pleasure to see so many accounts of my fellow climbers' exploits collected in one wonderful volume. There is a grand tradition of mountaineers recording their adventures for posterity; each tale has its unique moments of danger, despair and delight that can be enjoyed not just by those of us in the climbing fraternity, but by anyone who is thrilled by boys' (and girls') own stories and who wonders at the sheer daring and determination involved in such endeavours.

I have personal experience and fond memories of meetings with several of the mountains featured in this book. I have attempted Everest by three different routes, reaching the summit myself in 1985 at the age of 50. I was a member of the team that first climbed Mont Blanc's Central Pillar of Frêney in 1961, the same year that I also climbed the North Wall of the Eiger. In 1974 I led the first ascent of Changabang, and in 2001 I was at base camp with another Indo-British team, praying with the monks for the safe return of the two Marks, Richey and Wilford, from their daring raid on Yamandaka. And, of course, I will never forget our epic retreat from the Ogre when Doug Scott broke both his legs on the summit.

I have known the author, Stephen Venables, for many years and, in 1992, he was in the team that I joint-led, which made several first ascents in the Indian Himalaya, including Panch Chuli V; we have also rock-climbed together in Britain on several occasions. I respect Stephen both as a mountaineer with many first ascents under his belt and as an authoritative author, and in this page-turner of a book, he has collated spell-binding tales, some of which are iconic chapters in mountaineering history, others of which are less well-known but still deserving of epic status. Every mountain has its own unique personality and a big part of the allure lies in the human tales lived out on its slopes.

I hope you will join me in celebrating these heroes and the mountains that lure them.

Sir Chris Bonington

**Climbers below the
Aiguille des Drus,
in the Mont Blanc
Range, French Alps.**

Introduction

'Great things are done when men and mountains meet; this is not done by jostling in the street.' In that famous couplet the poet William Blake put his finger on the thrilling quality of mountain scenery—the sense of otherness, of remoteness from humdrum everyday life.

Mountains have always fascinated the human imagination. Alpine shepherds and farmers feared the icy peaks towering over their wooden chalets. Buddhist and Hindu pilgrims prostrated themselves before the greatest mountain range on earth—the Himalaya. In the Andes of South America Inca priests made sacrifices on summits over 20,000 feet (6,000 m) above sea level, five centuries before 'mountaineers' dreamt of climbing these peaks for fun.

Then in the eighteenth century that fearful awe began to change into a more appreciative fascination. In 1732 the Swiss scientist Albrecht von Haller published a poem extolling the beauties of the Alps. Sixty years later William Wordsworth recorded crossing the Alps in his narrative poem *The Prelude*. He was followed by painters such as Turner, Inchbold and Ruskin, all of them mesmerised by the power of mountain scenery. In North America the same awed response to the 'Sublime' inspired Alfred Bierstadt's pilgrimage to the Yosemite valley to paint his gorgeously luminous canvases of Sentinel Rock and El Capitan—the gigantic granite monoliths which would later enthral rock climbers.

But what of climbing, or 'mountaineering', to use its all-encompassing term? When did mountaineers begin to grapple with the vertical landscape so admired by poets and painters?

Mont Blanc, the highest peak in Western Europe, was first climbed in 1786, after a Swiss scientist offered a reward to the first people to stand on its white-domed summit, but it was only in the mid-nineteenth century that alpine climbing really took off, with local farmers and hunters working as 'guides' for mainly British gentleman climbers, enjoying the long summer vacations away from their legal chambers, church parishes and university colleges.

Those Victorian pioneers were fantastically energetic enthusiasts and they invented a pastime which has grown and blossomed all round the world, with today's climbers performing feats of technical brilliance and daring unimaginable 150 years ago. Some people call mountaineering a 'sport'. But it has no written rules, no overt competition, no fixed location. It is infinitely varied and diverse; but at its heart, I think, there is still the same feeling of wonder which inspired those first poets and painters—an awed sense of man's tiny place in an immense landscape.

For any intelligent mountaineer, that sense of wonder is tinged with respect, and even fear. Mountains are unquestionably dangerous and the mountaineer always has an acute feeling of trespassing in a forbidden world, knowing that sooner or later he may well be forced to make a desperate escape. Several of the stories in this book describe such escapes: Doug Scott's astounding retreat, with two broken legs, from the Ogre; Catherine Destivelle's similar escape from a remote summit in Antarctica; Walter Bonatti's harrowing retreat from Mont Blanc's Central Pillar of Frêney, when only three of seven men returned alive. They are salutory

tales, but they are also inspiring, uplifiting demonstrations of the human spirit triumphing over adversity.

Not all the stories here are of injury and rescue. I was determined also to celebrate the innate joyfulness of great mountain adventures; hence the inclusion of John Barry and his friends romping garrulously up Deborah's East Ridge; Voytek Kurtyka's meditative journey up the Shining Wall; Lynn Hill's balletic grace on El Capitan; Barry Blanchard's brilliant triumph on Canada's fearsome North Twin, with his exuberant partner Dave Cheesmond. And some of the mountain climbs featured here, such as the Antarctic summit climbed by Irene Oehninger and Cestmir Lukes, are not particularly hard: they are just intensely satisfying journeys to mountains of extraordinary beauty and remoteness.

Everest had really to be included, in particular the first ascent by Edmund Hillary and Tenzing Norgay—the man who was born and lived all his early life within sight of the mountain. I have complimented that 1953 ascent with the 35th anniversary expedition I took part in. I make no apology for that authorial bias; nor for including several other mountains which I have climbed. Mountaineering is an intensely personal experience, and in collating tales from peaks and climbers all round the world, it made sense to maximise my own store of adventures which, while they might have seemed harsh and brutal at the time, provide a legacy of lasting fulfilment which nothing will ever destroy

Stephen Venables

Europe

Mont Blanc
Finsteraarhorn
Eiger
Vågakallen

Mont Blanc

Height
4,807 metres (15,771 ft)

Location
Mont Blanc Massif,
French-Italian Alps

Origin of name
The White Mountain,
known as Monte Bianco
on the Italian side.

First ascent
8 August 1786: Jacques

Balmat/ Michel-Gabriel
Paccard

Other key routes
Goûter Ridge 1861: Leslie
Stephen/F. Tuckett/M.
Anderegg/J. Bennen/P. Perren

The 'Old Brenva' Spur 1865:
G. Matthews/A. Moore/F. &
H. Walker/J. & M. Anderegg

Route Major (Brenva Face)
1928: Thomas Graham

Brown/Frank Smythe

Peuterey Ridge 'Integrale'
1953: Adolf Göttner/Ludwig
Schmaderer/ Ferdinand
Krobath

Central Pillar of Frêney 1961:
Chris Bonington/Ian Clough/
J. Djuglosz/Don Whillans

1984 Divine Providence:
Patrick Gabarrou/
François Marsigny

Interesting facts
Mont Blanc is the highest
mountain in the Alps, and
also the highest in Western
Europe. It was one of the
first alpine summits to be
climbed, when the wealthy
Genevan scientist, Horace-
Benedict de Saussure,
offered a reward to the first
successful summiteers.

In July 1961, Walter Bonatti, one of the greatest mountaineers of the twentieth century, led a team to within a whisker of success on the most remote, demanding pillar of Mont Blanc. After a ferocious snowstorm pinned them down for two days, they were forced to retreat down one of the most dangerous glaciers in the Alps. Out of seven men only three returned alive.

The Fatal Pillar
Walter Bonatti (1961)

When dawn broke on Friday, 18 July 1961, the storm had been raging for sixty hours. Everything was blanketed in snow. Even the undersides of the overhangs were plastered white. All chance of fighting through those overhangs and over the summit of Mont Blanc was gone and the only hope now lay downward – down 3,000 metres (10,000 ft) of rock precipices and chaotic, jumbled ice. As the seven men struggled to get ready, shivering inside the stiff armour of their frozen clothes, fumbling with numb fingers, peering through tight-screwed eyelids at the wind-whipped vortex into which they were about to descend, they all acknowledged silently that their only hope for finding their way out alive lay with Walter Bonatti.

Bonatti grew up near the northern Italian town of Bergamo. He had a tough childhood and adolescence, struggling through the horrors of the Second World War, witnessing the execution of Mussolini and, in 1948, at the age of eighteen, discovering the joy of climbing, in the limestone pinnacles of the Grigna near Bergamo.

From then on, as Bonatti later recalled, 'I was devoted heart and soul to rock faces, to overhangs, to the intimate joy of trying to overcome my own weaknesses in a struggle that committed me to the very limits of the possible.'

By nineteen he had repeated ascents of some of the hardest mountain faces in the Alps. Then, in 1951, he astounded the climbing world by making the first ascent of the stupendous overhanging east face of the Grand Capucin, a spectacular rock obelisk in the Mont Blanc massif.

Overseas in Pakistan it was he who carried the vital oxygen cylinders that helped his compatriots reach the summit of K2 in 1954; five years later he returned to Pakistan to make the first ascent of Gasherbrum IV. But his greatest legacy of new climbs was in the Alps, where from 1957 he made his home in the town of Courmayeur, immediately beneath Mont Blanc.

Bonatti earned his living as a mountain guide, taking clients countless times up the classic routes of Mont Blanc and its satellite peaks. In his spare time he pioneered new routes, in summer and winter, pushing himself to the limit. He probably knew Mont Blanc better than anyone else alive and, in particular, he knew its wild southern side. For nearly ten years he dreamed of attempting a rock pillar high on this Italian face – the Central Pillar of Frêney – 'which posed a problem of indubitable interest due to its imposing beauty, high altitude and complete isolation, even aside from the great technical difficulty that the climb presented.'

The chance to attempt this highest, hardest rock climb in the Alps finally came in July 1961, just a week after Bonatti and his companion Andrea Oggioni had returned from making the first ascent of Rondoy North, in Peru. With a third Italian, Robert Gallieni, they made their way up to the Col de Fourche bivouac, a tiny wooden hut perched on the French-Italian border, just to the east of Mont Blanc. Rather than ascend directly up the hideously jumbled Frêney Glacier, they planned to reach the remote foot of the pillar by an oblique approach. Before even setting foot on the pillar, they would have to do a major ice climb to a saddle called the Col de Peuterey. And to complicate matters they found four Frenchman at the bivouac hut, also bound for the prestigious pillar.

The three Italians agreed to join forces with Robert Guillaume, Antoine Vieille, Pierre Kohlman and the well-known Parisian politician and alpinist, Pierre Mazeaud. They left soon after midnight, climbed 800 metres (2,600 ft) of steep ice, and by dawn on Tuesday, 11 July, they were already at the Col de Peuterey, walking across deceptively easy snow slopes to the foot of the pillar – deceptive, because from here there was no easy retreat.

Walter Bonatti at the height of his powers – one of the greatest mountaineers of all time.

But the weather was fine, and there was no talk of retreat. The seven men climbed quickly up the initial 500 metres (1,600 ft) of the pillar. The rough red granite, baked warm by the sun, offered good friction and comparatively easy climbing, so by midday they had reached a pedestal at the foot of the Chandelle. This monolithic candle of smooth, vertical rock was the real crux of the route – the challenge that made the pillar such a coveted prize. The extreme difficulties would last only for about 80 metres (260 ft) before easier slopes led to the summit, which Bonatti knew as well as his own house. But already as he started to make his way up a thin vertical crack, hammering in steel blade pitons to make progress, wispy clouds began to drift across the top of the pillar.

Snow began to fall, forcing Bonatti back down to the pedestal, where the other men were organizing shelter. The air was now humming with electricity, and a sudden flash caught Kohlman on the face, almost knocking him off the mountain. Securing themselves to pitons, the men huddled down on three ledges. The three Italians had a sack-shaped tent to drape over themselves; the Frenchmen had only individual plastic sheets, and one of them, the shaken Kohlman, had to make do with a ledge on his own.

Bonatti wrote later, 'We were smack dead on the pillar that forms the lightning rod of Mont Blanc.' Time after time the men's frightened faces were lit up by bright flashes as electric discharges lifted them off the ledge. The thunder eventually moved away to be replaced by the inexorable patter of snow, pressing down on the huddled men. 'We were almost suffocating. We ripped a hole in the fabric of the bivouac sack and gasped for air. By now we were practically buried in snow, and the warmth of our breath inside it created a dense humidity that, depending on the variations of temperature outside, transformed itself into drops of water alternating with crystals of ice.'

On Wednesday there was a slight clearing, and Bonatti noticed fresh snow on the normally green pastures 3,000 metres (10,000 ft) below. He still hoped that the storm would pass and allow him to lead his companions up the remaining Chandelle and across the summit of Mont Blanc to the easy French descent route – the shortest route to safety. But the storm returned and continued to bluster through the second night.

On Thursday there was no abatement, no relief from the torture of cramped confinement. That night Bonatti gave up all hope of the summit and at 3:30 A.M. on Friday shouted to his companions to tell them that they would have to go down – down the route that so terrified him.

It took a whole day to descend the Pillar, abseiling rope length by rope length. The shrieking wind drowned their voices, so that on one occasion Bonatti, descending first, found himself alone and without a rope on a ledge in the middle of the wall, until Mazeaud appeared out of the gloom to reunite him with it. That night they all crawled into a crevasse on the Col Peuterey. All night long they were tormented by claustrophobia and thirst, unable to light their stove to melt snow, because there was not enough oxygen inside their suffocating shelter. When Bonatti handed the fuel bottle to Kohlman to rub on his frostbitten hands, Kohlman tipped the poisonous liquid down his throat. Delirium had taken hold.

There was no abatement in the storm on Saturday morning as Bonatti led the way, wading across a treacherous snow slope towards the Rochers Grubers, the only safe rock descent onto the Frêney Glacier. The others failed to follow across the snow trench. Then a shout summoned Bonatti back to the huddled group, where Vieille was breathing his last gasp. They left his body tied to a piton and continued, abseiling down the Rochers Grubers, finally reaching the Frêney Glacier at 5:30 P.M. Since leaving the Chandelle the previous morning, they had made about fifty abseils.

It was at this time that Bonatti heard voices, but there were no tracks on the glacier and the voices receded. So Bonatti continued wading, up to his waist in fresh snow, relying on his immense knowledge and instinct to weave a route through the notorious maze of crevasses and tottering ice towers that make the Frêney Glacier so dangerous, towing his five companions on the rope. To escape from the great trench of the glacier, he had then to climb *up* to another pass, the Col d'Innominata. This steep climb,

The Central Pillar of Frêney (1) on the south side of Mont Blanc, the highest, remotest rock climb in Europe, rises from the snow saddle of the Col de Peuterey (2). Bonatti's party approached this from the right in fine weather, but during their desperate retreat through the storm, the only possible escape was down the Frêney Glacier (3) and over the Col de l'Innominata (4). Only three of the seven men made it back to the Gamba Hut (5) alive.

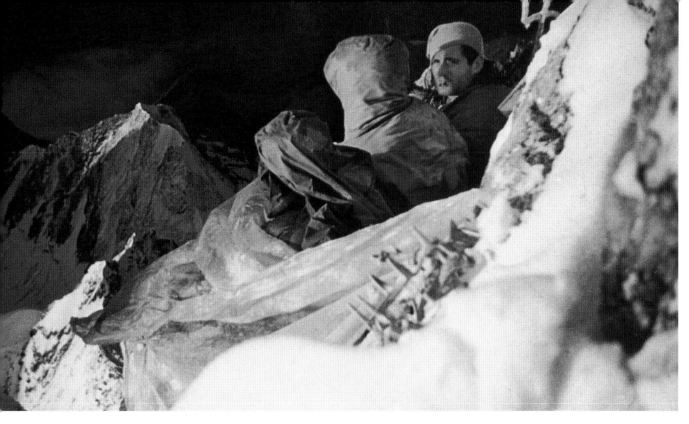

After a horrendous night huddled on their ledge, the three Frenchmen – Guillaume, Vielle and Mazeaud (right) emerge from their tent-sack during a lull on 12 July, but the storm returned that afternoon and continued to rage unabated. At dawn on 14 July the men began their desperate retreat from the highest mountain in Western Europe.

normally broken rock, was now a smooth, icy funnel, and halfway up the ascent Bonatti's old friend Oggioni collapsed, unable to unclip himself from the piton to which he was attached. Desperate to get help, Bonatti told Gallieni to untie from Oggioni and follow him up over the pass. But as they set off into the night, they suddenly found Kohlman with them shouting deliriously. Unable to leave him alone, they tied him onto their rope, but he stumbled around in the deep snow, dragging them backward and forward.

'Hurry! There's another one of us outside! The others are in the Innominata gully! Hurry!'

They realized eventually that they would have to escape from the crazed man, but since they had no knife they had to loosen their frozen breeches and pull the looped rope down over their feet, leaving Kohlman raving in the snow. Within moments Bonatti was waking the guides at the Gamba Hut and shouting, 'Hurry! There's another one of us outside! The others are in the Innominata gully! Hurry!' It was 3:00 A.M. on Sunday morning.

A rescue party set off into the dark, while others helped Bonatti and Gallieni into dry clothes and warm bunks, where they fell fast asleep. 'When I awoke,' recalled Bonatti, 'about three hours had passed and it was light. The door creaked open. The dark silhouettes of two men were outlined against the greyness on the other side of the threshold. One of them was my friend Gaston Rébuffat, who had just arrived in a helicopter from Chamonix. Then he spoke – words I will never forget for the rest of my life: "Oggioni is dead! They're carrying him down now." I was overcome by uncontrollable grief. The bodies of my poor companions were recovered one by one, except that of Vielle, which remained unreachable for another six days. Dear Mazeaud, the only one they found alive, embraced me and wept with me.'

Only three men returned alive; without Bonatti's superhuman drive and route-finding skills, perhaps none would have survived. As for that final, beautiful, bewitching candle of rock near the top of Mont Blanc, it was climbed successfully, a few weeks later, by a British-Yugoslav team. Nowadays the Central Pillar of Frêney is considered a reasonable proposition for competent alpinists. It has become a classic, but it remains a serious challenge, and mountaineers approach it with extreme caution, knowing just how hard it can be to escape from the remote pillar when a storm sweeps across the highest mountain in Western Europe.

The storm breaks as the team joins Bonatti at the base of the final overhang on the afternoon of 11 July.

Finsteraarhorn

Height
4,273 metres (14,019 ft)

Location
Berner Oberland, Swiss Alps

Origin of name
Finster means 'dark'. The river Aar, a tributary of the Rhine, flows from the east side of the mountain. So it is the Dark Mountain of the Aar.

First ascent
10 August 1829: Jakob Leuthold/Johann Währen by Northwest Ridge

Other key routes
Southeast Ridge 1876: H. Cordier et al.

Northeast Rib 1904: Gustav Hasler/Fritz Amatter

East Rib 1929: O. Brügger/ H. Winterberger/H. Kohler

Interesting facts
The Finsteraarhorn is the highest peak in the alpine region called the Bernese Oberland (after the nearby Swiss capital city Berne). The summit is a watershed: the snows on its northeast side melt into the Aar, and ultimately the Rhine, which flows into the North Sea; its southwestern snowmelt drains into the Rhône, which

flows into the Mediterranean. The guides who made the first ascent were working for the Swiss glaciologist, Franz Joseph Hugi. Another scientist associated closely with the Finsteraarhorn was Louis Agassiz, who in 1841 spent three weeks camped on the glacier below the mountain. He later emigrated to America where he became a professor at Harvard.

The first alpine climbers sought the easiest routes to the summits. But once all the alpine peaks had been climbed, people began to look at the harder routes, in particular the steep, shattered, ice-carved north faces. Virtually none of the great north faces was attempted before the 1930s. But there was one – the Northeast Face of the Finsteraarhorn – which was tried as long ago as 1902. It was a climb far ahead of its time and, even more remarkably for those days, it was made by a woman.

A Formidable Wall for a Formidable Woman

Gertrude Bell (1902)

Gertrude Bell was an Oriental scholar, archaeologist and diplomat who spent much of her life travelling in the Middle East. The Baghdad Museum was her legacy, as was indeed that disputatious line in the sand: the frontier of the modern state of Iraq, which she helped to establish after the First World War. One Arab sheik is reputed to have remarked after meeting her, 'If British *women* are this tough, what are the *men* like?'

She *was* tough. And her huge range of talents also extended to mountaineering. In 1899 she made what was then a rare traverse of the Meije in the French Alps. Returning to the Alps in the summer seasons of 1901 and 1902, she concentrated her formidable energies on the Bernese Oberland. This is the celebrated range at the heart of Switzerland, with such famous summits as the Eiger, Jungfrau and Wetterhorn. But Gertrude Bell was a connoisseur of the esoteric – a true explorer – choosing to inscribe her name on some of the obscurer, previously untouched walls and ridges of the range.

Like most of the British pioneers of that time, she employed local guides, and all her Oberland climbs were done with the brothers Ulrich and Heinrich Fuhrer. This partnership succeeded on several first

ascents, but the climb that left the greatest impression on Miss Bell – and on subsequent generations of mountaineers – was actually a failed attempt to climb the mighty northeast face of the Finsteraarhorn.

The Finsteraarhorn is the highest peak in the Bernese Oberland and arguably the finest – a spectacular spire towering above the Aar valley. Most impressive of all is its 1,000-metre (3,300-ft)-high northeast face, dominated by a single spur, or arête. By 1902 several ambitious mountaineers had eyed it up, but none had made any impression on what was a futuristic and, frankly, dangerous project, as Gertrude Bell explained in a letter to her brother: 'The arête, the one which has always been discussed, rises from the glacier in a great series of gendarmes and towers, set at such an angle on the steep face of the mountain that you wonder how they can stand at all and indeed they can scarcely be said to stand, as the great points of them are continually over-balancing and tumbling down into the couloirs. The game was beginning even when we crossed an hour after dawn.'

It was the morning of 1 July 1902. Huge blocks, frozen temporarily in place by the night frost, were breaking loose as Bell and the Fuhrer brothers scurried across a gully to gain the comparative safety

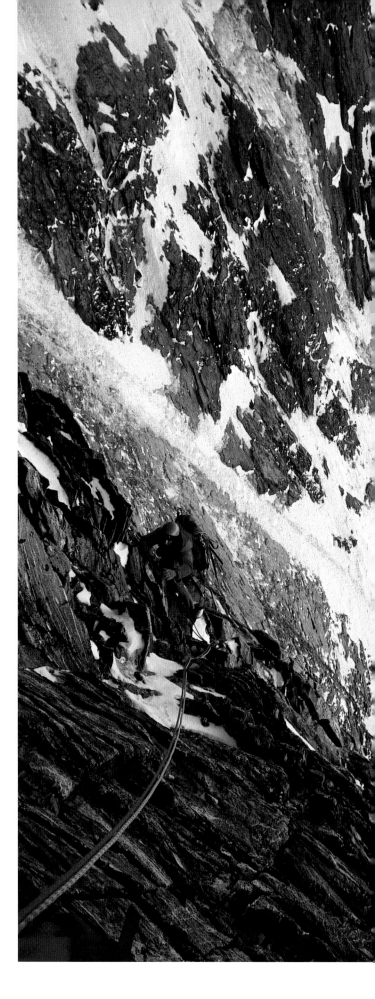

of the projecting spur. All day they worked their way up a series of towers 'which multiplied like rabbits', getting progressively steeper until they were halted by 'a great tower leaning over to the right and made of slabs set like slates on top'.

They had reached the Grey Tower, over 600 metres (2,000 ft) up the face. Smooth and undercut, it seemed to block the way completely. Ulrich Fuhrer tried traversing out to the right but drew a blank. Then he tried a steep gully on the left, chipping at 70° steep ice with his adze to create little nicks for his nailed boots. Then snow began to fall, and by mid-afternoon the climbers were in the thick of a raging storm. The only option was to retreat all the way back down those terrible towers.

Three days later, in a letter to her brother, Bell wrote, 'I shall remember every inch of that rock face for the rest of my life.' Soon after starting the retreat, they had to bivouac, soaked to the skin, huddled together in a violent thunderstorm, with rocks fizzing and crackling all around them. 'It was a curiously exciting sound and rather exhilarating, and as there was no further precaution possible, I enjoyed the extraordinary magnificence of the storm with a clear mind. It was worth seeing.'

> **'**It was a curiously exciting sound and rather exhilarating, and as there was no further precaution possible, I enjoyed the extraordinary magnificence of the storm with a clear mind. It was worth seeing.**'**

On 1 August they rose stiffly at 4:00 A.M. to spend the next sixteen hours descending continuously, most of the way in 15-metre (50-ft) abseils on their shortened rope, cut by falling rocks. At 8:00 P.M. they finally escaped off the spur. However, wet matches refused to light the lantern for a descent of the crevassed Unteraar Glacier, so they had to resign themselves to another night in the open. Bell consoled herself by thinking of a friend on service in the Boer War and how he had slept out in the rain and been 'none the worse'.

What magnificent sangfroid! And modesty about such a bold attempt at a mountain climb that was way ahead of its time. The northeast face was climbed two years later, by Gustave Hasler and Fritz Amatter. They were luckier with the weather and managed to continue beyond the Grey Tower to the summit. Hasler said years later that he considered the route 'a very serious proposition'. The American climber, Miriam O'Brien, who made the third ascent in 1930, wrote, 'It is the only climb I have ever done which I cannot think about with pleasure. Not that it was the only occasion in the mountains when I have been frightened, but it was the occasion when I was most badly frightened, and for the longest period.'

Nowadays most parties, my own included, climb the route in winter, when everything is frozen solidly in place. But the northeast face of the Finsteraarhorn still gets only rare ascents, and it remains an outstanding memorial to that tough woman who first dared to attempt it.

Eiger

Height
3,970 metres (13,025 ft)

Location
Berner Oberland,
Swiss Alps

Origin of name
Eiger is thought to mean
'Ogre', forming a triptych
with the Mönch (Monk) and
Jungfrau (Maiden).

First ascent
11 August 1858: Charles
Barrington/Christian Almer/
Peter Bohren by West Flank

Other key routes
Mitetellegi (East) Ridge
1921: Yuko Maki/Fritz
Amatter/Fritz Steuri/
Samuel Brauwand

Northeast Face 1932: Hans

Alexander Graven/Joseph
Knubel

Northwest Face (Eigerwand)
1938: Anderl Heckmair/
Ludwig Vörg/Fritz Amatter/
Heinrich Harrer

Eigerwand Direct – 'Harlin
Route' 1966: Dougal Haston/
Sigi Hupfauer/Jörg Lehne/
Roland Votteler

Interesting facts
The Jungfraujoch rack
railway climbs a spiraling
tunnel inside the Eiger, with
windows piercing both the
north and south faces. Thirty
workers, mainly poorly paid
Italians, were killed during
its construction between
1896 and 1912.

In 1966 American climber John Harlin II plunged 1,500 metres (5,000 ft) to his death when a rope broke on the new Eiger Direct route he had initiated. Almost forty years later, his son and namesake (who was just nine years old when his father died) set out to experience for himself the challenges of the mountain face where his father had perished – the biggest, most famous and arguably most dangerous precipice in the Alps, the North Wall of the Eiger.

In His Father's Footsteps
John Harlin III (2005)

John Harlin III was nine when the rope broke that sent his father plunging 1,500 metres (5,000 ft) to his death. His world was torn apart, and he could have been expected forever after to hate the mountains. But living in the Alps, he had skied and climbed almost before he walked; the mountains were in his blood, and later, as a student in California, he became a highly proficient alpinist before starting a successful career as an outdoor writer. He promised his mother to be careful, but he knew that sooner or later he would want to experience for himself the mountain where his father had died.

The chance finally came in 2005, the thirty-ninth anniversary of his father's death. As John Harlin put it, 'My sister never really forgave my father for dying. With me it was different. Of course it was hell – losing a father – but my sadness was tinged with admiration. Admiration for his boundless passion, his bold vision, his drive, his determination to make his mark here, at the heart of Europe, amongst the mountains where men first climbed. I've followed my own path, climbed different mountains, but there was always a part of me that wanted to experience this one particular, unique mountain.' That mountain – or mountain face, to be precise – was the biggest, most famous, arguably most dangerous precipice in the Alps: the North Wall of the Eiger.

Unlike the Matterhorn, the Eiger does not stand in proud isolation. Nor does it have the elegant nobility of the two peaks with which it makes such a famous triptych – the Mönch and the Jungfrau. No, the Ogre seems squat and graceless beside the Monk and Maiden. But even if it lacks beauty and its summit does not reach 4,000 metres (13,200 ft), the Eiger's immense, dark, scooped, northwest-facing concavity, rising improbably for almost 1,850 metres (6,000 ft) above the grassy meadows of Kleine Scheidegg, has a mesmerizing fascination. By the early 1930s, when Europe's finest alpinists were beginning to attempt the hardest, steepest, iciest north faces, the north face of the Eiger had become the most celebrated prize – the ultimate test of courage and skill.

In 1934 two German climbers made the first foray onto the face, before escaping, low down, into a window that leads strangely into the railway tunnel inside the mountain. The first serious attempt came the following year, when Max Sedlmayer and Karl Mehringer reached a point two-thirds of the way up the wall before succumbing to a prolonged storm and freezing to death. Undeterred, in 1936 four men almost reached the same point before turning back, probably because one of them had been injured by the Eiger's murderous stonefall. No one will ever know exactly what happened the next day; all we know is that one man was detached from his rope and fell to the bottom of the wall. The other three, roped together, were plucked from their stance; two were killed instantly, but the third, Toni Kurz, remained

alive, dangling beneath a huge overhang. Rescuers appeared from the railway window and promised to return in the morning. Kurz survived the night – his fourth night on the wall – hanging in space. When the rescuers returned in the morning, icicles hung from his boots, and one of his hands was a frozen claw. He managed, amazingly, to lower a line and pull up further rope and equipment. But then his strength gave out. He mumbled, 'I am finished' and slumped lifeless on the rope. His dead body had to be cut down with a knife tied to a pole.

In 1937 Ludwig Vörg, with Matthias Rebitsch, managed to get higher on the face than any previous party, and when an inevitable storm closed in, made a brilliant retreat – the first contenders to return alive. A year later Vörg returned with fellow German Andreas Heckmair. Overtaking two Austrians, Heinrich Harrer and Fritz Kasparek, who had already started up the wall, the strongest climber, Heckmair, agreed reluctantly to join forces and, over three days, found a route up the wall, emerging alive on the summit. The Eiger's north face was finally climbed.

The 1938 route up the Eigerwand (Eiger Wall) was a triumph of intuition, weaving an improbable zigzagging line following a series of chimneys, ramps and ledges between smooth overhanging walls. Most remarkable was the fact that on the last two days Heckmair had to lead the team through a harsh storm, battling snowfall and avalanches, literally fighting for life, knowing that the only escape was over the top.

The Eigerwand climb was repeated in 1947. Then, gradually, more and more teams made the nervous pilgrimage to Kleine Scheidegg to pit themselves against the wall. But frequent deaths from rockfall, avalanche, falls and hypothermia only reinforced the Eiger's fearsome reputation. In 1962, when John Harlin II made the first American ascent, it was still regarded as the ultimate alpine climb for any seriously ambitious mountaineer, but Harlin and others were also dreaming of new possibilities: a direct route straight up the middle of the face. That dream was realized by a joint German-British-American team in 1966, laying siege to the face with a line of fixed ropes, like a big Himalayan climb. It was on the final push to the summit that one of the ropes broke, sending John Harlin, the leader, plunging to his death.

The 1938 route weaves a brilliant line, exploiting the most climbable weaknesses in the Eigerwand's formidable defences.
1: Hinterstoisser Traverse; 2: Second Icefield ; 3: Flatiron/ Death Bivouac ; 4: The Ramp; 5: Traverse of the Gods; 6: The Spider; 7: Exit Cracks

and the face well plastered with hard frozen snow, locking the infamous loose stones in place. This late in the autumn, the sun would hardly touch the wall. Conditions looked perfect.

In this fine weather the first 700 metres (2,300 ft) were straightforward, until the trio reached the famous Difficult Crack. John led this near-vertical pitch, following the polished scratch marks where countless crampon spikes had gouged the grey limestone. Then, at about 3:00 P.M., the team made camp on a long, narrow ledge and settled down for the night. The real meat of the climb was still to come.

In the morning they were on the move before dawn, traversing leftward beneath a huge overhanging cliff called the Rote Fluh. Unlike the very first Eiger contenders, who imagined wrongly that this could be a pure rock climb, this team wore crampon spikes all day and made the most of the Eiger's icy carapace. John relished the rising traverse: 'The iced crack and mixed snow and rock was delicious. I just love that kind of stuff.' It took him to the start of the Hinterstoisser Traverse where, in 1936, Anderl Hinterstoisser used the rope to pendulum across a 75° slab of smooth limestone. Hinterstoisser left the rope looped across the traverse for his three companions to swing across but then pulled the rope through. Returning three days later on their desperate retreat, with no rope left in place, they found themselves unable to reverse this key passage, so they were forced to try descending direct, resulting in the accident that killed three of them and left Toni Kurz dangling in space.

In 2005 the Hinterstoisser Traverse was laced with ropes, old and new, but John climbed most of it 'free', tiptoeing across the white ice plastered to the

Forty years later, in the cool blue early morning light of 23 September 2005, John Harlin III finally set foot on the wall where his father died. Like his father, he is an internationalist: his German companions, Robert and Daniela Jasper, live just a few miles from the Eiger; Robert, in particular, knows the wall intimately and has already climbed it many times, by several of the twenty or so routes that now crisscross the face. But on that September day they were bound for the original classic line – Heckmair's 1938 route.

They had to wait for two weeks of bad weather to clear. But at last the sky was clear, the forecast good

'Kurz survived the night – his fourth night on the wall – hanging in space. When the rescuers returned in the morning, icicles hung from his boots, and one of his hands was a frozen claw.'

rock, only pulling on the rope towards the end, when the ice ran out. The pilgrimage continued as each famous feature, logged into the consciousness of every mountaineer, revealed itself: the little hollow of

Above: John Harlin II in his element, a short while before his sudden death in 1966.

Right: John Harlin III. nose grazed by rockfall, climbing in the Canadian Rockies, November 2000.

Approaching the famous Traverse of the Gods. The base of the wall can just be glimpsed where the Eigerwand casts its shadow on the meadows, over 1,300 metres (4,000 ft) below.

the Swallow's Nest, the First Icefield and then the Ice Hose. 'Robert led it without any protection. This seemed awesome until Daniela and I followed, and I found that conditions were perfect, with sinker-soft ice the whole way up.'

This climb, which John had dreamed about for so many years, was proving to be perfect. But also heavy with the weight of history. At about midday they reached Death Bivouac. This is where Sedlmayer and Mehringer froze to death in 1935. It was also from a snow cave at this spot that John's father set off up the fixed ropes of the Eiger Direct on the last day of his life. John Harlin III had been dreading this moment. 'But anxiety and panic attacks didn't happen. As I traversed across the Third Icefield, I looked up the wall above to where Dad's rope broke, and thought about where he must have hit, but I was just looking at it rationally, as a climber, not letting the memories detract from the pleasure of being in the moment. I guess I must have some real climber's blood in me.'

Having crossed the line of the Direct Route, the original 1938 route now slanted left, up the Ramp – a great, slanting gash, straightforward at first, then narrowing to an overhanging bottleneck that in warm weather gushes water. Thankfully, the Waterfall Chimney was frozen. 'Robert led it beautifully, then

Daniela and I followed simultaneously on the two ropes, Daniela just in front of me, as usual. The ice was sparse, and we mainly hooked the rock with our axes. Then another, harder pitch, where Daniela dangled, and then I popped off to land on the snow ledge below as the rope came tight.'

Late that afternoon they escaped towards the right of the Ramp, onto the shattered Brittle Ledges, where they stopped to bivouac. In the morning the sky was still clear, and they continued right towards the Traverse of the Gods. 'Robert led; then I stayed at the belay while Daniela crossed over, clipped to my

rope for a running belay. Then I unclipped from my belay and followed, looking across at the potential pendulum should I screw up over an infinity of space through which Dad tumbled to his death.' The dizzy traverse led right back into the heart of the concave wall, where the incipient snowy cracks and gullies radiated from the icefield called the Spider.

As they climbed out of the top corner of the Spider, following a complex sequence of cracks and gullies, John marvelled at the genius of Heckmair, the man who found this route in 1938, groping his way intuitively through the dense cloud, fighting the smothering violence of spindrift avalanches. Although in 2005 the weather was ideal, the climbing was still hard as John led the Quartz Crack. 'It was glazed in thin ice on the left, with dry rock on the right, and I bridged across between the two, totally stoked up, eager for the final Exit Cracks.' And when he got there and found just an open, blank, square-cut chimney, with virtually no cracks at all to take protecting steel pegs, he marveled again at Heckmair teetering his way up through the storm.

Two rope lengths and the three climbers emerged onto the final summit icefield. Even there, where a careless mistake could have sent them plunging 1,700 metres (5,600 ft) back down the wall, they moved with infinite care. For the first time in three days they were in bright sunshine, and as they reached the knife-edge summit ridge, John was totally fulfilled. 'It is probably the most spectacular I've ever walked. So thin, and dropping so far to each side. I'm not sure how much the glory of that ridge comes from actual exposure and how much from my thrill in being there, but to me it seemed like the finest ridgewalk in the world.'

Perhaps the last word should rest with his father. When he first climbed the face in 1962, John Harlin II had a final bivouac in the Exit Cracks, reaching the summit in the early morning. This is how he described that glorious moment: 'Clouds completely undercast the landscape, with only mountain masses penetrating the blanket. The sun was still low, giving relief, yet more intense because of the reflecting layer below. Thus the snow ridge leading to the summit cornice had the fantastic brilliance of a jewel lit from within. Chips of ice from axe blows were caught in the air and gleamed in the sun against an impeccable blue.'

Vågakallen

Height
942 metres (3,090 ft)

Location
Southern tip of Austvågøy,
Lofoten Islands, Norway

Origin of name
There are various explan-
ations: In one Norwegian
dialect 'kall' means old man
and may be the origin of the
legend of Kallen, the troll

Another theory is that the
name derives from the Same
word 'gaille', meaning 'high
mountain', and the northern
town of Vagar.

First ascent
1889: Martin Ekroll/Angel
Johannesen by South Face

Other key routes
North Ridge 1939: Arne
Randers Heen/Lars Nordby

Storpillaren ('The Great
Pillar') 1980: Finn Tore
Bjørnstad/Arild Meyer/
Kjell Skog

Freya 1998: Daniela &
Robert Jasper

Stormpillar 2003: Louise
Thomas/Twid Turner

Interesting facts
Centuries ago, local
fishermen believed
Vågakallen to be one of
the highest mountains in the
world. Young fishermen on
their first visit to the winter
fisheries around Lofoten
had to doff their hats to
Vågakallen to ensure
good fishing.

The locals once believed that it was one of the highest mountains in the world. In those days they never dreamed of *climbing* mountains. They were fishermen, not mountaineers. Young apprentices, rowing past on their way to the world's most prolific cod fishery, would doff their hats to the great granite monolith rising out of the sea, for Vågakallen was a mountain steeped in legend, where trolls were turned to stone.

Traversing the Land of Trolls

Martin Ekroll and Angel Johannesen (1889)

The Lofoten Islands are sometimes referred to as the Magic Islands. From Norway's arctic coast they appear as a line of jagged peaks piercing the western horizon. During the constant daylight of midsummer, the mountains glow above a glittering sea, and it is sometimes sunny for weeks on end. But the luminous green of the lush ferns and mosses that cloak the island's slopes – and the piebald patterns of snow on rock, higher up – betray the prevailing dampness of the frequent storms that sweep in from the North Sea. These mountains are often sombre, dark and brooding. As for the seashore villages below, flat ground is sometimes so scarce that the timber houses are built on stilts, hanging out over the water. The traditional livelihood here is fishing: in particular, the cod that congregate every winter in the Henningsværstraumen, a broad channel between the islands of Vestvågøy and Austvågøy. The village of Henningsvær watches over the global epicentre of cod fishing. And watching over the village is a mountain called Vågakallen.

There is a legend about a troll named Kallen who lived on this mountain and went out fishing with his wife one night. They fished at night because if the rays of the sun hit them, trolls were turned to stone. Just before dawn a strong wind blew up from the northwest, making it a terrible struggle for them to get back to shore before sunrise. They almost made it, but as Kallen was running ashore with the sail over his shoulder, the sun caught him and he was turned into a fisherman-shaped rock that sits on a ridge near the top of Vågakallen. (His wife was also caught by the sun and turned into another rock formation, called Kjerringa.)

When real human beings began to climb Norway's mountains towards the end of the nineteenth century, British mountaineers played a prominent role. One man in particular, a Yorkshireman called Cecil Slingsby, preferred Norway's empty wilderness to the more traditional playground of the Alps. On the mainland his ascent of Store Skagastølstind in 1876, completed solo, was one of the most celebrated early Norwegian climbs. He finally came to the Lofoten Islands during the summers of 1903 and 1904 with his regular climbing partner, Professor Norman Collie. Camping wild in deserted glens and using fishing boats to get around the roadless islands, they made several first ascents, including a mountain called Rulten, considered one of Lofoten's finest.

The British may have helped awaken Norway's interest in mountaineering, just as Arnold Lunn was later to turn the ancient Nordic art of skiing into an alpine sport, but there was no shortage of home talent. In fact, the most celebrated early ascent

in Lofoten took place sometime before Slingsby arrived – the first ascent of Vågakallen by Martin Ekroll and Angel Johannesen.

The two men lived on the tiny island of Skrova, 16 km (10 miles) east of Austvågøy. One bright sunny day in the summer of 1889 they set off in their open boat to row across to Austvågøy. Having secured their boat on the shore beneath Vågakallen, the great granite pyramid that everyone thought was unclimbable, they started up the south face, first thrashing through the chest-high ferns for which Lofoten is famous, then padding over mossy slabs spangled with the bright, creamy blooms of cloudberry plants, then on to rockier terrain. History does not relate whether the gully above was still choked with the damp remains of winter snow or whether they had to scrabble up loose scree. What we do know is that they reached the rocky crest of the west ridge, which narrowed to a knife edge, where they had to sit and shuffle, *à cheval*, with nailed boots scrabbling the smooth rock either side. Then they were on the upper south face, climbing another gully, then linking a series of ledges and grooves in the rough crystalline granite, leading eventually to the summit.

More than fifty years later the famous Arne Randers Heen found Ekroll's calling card under the summit cairn – definitive proof of the first ascent in 1889. Heen, perhaps Norway's most famous mountaineer, was a tailor from Åndalsness, in Romsdal, who came regularly to the Lofoten Islands to sell his goods to the cod fishermen. Other famous visitors included the Oslo climbers Ferdinand Schjelderup, Alf Bryn and Carl Wilhelm Rubenson. In 1910 they made the first ascent of a spectacular anvil-shaped peak near Narvik, called Stetind. (Slingsby, perhaps piqued because he had narrowly missed making the first ascent himself, called it the 'ugliest mountain in the world'.) Flushed with their mainland success on Stetind, Schjelderup, Bryn and Rubenson took a boat across to Austvågøy, landing at the harbor of Svolvær, right beneath the Svolværgeita – the Svolvær Goat.

This fine granite pinnacle culminates in two curved prongs separated by a wide, deep gap: the Goat's Horns. Until 1910 no one had dared climb them, but now the three Oslo climbers found a route to the top. Their line up the steep wall on the back side is now a popular outing for guided novices, many

American climber, Ed Webster, and commissioned by Thorbjørn Evenold, who runs a climbing school at Henningsvær with his wife, Lutta, great-great-granddaughter of Angel Johannesen, one of the two fishermen who first climbed Vågakallen. The original route up the south face of Vågakallen remains a popular outing, but ambitious rock climbers looking for something in the modern idiom make their way to Vågakallen's huge, sombre north face. It is dominated by the Storpillaren – the Great Pillar – first climbed during a twenty-six-hour stint in 1980 by Arild Meyer, Kjell Skog and Finn Tore Bjørnstad. The twenty pitches of continuously hard climbing were not repeated for thirteen years and still today the route commands respect. In the best Lofoten traditions of pioneering courage, the route has no bolts drilled into the rock and can be safeguarded only with 'natural' protection – pitons or removable alloy cams and wedges – and near the top there is a completely unprotectable smooth slab, impossible to climb unless completely dry.

As the fame of Lofoten's hardest 'big wall' spread, foreigners inevitably arrived to attempt the Storpillaren. And to add new routes to the wall. In 1998 the German couple Daniela and Robert Jasper spent their honeymoon weaving a new line up the wall, which they called Freya after the Nordic god of fertility. In 2003, fighting rain, sleet and snow, the Welsh couple Louise Thomas and Twid Turner added another new route, which they called Stormpillar.

There are hundreds of mountains in the Lofoten Islands. Many of them can only be reached by walking for several days or by sailing into one of the many fjords. Some summits have probably only had one or two ascents. For the most part, the Lofoten mountains are wild and deserted. Vågakallen is different. It is so famous and so close to the busy fishing village of Henningsvær that it will always see a certain amount of traffic. It – and the surrounding cliffs, such as the great dome of Presten – also offers some of the soundest granite in Europe. It is a real climbers' paradise.

of whom find it terrifying. Most terrifying of all is the optional extra – the feat first performed by Arne Randers Heen in 1930, which involves jumping from the tip of one horn to the other. Jumpers are roped

'Jumpers are roped for safety; nevertheless, it is nerve-racking, leaping from the higher horn and trying not to glance down at the tiny boats and houses in Svolvaer harbour, several hundred meters directly beneath.'

for safety; nevertheless, it is nerve-racking, leaping from the higher horn and trying not to glance down at the tiny boats and houses in Svolvaer harbour, several hundred metres directly beneath.

Nowadays all these routes are recorded in an English-language guidebook authored by the

North America

Mt Deborah

Height
3,761 metres (12,339 ft)

Location
Alaska Range

Origin of name
James Wickersham, Alaska's delegate to Congress, named the mountain after his wife, Deborah, in 1907.

First ascent
1954: Fred Beckey/Heinrich Harrer/H. Meybohm by Southwest Ridge

Other key routes
North Face 1977: David Davis/Dakers Gowans/Charles Macquarrie/Eric Reynolds

East Ridge 1983: John Barry/Dave Cheesmond/ Rob Collister/Roger Mear/ Carl Tobin

Interesting facts
The Alaska Range forms an arc 644 km (400 miles) long separating southern Alaska from the great plateau of the interior. The highest peak, Denali, is 6,195 metres (20,329 ft) and is the highest in North America. The arctic climate, the fierce storms which blow in from the Pacific dumping huge amounts of snow, and the sheer scale of peaks and glaciers, make climbing here as serious as (perhaps more serious than) in the Himalayas. Most climbers reach them by light aircraft, bypassing great tracts of tundra wilderness, to land direct on the glaciers.

Mt Deborah's outrageous East Ridge is a fantastic twisting ribbon of snow-encrusted rock, blocked halfway up a crumbling cliff which earlier unsuccessful contenders had called Nemesis Wall. In 1983 a British-Canadian team succeeded in scaling it on the climb of their lives, regaled all the way by the iconoclastic humour of an ex-Marines officer, John Barry.

A Ribbon on Edge

John Barry et al. (1983)

As with many adventures, this one started with a photo, along with eloquent prose that described 'a serpentine wisp of snow, like the curl of a ribbon on edge'. Then, the prose expounded the moment of defeat: 'The crumbly brown rock towered flat and crackless a few degrees less than vertical. A thin splotchy coating of ice overlay most of the rock … I had never seen a mountain sight so numbing, so haunted with impossibility and danger.'

The author was Dave Roberts. The mountain was Deborah, first climbed in 1954 by Eiger veteran Heinrich Harrer, his friend Meybohm, and one of America's greatest mountaineering pioneers, Fred Beckey. They described their route up the southwest ridge as the 'most sensational' ice climb of their careers. And that was the easiest way up the mountain: quite different from the east ridge, which later defeated Roberts and several other contenders. Deborah, one of Alaska's grandest, wildest, most beautiful mountains, had thrown down the gauntlet that in 1983 was picked up by an unlikely team of mountain guides from North Wales.

John Barry was a self-confessed redneck, former officer in the Royal Marines, and an Irishman – all blarney and bluster on the surface, concealing unconvincingly a highly intelligent, sensitive soul. Roger Mear, a student in the art of suffering, had already climbed Denali's epic Cassin Ridge in winter and made the first unsupported trek to the South Pole. Rob Collister was, in Barry's words, 'a man of culture, a man of peace, a Renaissance man, all the good bits from *Chariots of Fire*, arrow alpinist, and as fit as a butcher's dog – a deliberately inappropriate metaphor for a conscientious vegetarian'. He was also a hugely experienced mountaineer, with a prodigious string of first ascents to his bow.

They arrived in Alaska, and the Cessna pilot said, 'I can fly you to hell, Deborah, or both'. When they were deposited on the glacier beneath the east ridge, Barry's hope crumbled: 'Cliffs loomed, cornices arched on cornices as I had never seen in the Alps or Himalayas, as Roger had said they would. The snow lay feet deep and I was cold and frightened.'

Action helped galvanize them. With their grain shovels they excavated a huge snow cave, then relayed loads 760 metres (2,500 ft) up to the col – the saddle – from which the east ridge reared so monstrously. Here, as Roger Mear explained in the *American Alpine Journal*, they made a secure advance base: 'We cut a cave of luxurious dimensions. Enormous blocks of wind slab formed its lintelled entrance. Rob, between bouts of sunbathing, demonstrated the art of drystone walling and built a windbreak to make any Welsh farmer proud.' Then, as Barry recorded in his

diary, they set to work on the first horizontal stretch of the ridge, 'tip-i-toeing along as far as the first steepening – a couple of hundred yards or so. I think none of us much liked what we saw. Ribbons on edges of ribbons, great meringues of snow, and crevasses where no crevasses should have been'.

Reflecting later on that tottering ridge, Roger wrote: 'We had brought with us two 100-metre (328-ft) ropes (standard ones are 50 metres/164 ft) especially for this belayless terrain, hoping that the

For the moment, they were spared the reality of having to face it, as a storm pinned them down on the col for four days. 'Rob's wall sank without trace on the first day under feet of snow and we only left our sanctuary to dig out the entrance or perform our morning duties. Anecdotes and parlour games and John's Irish-rebel songs punctuated the dreaming. Yet always present was the thought that the last team had spent fourteen storm-bound days on this same col.'

They were spared a fourteen-day wait. On the sixth day the sun returned, but their isolation was shattered by the roar of a Cessna, which circled over the ridge, dropping loads near the cave and two climbers down on the glacier. The labelling on their air-dropped boxes proclaimed that they were two of North America's finest – the American, Carl Tobin, and the South African turned Canadian, Dave Cheesmond. They were heading for the same prestigious 'last great problem'.

At this time the Brits were ahead, getting to grips at last with the ridge proper. 'Short outcrops of horizontally bedded shale were linked together by knife-edge arêtes of snow or more improbable cornicing. Breaking trail on this terrain was extremely harrowing, as we expected each step to trigger the collapse of these tensile structures and listened with intent for those sounds that tell of equilibrium disturbed.' Nevertheless, they fixed 274 metres (900 ft) of rope that day, before abseiling back down to the cave. 'John was in fine form that evening having completed some hard pitches and we were all satisfied to have the serpent by the tail at last.'

The next day, 7 May 1983, while the Brits advanced back up their ropes carrying food for six days, intent on continuing up the ridge, the Americans arrived to collect their air-dropped gear ('it had taken us thirteen days to get this far', observed a rueful Roger), and prepared to climb up the British ropes and join the race. For the moment, the Brits were ahead, above the fixed lines, exploring some terrifying new ground. Roger Mear described one particularly memorable pitch:

'Tip-i-toeing along as far as the first steepening – a couple of hundred yards or so. I think none of us much liked what we saw. Ribbons on edges of ribbons, great meringues of snow, and crevasses where no crevasses should have been.'

greater distance between each man would give us greater assurance.' As they approached the main steepening of the ridge proper, he saw: 'Steep walls of frost-shattered shale, plastered with the most improbable structures or rime and wind-impacted snow. More cornices creamed in all directions and above these loomed the cliff that Roberts had named the Nemesis Wall, the biggest question mark of all, guarding access to the upper ridge.'

'We gathered together beneath the next imponderable, a grossly bulging mushroom of rime, its crystal lattice too brittle for pick or axe shaft. To the left, a steep rotting wall of red shale. Between the two was formed a shallow cleft. The chimney led to a macabre cul-de-sac. The way ahead was barred by yet another bulging wall of shale clothed in a mantle of rime feathers. To either side great vertical fins of rime jutted into the white clouded space. Like a mouse brought up short in its journey through a cardboard maze which breaks the rules set by its unseen observers and begins to gnaw through the walls of the passage, I tensioned across the steep face of the right fin and cut a notch in its vertical edge, gaining entry into the adjacent scoop. I progressed up a rotting bookcase of shale, each shelf piled with volumes laid flat and loosely covered with soft snow.'

And so it went on. On 8 May Barry wrote in his diary, 'Snowed all night. Two feet or so over tent by morning. Lie in wondering what to do. After much dithering get going about 11ish – more to avoid being suffocated than desire to climb. Jumar up to high point past American team who stay ensconced in their tent all day, occasionally shouting encouragement, 'Yeah man, everything's gonna be all right,' through half an inch of unzipped door. (They must be possessed of some sort of psychological sixth sense, for their cry always comes floating up just when we are convinced everything is far from all right.)'

While the Americans bade their time, the Brits worked that day on fantastically steep terrain, including a traverse that they thought made the Eigerwand's notorious Traverse of the Gods 'look like a garden path'. In a bizarre kind of way, despite the trepidation, they were enjoying themselves, thrilled now to have reached the crumbly rock band – the Nemesis Wall that had defeated Roberts's team. The next day, 9 May, Cheesmond and Tobin were away early, at 3:00 A.M., stealing a march on the Brits. But later in the day the two teams worked together,

The gigantic North Face of Mt Deborah. The East Ridge is on the left skyline. On the previous page the East Ridge appears as a slender twisting ribbon of ice, descending directly from the summit towards the camera.

Huge cornices overhang dizzy depths as the team nears the top of the great East Ridge.

sharing the glory of leading a succession of insecure pitches through a gully system on the right that proved the key to the Nemesis Wall. Late that evening, Barry and Collister followed a rope across a long traverse back left. It was dark by the time they reached Mear, chopping out a notch for their little tent; only at midnight did they light the stove to melt snow for supper, finally getting to sleep at 3:00 A.M.

On 10 May Barry woke to a gorgeous surprise. 'Sun! We are east-facing – warm. Sun dries bags and boots, warms the soul. Brew and snooze, snooze and brew. The best morning of my life.' That gloriously primal, animal joy in simple pleasures is one of the many rewards of a great climb – a delight in sheer physical well-being, won through hard toil and creativity. That, and the exhilaration of living, breathing, sleeping, waking in the most sensational

surroundings. Just to the left of the three Britons, Cheesmond and Tobin's tiny dome tent was perched on an even tinier blob of snow. As they dismantled the tent and sat atop the blob, their boots hung over an immense void – a fantastic abstract in snow, ice and rock.

Collister and Cheesmond returned heroically, across the previous night's traverse, to collect climbing gear that had been left behind. Then eventually, at 11:00 A.M., the combined team started the final push for the summit, only to be brought up short by what Roger called 'the most absurd of spectacles. The underbelly of a great ice whale, clothed in barnacles of rime, overhung our path. Rob, being a father of three and the custodian of sanity, immediately abseiled off the ridge in search of more reasonable alternatives. Carl, with brain addled

by years spent in pursuit of 'altered states', viewed the prospect with relish and began to weave a web of possibility up the underside of the beast.' As the Brits sat down to gawp, John Barry was hugely impressed. 'It was a tour de force by Carl, climbing 70 ft [21 metres] of overhanging ice on horizontally driven snow stakes, all the while dangling in space with 5,000 ft [1,525 metres] free beneath him. What frightened me most was the way he could withdraw each stake by hand, like an arrow from a quiver. It was as spectacular a feat of mountaineering as I ever hope to witness.'

Collister returned from ploughing his abortive lonely furrow and joined the others, jumaring dizzily up the free-hanging rope fixed by Tobin. Once they were all over the ice overhang, the climb was virtually in the bag, and a little later, in the serene light of the Arctic spring evening, they all arrived together on the summit at 9:30 P.M.

As they prepared in the morning to descend the original Harrer-Beckey route, the satisfaction began to glow, as Barry recorded:

'In the last hours of the previous day, as we neared the top, the cold clamp of seriousness had begun to melt away. But the dark, cold and sleep came before it had melted fully away, so that a brewing contentedness never quite bubbled that night. But it boiled busily in the morning when, released by the sun's rays, a greater inner joy burst, enough for some to spill over to the outside. In the cold clamp we had worked well as a team. Now we were happy. On that day, on that mountain, it would have been impossible to be anything else. It was a great adventure and the memory of it is unblemished: a perfect reflection.'

'The underbelly of a great ice whale overhung our path.' Hanging from driven aluminium stakes, over a 1,500-metre (5,000-ft) drop, Carl Tobin does battle with the underbelly.

Mt Lucania

Height
5,226 metres (17,146 ft)

Location
St Elias Mountains, Yukon, Canada

Origin of name
The first recorded sighting of the peak was by the Duke of Abruzzi, from the summit of Mt St Elias on 31 July 1897. He named it after the ocean liner that had carried him across the Atlantic.

First ascent
9 July 1937: Robert Bates/ Bradford Washburn

Other key route
North Ridge 1967: Jerry Halpen/Gary Lukis/Mike Humphreys/Gerry Roach

Interesting facts
Lucania is the third highest mountain in Canada. The two first ascenscionists went on to have distinguished careers. Bob Bates took part in the 1938 and 1953 expeditions to K2, on the latter attempt surviving an epic retreat from the mountain, during the attempt to save the life of Art Gilkey stricken with a pulmonary embolism. Bradford Washburn pioneered the standard West Buttress route on Denali and made the first ascent of Mt Bertha during his honeymoon with his wife Barbara; from 1939 to 1980 he was Director of the Boston Museum of Science and in 1988 masterminded the National Geographic 1:50,000 map of Mt Everest.

Even if everything had gone to plan, the first ascent of Lucania would have been a brilliant achievement. As it turned out, events did not follow the plan and Bradford Washburn found himself not only climbing the third highest summit in Canada, but also having to improvise a desperate escape from one of the most remote wildernesses on earth.

Surviving on Squirrel Meat
Bob Bates and Bradford Washburn (1937)

The clouds dropped and a wild thunderstorm was followed by torrential warm rain all night. For two days it poured and snowed intermittently and thick impenetrable fog covered the glacier: the plane was hopelessly bogged in. ... The short landing strip we had trampled was sliced nearly in half by myriad crevasses. On the 20th Bob tried to take off, but the slush was too deep and loose, and as he was taxiing back towards camp his left ski plunged into a deep hole in the treacherous slough. The left wing tip disappeared beneath the surface.'

It was June 1937, and Bradford Washburn's bold, futuristic plan to make the first plane landing on one of Canada's most wild, remote glaciers had backfired. But he had always been a bold entrepreneur: publishing his first book – on alpine climbing – when he was seventeen; paying his own way through Harvard; and then, in 1935, when he was only twenty-five, carrying out a major aerial photographic survey of the St Elias Range for *National Geographic*. It was that expedition that sparked his interest in Mt Lucania. The following year, when a rival, Walter Wood, attempted the mountain and pronounced it unclimbable, the interest became an obsession. It was the highest unclimbed mountain in North America. And also one of the most remote – 160 km (100 miles) from human habitation and guarded by some of the greatest glaciers on earth.

Any approach on foot would involve prohibitively expensive travel with pack animals. So Washburn decided to do what would later become standard practice for mountaineers in the Yukon and fly in.

In May 1937 the pilot Bob Reeve made three flights to the Walsh Glacier, immediately beneath Lucania, to cache stores and equipment. Then, on 18 June he took off again from Valdez Flats, this time carrying Washburn and his ex-Harvard climbing companion, Bob Bates. The plan was to put them down beneath Lucania, 300 km (185 miles) to the east, then return to fly in the other two team members. A few weeks later, once all four members had made their attempt on Lucania, Reeve would return to collect them.

That was the plan, but unseasonal rainstorms turned the glacier's snow surface into a slushy quagmire, riddled with half-opened crevasses. As the Fairchild 51 came in to land, it sunk up to its wing strut. Bates and Washburn had to spend hours digging out the plane. Two days later Reeve crashed trying to take off. Again the two climbers laboured to excavate the plane. Rather than risk another crash, Reeve now waited, hoping desperately for temperatures to lower and freeze the snow surface.

After two days, according to Washburn, 'We'd got an inch of crust on top of this fathomless bullshit, and Reeve said he would give it a try. He said, "You guys

Washburn's bold, innovative plan to fly in to the base of Lucania nearly ended in disaster when the Fairchild 51 got bogged down in fathomless, mushy snow. When pilot Reeve finally managed to take off, he made it clear that he wasn't coming back: Washburn and Bates would have to get out on their own.

can skin your own skunks and I'll skin mine; I'm getting out of here and I wouldn't land again in this goddam place for a million bucks.' This time, his fourth attempt, the pilot just managed to scrape clear of the glacier and escape, leaving Bob Bates and Bradford stranded with a one-way ticket and 'a hundred-odd miles of desolation between us and all civilization'.

So there they were – two climbers instead of the planned four, marooned at the heart of North America's greatest mountain wilderness, with no chance of a pickup. It was a grim situation, but they were young and resourceful, and they had ample stocks of food and fuel. The nearest exit from the St Elias

> **'One thing was clear: if we could not use snowshoes most of the time, we were licked. I took mine off for a second to test the snow and went in halfway up to my chest. …'**

mountains was to the east, at Burwash Landing on Lake Kluane. The only problem was that imposed between them and their escape route was the gigantic bulk of Canada's sixth-highest peak, Mt Steele. They would simply have to climb it. 'It would be a grim business,' wrote Washburn many years later. 'For the

first time in our lives we knew what it was like to be really up against it: we were not *trying* to make a first ascent of the west face of Steele – we *had* to.'

From the Walsh Glacier they faced a climb of nearly 3,000 metres (10,000 ft), trudging backwards and forwards, relaying loads of food, fuel and survival gear, relying on snowshoes to plough through soul-destroying soft snow, either struggling under the glare of the sun or, more commonly, navigating through thick fog and fresh snowfalls, scrutinizing the maps and aerial photographs they had brought with such canny foresight.

After reluctantly abandoning nearly all their photographic and survey gear, they set out on 25 June with fifty days' food, first dragging a ski sledge, then, when the ground became steeper, relaying loads in rucksacks. By 7 July they had made their eighth camp on the pass between Mt Lucania and Mt Kling. Soon they would be on the summit of Mt Kling, and from there they could head down the east ridge, which Wood's party had climbed the previous year. Never a man to suffer from false modesty, Washburn was confident that 'anything Walter Wood could get up, we could get down'. In fact, he and Bates were so pleased with progress so far that they began to think again. 'Our only plan until that moment had been to save our skins by a speedy retreat to civilization over the top of Mt Steele. … But finding ourselves with about ten days' more food than we needed or could carry … tempted us to think again about Lucania. Rather than simply abandoning our climbing plans, why not make one desperate bid to 'bag' it?'

This was mountaineering at its spontaneous, improvisatory best – planned siege transformed into brilliant commando raid. Superlatively fit, the two young men left a cache of fuel, packed their rucksacks and trudged towards their objective, being forced to *descend* 300 metres (nearly 1,000 ft) to reach the huge plateau at the foot of the final pyramid of Lucania's massive bulk. The following day, 9 July, they left their tent to wallow up the final slope. 'One thing was clear: if we could not use snowshoes most of the time, we were licked. I took mine off for a second to test the snow and went in halfway up to my chest. … We took turns… breaking trail for fifty steps, then climbing aside for the other to lead; and after nearly eight hours of continuous climbing, we finally stood on top at 4:45 in the afternoon.'

Lucania, against all odds, had been conquered. But that was only the beginning. 'Sixty miles of mountain, glacier and muskeg, as well as the summit of Steele, still lay between us and our next sound sleep in a bed.'

On 10 July an icy wind kept them locked in their tent, and it was only on 11 July that they got away, ploughing with 34-kilo (75-lb) loads up to the shoulder of Mt Steele, which marked the top of the vital east ridge. Here they temporarily left loads to bag Steele's summit as well, finding Walter Wood's willow wands still rammed into the final wind-scoured snow cone. Then back to the loads to start the long descent of the east ridge, first jettisoning excess fuel, food, spare clothing, shovel – even ripping out half the tent groundsheet – to reduce loads to a manageable skeletal survival kit. At 3:20 P.M. they started down the ridge; by 8:35 that evening they were camped on the Wolf Creek Glacier, nearly 3,000 metres (10,000 ft) below, yet another display of astounding skill and stamina.

The following day, they headed on down the glacier, longing to gorge themselves on a food cache at Walter Wood's old advance base, but when they got there, they found that bears had destroyed

everything, leaving just one untouched jar of peanut butter. Now incredibly hungry, they slogged another 32 km (20 miles) east on 13 July to the Donjek river. In the grim light of morning they realized that its icy current was suicidal, so they had to make a 32-km (20-mile) detour upstream to find a safe crossing place. Then they spent the next night huddled in the rain, wrapped in the poleless tent. On the far side of the river, they managed to shoot a rabbit and a red squirrel and found some mushrooms to supplement the scrawny meat ('just like eating piano wire').

At last, on 19 July, struggling across a swamp on the way to the final pass, they met a pack train. 'These guys came up and asked, 'Where are you going?' and we said, 'We're going where you're going.'

The men helped the mountaineers to a cabin, where they feasted for twenty-four hours before being loaded onto the packhorses for the final leg of their long escape to Burwash. Sixty years later that final passage still stuck vividly in Brad Washburn's memory as 'the most excruciating torture I have ever endured'.

Bob Bates (left) and Bradford Washburn – the first people to reach the summit of Mt Lucania. Now all they had to do was climb another mountain and tramp 160 km (100 miles) back to civilization.

Mt Logan

Height
5,959 metres (19,550 ft)

Location
St Elias Mountains, Yukon, Canada

Origin of name
Named after William Edmond Logan, first director of the Geological Survey of Canada

First ascent
23 June 1925: Allen Carpé/ William Foster/Fred Lambert/ Albert MacCarthy/Norman Read/Andrew Taylor, from the north

Other key routes
East Ridge 1957: Dave Collins/Don Monk/Cecil Oullette/Gill Roberts/ Kermith Ross

Hummingbird Ridge 1965: Paul Bacon/Frank Coale/ John Evans/Dick Long/Allen Steck/Jim Wilson

Interesting facts
Mt Logan is possibly the largest mountain on earth, in terms of volume and elevation – a greater single mass than any Himalayan peak. The Hummingbird Ridge, for instance, rises over 4,000 metres (13,000 ft) from glacier to summit. The glaciers in the region are the largest non-polar glaciers on earth. The weather, close to the Pacific Ocean, is notoriously stormy.

The irony didn't escape the men trapped by a vicious snowstorm on Canada's tallest mountain: they were members of a search-and-rescue team, off duty. Now their lives were in the hands of others.

Trapped on Mt Logan

Erik Bjarnason, Don Jardine and Alex Snigurowicz (2005)

As he did on every climbing trip, Erik Bjarnason pulled a plastic-wrapped picture wrapped of his two children from his jacket and taped it to a bamboo pole used to mark his route. This time, he was climbing Mt Logan. At 5,959 metres (19,550 ft), it's Canada's highest mountain and the jewel of the Yukon's Kluane National Park and Reserve.

Bjarnason, whose day job was fighting fires, had been climbing for three weeks with other members of a volunteer search-and-rescue team, to celebrate the team's 40th anniversary. He was close to the summit, but the route was turning treacherously icy. Tired and cold, he and three companions decided to turn back.

The next morning, Wednesday, 25 May 2005, was clear. A mild disturbance was forecast. Bjarnason saw off Gord Ferguson and Linda Bily, who wanted to continue to the summit. Bjarnason started his descent at noon with Don Jardine and Alex Snigurowicz. There was plenty of time for the four-hour ski trip to the next campsite – the long spring days at that latitude meant it would not be dusk until after 11 P.M.. Others from their group were already well down the mountain, and just below them were Barry Mason and Isabel Budke.

By 2 P.M. the trio was approaching Prospector's Col, an exposed pass they'd have to cross. Jardine noticed the wind picking up and broken clouds scudding across the sky. An hour later it was as if they

had suddenly stepped into a howling white hell. A roaring headwind pushed them back on their skis. and granular snow peppered their faces. Jardine had never seen weather change with such frightening speed. He spotted a large rock, and they dashed for it. Hunkering down, they took off their skis while Jardine fished out the tent fly to cover them.

Mason and Budke had already crossed Prospector's Col and were continuing their descent. Jardine radioed and told them Bjarnason's hands were cold so they were stopping to warm up. Within 20 minutes, winds of over 100 km (62 miles) an hour were shrieking over the col. They continued their descent on foot.

Towing a sled loaded with gear, Jardine suddenly felt his feet slide from under him. Slithering down a slope towards crevasses below, he flung his weight onto his ice axe, but the axe penetrated only a few millimetres into the icy ground. 'Alex! Erik!' he screamed. The pair grabbed his sledge and hauled him back up. With ice forming around their eyes and frozen goggles, it was impossible to see where they were going. 'Let's get the tent up,' Bjarnason yelled.

They retreated to the rock, took off their bulky overmitts and assembled the poles, their fingers stiffening as they struggled to hold the tent down. By the time they got it up, secured their packs to it and crawled inside, they were painfully cold.

As afternoon turned to evening, gusts repeatedly lifted the men completely off the ground. Jardine crawled out to better anchor the tent, struggling for 30 minutes to secure it with ice screws. Fearing the wind would soon rip apart their flimsy shelter, the men stayed dressed with their boots on and kept each other awake with conversation. They had some radio contact with Budke and Mason, waiting about 700 metres (2,300 ft) below them, but they couldn't reach Ferguson and Bily above them.

By the next morning, the three men were weary from lack of sleep, dehydration and hunger. They managed to get the stove going and melted ice for drinks. At noon, the storm still at its peak, Jardine went outside to see how the tent was faring after 20 hours of stress. It was beginning to shred. 'We have to dig a snow cave as backup,' he told the others. Unable to use a shovel because his hands were now frostbitten, Bjarnason stayed in the tent, melting snow and ice for drinking water while Snigurowicz and Jardine went out to find a spot for the snow cave, leaving their shovels behind for the moment.

Without the weight of the two men, the wind soon ripped out the tent's ice-screw anchors. Bjarnason fell onto his back as the tent rolled towards the edge of the slope. His upper body fell through the opening, leaving his legs tangled in billowing nylon. Snigurowicz reached him first and dived onto the tent. Bjarnason scrambled out and Snigurowicz hung on to the tent, but the wind snatched it away. They watched as it sailed off, carrying with it their shovels, the stove, two packs – almost everything they needed to survive.

'Erik, take shelter behind the rock while we dig a snow cave,' Jardine shouted. Their only tools were an ice axe and a pot lid. Three hours later as Bjarnason lay alone, his thoughts turned to his kids, in particular his 17-year-old daughter who he had last seen when she was a toddler and might never see again.

Around 7 P.M., after huddling behind the rock for over six hours, Bjarnason stopped shivering. His rescue training told him he was sinking into the first stages of hypothermia. Suddenly surprised by shouts from Jardine and Snigurowicz, he raised his head. 'Erik! Come on, time to go!' They showed him to their new shelter. He was expecting a cave with a low entrance to trap heat. When he saw a hole in the snow, his heart fell. It looked more like a grave. They crammed in and lay sideways, curled like spoons.

Jardine and Snigurowicz had frostbitten toes and fingers. When Bjarnason tapped his fingers together they sounded like blocks of wood, and he could feel nothing up to his wrists. He was convinced that if he survived, he would lose his hands. The men were battered, but for the first time in almost seven hours they were mercifully out of the wind.

Around midnight, Jardine got up and went outside. The snow cave felt like a tomb, and he could bear it no longer. Unless the storm broke soon, they had no chance. Bjarnason and Snigurowicz were not sure why he had left the snow cave, but without him it was getting colder. 'We need your heat,' Bjarnason shouted to him. Jardine crawled back in. They put him in the middle so he couldn't leave again.

By about 3 A.M. the storm had subsided. Mason and Budke, who had been caught in the same vicious weather, were hungry and exhausted from two sleepless nights huddled in their tent. But they were worried

This photo by local expert Joe Josephson, captures the gigantic scale and complexity of Mt Logan, which is possibly the largest mountain in the world. The picture on page 44 shows the vastness of the glaciers that surround it.

about the trio above, having received desperate radio calls. A few hours later, they set off to reach their companions above. But with more than 1 metre (3 ft) of fresh snow, it took them almost an hour to move just 300 metres (10,000 ft). Realizing that the only thing that would save the men now was a helicopter, Mason and Budke reluctantly decided to descend the mountain to find a satellite phone.

At 6 A.M. the sun drew the men out of their snow cave. They staggered around trying to get circulation into their frozen limbs. The clear weather finally enabled radio contact between the trio and the two climbers above. Ferguson and Bily had sat out the storm in their tent, unaware of the disaster. They had a satellite phone and were able to call for help. Almost simultaneously, Mason and Budke used the phone of a generous French team to call Kluane National Park and NSR's search manager for immediate assistance, and realyed information about their teammates and weather conditions throughout the rescue effort.

Officials at Kluane National Park had a helicopter that could reach the site, but because of ongoing weather concerns they called for the help of their American counterparts at Denali National Park in

Bjarnason's hands were a deathly grey, his fingers split open and swollen up like sausages.

The men were beginning to despair that no rescue was coming when, around 8 P.M. they were startled by a roar. An American HC-130 plane swooped down and began circling overhead, providing a link with rescue crews. Thirty minutes later the Lama and the Parks Canada Jet Ranger clattered towards them.

Bjarnason was the first to be whisked off the mountain. Facing backward, he was awestruck by the

Two days prior to the storm, Mike Danks (left) and Barry Mason thank North Shore Rescue for their support before climbing the remaining exposed metres of the west summit and continuing to the main summit of Mount Logan.

> **'When Bjarnason tapped his fingers together they sounded like blocks of wood, and he could feel nothing up to his wrists. He was convinced that if he survived, he would lose his hands.'**

beauty of soft, pink alpenglow bathing the peaks. Jardine arrived next, then Snigurowicz as the sun was setting. The Pave Hawk crew gave them warm gloves, blankets and earplugs, then lifted off into the dusk and headed for Anchorage, Alaska. As they looked back at the

Alaska. A cross-border, multi-aircraft rescue was quickly organized from over 500 km (310 miles) away.

Hypothermia, thirst and lack of nourishment were taking a toll. Bjarnason realized they were all sliding in and out of delirium. Snigurowicz had stopped talking and was rocking back and forth. He had began to fall in and out of consciousness, his body twitching. 'Gord, we're losing Alex.' Jardine radioed.

At Denali the Lama lifted off at 3:40 P.M. local time for the long haul to Mount Logan. Meanwhile, Ferguson and Bily reached Prospector's Col and quickly pitched their own frayed tent. They hustled the cold and confused climbers inside and covered them with sleeping bags. The trio were in bad shape. They talked uncontrollably, but made little sense.

mountain that had tried so hard to kill them, the three men exchanged weary grins and gave a thumbs up.

At Providence Alaska Medical Center the next morning, Snigurowicz and Jardine were told they might lose toes. When Bjarnason learned he would lose all his fingers, the exhilaration of survival evaporated as he realized that his days as a firefighter were over.

Before flying home on 2 June the trio learned that Mason, Budke, Ferguson and Bily had all reached base camp – tired and hungry, but safe. For Jardine, Snigurowicz, and especially Bjarnason, now reunited with a daughter he had not seen for fifteen years, the close brush with death on Mt Logan had given them a new appreciation of what's important in life. As Bjarnason says, 'I don't need my hands to hug my kids.'

Mt Waddington

Height
4,019 metres (13,186 ft)

Location
Coast Range, British
Columbia, Canada

Origin of name
The Mundays originally
called it 'Mystery Mountain'.
In 1930 it was named
officially after a nineteenth-
century entrepreneur and
mapmaker called Alfred
Waddington.

First ascent
1936 William House & Fritz
Wiessner, by Southwest Face

Other key routes
Northwest Ridge to
Northwest Summit 1928:
Don, Albert & Phyllis
Munday

Bravo Glacier Route 1950:
O. Cook/R. Houston/
W. Long/R. de Saussure

Risse Route 1987: Steven
Risse/Andy Tuthill

Cowboy Way 1995: John
Harlin III/Mark Jenkins

Interesting facts
Mt Waddington is the
highest point along the
western seaboard of North
America between Mt
Ranier, near Seattle, and
Mt Fairweather in Alaska.
Bill House and Fritz
Wiessner, who made the
first ascent, later attempted
the world's second highest
mountain, K2. In 1939 Fritz
Wiessner got to within about
250 metres (820 ft) of K2's
summit with Sherpa Pasang
Dawa Lama.

This is a story of two people, husband and wife, and their shared passion for a single mountain – their 'Mystery Mountain' – protected by sea, forest and glacier, unmapped, unexplored and, until they spotted it on the far horizon, one summer's afternoon, unknown to man.

Mystery Mountain of the Coastal Range

Don and Phyllis Munday (1925)

Don and Phyllis Munday met while climbing the mountains that filled the skyline of their home city of Vancouver. One June afternoon in 1925, returning from an attempt on a peak on Vancouver Island, defeated by deep wet snow but still content, they stopped to look across to the Canadian mainland.

'We paused for a meal in welcome evening sunshine on a mossy shelf near the timber line. The Coast Range towered in a violet wall out of the Georgia Strait. Shining upper levels merged with bright clouds piled mountainously along nearly 200 miles [320 km] of the range. Only the known, nearer summits shouldered the clouds aside. Phyl's eyes shone as she handed me the binoculars and pointed to a tall mountain nearly due north though a new cloud rift. The compass showed the alluring peak stood along a line passing a little east of the head of Bute Inlet and perhaps 150 miles [240 km] away, where blank spaces on the map left ample room for many nameless mountains. Clouds refused to reveal its neighbours. It was the far-off finger of destiny beckoning. It was a marker along the trail of adventure, a torch to set the imagination on fire.'

At that time Canada's Rocky Mountains, 645 km (400 miles) inland near Calgary, were already well engrained in the national consciousness, its famous summits visible from the railway. But the Coast Range, stretching 1,450 km (900 miles) north from

Vancouver to Alaska, was virtually unknown. Apart from a few tough trappers, few people had penetrated the dense forest protecting the mountains. No one had set foot on the upper glaciers, and no one knew the exact height of the Mundays' Mystery Mountain.

That autumn they took a boat and made the first of many journeys to solve the mystery. When Don Munday later wrote up their adventures in his classic *The Unknown Mountain*, he included telling photos of 'the heroine' in breeches and shirtsleeves, pushing her way through tangled undergrowth, or sitting at the campfire. Another photo, captioned 'Mrs. Munday', shows her balancing over a raging torrent, side stepping along a natural bridge of fallen tree trunks with a 27-kg (60-lb) rucksack on her back. In the foreground, her brother-in-law, Albert Munday, holds tight a rope handrail, tensioned from a tree on the far shore. To remain self-sufficient long enough to reach the heart of the range, they had to relay heavy loads. And, as well as the notoriously awful weather in the Coast Range, which keeps the mountains shrouded in cloud most of the time, they had to be wary of bears and wolves.

The Mundays discovered that their Mystery Mountain lay at the heart of a whole cluster of peaks, rising from a complex tangle of glaciers. Approaching from the roadless wasteland to the east was out of the question, so they approached from the coast. From

The Mundays spent several happy summers exploring the forests and glaciers around Mt Waddington. In 1934 they succeeded in reaching the northwest summit of the 'Mystery Mountain', only to be met by the view on page 48 of the final, unattainable bastion. That ultimate prize was seized two years later by Bill House and Fritz Wiessner.

Georgia Strait, two deep inlets pierced the interior – Bute Inlet to the south of the mountain and Knight Inlet to the north. Into these inlets flowed the two immense rivers cutting through the Coast Range. In September 1925 the Mundays worked their way up the southern river, from Bute Inlet, working their way around to the east side of Mystery Mountain.

They returned in 1926, got a good view of their mountain and returned to Vancouver to be met by incredulity. 'It soon became clear that mountaineering circles in Vancouver for the most part greatly discounted the story we brought back of high peaks and mighty glaciers, and the next annual dinner of the British Columbia Mountaineering Club was made the occasion of an announcement that the actual height of our 13,000-ft [4,000-metre] Mystery Mountain was 11,884 ft [3,622 metres].'

That scepticism was prompted partly by the fact that Mt Waddington, as the mountain was later officially named, lay so far south and so close to the comparatively warm air currents of the Pacific Ocean. In 1927, when they took a boat up Knight Inlet and worked their way up the western side of the massif, the Mundays themselves were amazed at the size of the Franklin Glacier. They were also amazed by its complexity, as they fought their way over endless

humpbacks of ice, riven by torrents of surface meltwater racing through perilously smooth sluices, and made frequent diversions onto the many side glaciers that disrupted the main ice flow.

That summer they established that this western approach was their best chance of getting onto Mt Waddington, which they now realized was a complex peak with two main summits and several subsidiary turrets. The following summer, having once again relayed loads up the Franklin Glacier, Albert, Don and Phyllis Munday made their final camp beneath a windy pass they called Fury Gap. They slept briefly. Then: 'Icy wind raged through Fury Gap when I lit the primus at 1:15 A.M. Seemingly, moisture had condensed from the air inside it, and it balked horribly. We could not get away until 4:40 A.M.'

It was still dark, so they used lanterns to find their way up onto the Angel Glacier, which led eventually to their chosen route up Mt Waddington – the Northwest Ridge. Later that morning they had to cross slopes of dangerous windslab – new snow that was dumped by the wind without adhering properly to the old snow beneath. Higher up, Don had to scrape away loose powder with his axe to chop footsteps in the hard ice beneath. It took the whole day to work their way up the ridge, and evening was drawing in when they finally approached the northwest summit.

'Mentally and physically I was keyed up to the very high pitch which one reaches on certain occasions. This time I knew that the summit would be ours.'

'I had meant Phyl to be first on top, but so exacting was the work that I came unexpectedly to a short knife edge between two hornlike icy cornices flaring up and out. The fret of the rock showed a few feet below me on the other side. There was little room between the cornice tusks for the three of us to straddle the ridge.'

Beyond their summit the ridge plummeted into a deep gap separating them from the main summit: 'Eastward towered the tremendous eastern pinnacle of the mountain, still somewhat higher, and festooned with great masses composed partly of snow and partly of moisture congealed from wet winds.' It looked extremely hard, and at 7:30 P.M. there was no chance of continuing. They had been lucky to get one day's fine weather, and to stay longer on the summit ridge would be crazy. 'The eye was tempted to linger more on the glowing cloud fringes tossed aloft to snare the splendour of the sinking sun than upon their potency for breeding storm. Over the interior Plateau two thunder-headed masses trailed grey cloaks of rain; we lingered a mere fifteen minutes on that glorious crest.'

It was 2:00 A.M. when the Mundays returned to their high camp, exhausted but proud. In 1933 they made the first ascent of one of Waddington's most spectacular neighbours, Mt Combatant. Then in 1934 they had one final attempt at Waddington itself, repeating their route to the northwest summit and descending some distance into the gap beyond. But looking up at the final ice-decked crenellated tower, they became disheartened by this 'incredibly nightmarish thing that must be seen to be believed'.

The Mundays were brilliant explorers, but they were not great rock climbers. Now others, more technically proficient, were drawn by the challenge of Waddington. By 1936 it had become a race, with two teams – one from California and one from British Columbia – converging on the great unclimbed prize of the Coast Range. Then a third team arrived from the East Coast: Bill House and Fritz Wiessner.

Wiessner was born in Dresden and learned his climbing on the famous sandstone rocks of the Elbe valley, where rock-climbing standards were several grades ahead of anywhere else in the world. Before emigrating to America, he had made a name for himself as one of Europe's finest mountaineers, famous in particular for his rock climbs in Austria's Wilder Kaiser mountains. Now, faced with the challenge of Waddington, he and Bill House approached cannily, watching and learning while both the Californian and British Columbian teams failed.

All three teams tried the south face, realizing that this offered a more direct approach than the Mundays' route. The first two teams retreated when they could not reach the summit before nightfall. Then House and Wiessner had their turn, climbing the gully between the northwest and main summits, but they were defeated by ice-glazed rocks. The next day they tried again, setting off at 2:40 A.M., this time climbing up the rocks directly beneath the main summit. Undeterred by the rocks' steepness, Wiessner changed into special rope-soled climbing shoes, then popular in Europe. He had the technical expertise for the job; more important, he had the right mental approach: 'Mentally and physically I was keyed up to the very high pitch which one reaches on certain occasions. This time I knew that the summit would be ours.' Where his rivals had been over cautious, he was confident in his ability to find a line of weakness up this final bastion of Mt Waddington. And at 4:00 that afternoon he and Bill House stood on the summit, having completed the hardest climb in North America.

Phyllis Munday crossing a raging glacial torrent, belayed by her brother-in-law, Albert.

North Twin

Height
3,731 metres (12,241 ft)

Location
Columbia Icefield, Rocky Mountains, Alberta, Canada

Origin of name
Named by a visiting famous British climber, Norman Collie, in 1898. It is one of two linked peaks – South and North Twins.

First ascent
July 1923: Conrad Kain/ W. S. Ladd/J. Monroe Thorington by East Face

Other key routes
Northwest Ridge 1965: Henry Abrons

North Face original route 1974: Chris Jones/George Lowe

North Face right hand pillar 1985: Barry Blanchard/Dave Cheesmond

North Face central variation 2004: Steve House/Marko Prezelj

Interesting facts
North Twin is the highest mountain in Alberta and the third highest in the Canadian Rockies. Approaching from the Columbia Icefield to the east, it is quite a gentle, snowy mountain, which can be climbed on skis – utterly different from the dark northern aspect plunging to the Athabasca River. Despite being one of the world's most coveted objectives, during the thirty years from 1974 to 2004 the North Face had only three successful ascents, each by a different route or variation.

Fifteen hundred metres (five thousand ft) of sheer, black and north-facing limestone, steeper than the Eiger, one and a half times as high as El Capitan, with no possibility of rescue, Canada's most awesome wall was first climbed by Chris Jones and George Lowe in 1974. Barry Blanchard suggested that they had pulled off the hardest alpine route in the world. Eleven years later, with Dave Cheesmond, he set off himself to climb a companion route up 'the shadowland of North Twin'.

Sheer Heights

Barry Blanchard and Dave Cheesmond (1985)

And then I was falling and a black shadow charged over my right shoulder. For one horrifying instant I thought it was David. I snapped tight on the rope and saw the shadow twist and roar off into space, exploding into the glacier 3,000 ft [over 900 metres] below. Cheesmond was yelling to me to unweight the ropes, as I had fallen directly onto his harness. The shadow had been a 7-ft [2-metre] section of rock that had fractured from the belay.'

Barry Blanchard and Dave Cheesmond were committed totally to the overhanging wilderness of the north face of North Twin, the 'black hole' of the Canadian Rockies, which a former climber had found 'so dark, sheer and gloomy' that it was 'like a bad dream'. That same climber had also predicted, back in 1966, that this awesome wall 'must become one of the great face problems for the next generation'.

It was North America's answer to the Eigerwand: the same colossal height, the same dark triangular concavity, the same brooding menace, the same danger from falling rocks when the temperature rose above freezing. But there were also differences. North Twin's three great bands of striated limestone were steeper and more compact, with none of the zigzagging evasions offered by Switzerland's more famous wall. And North Twin was in the heart of the Canadian Rockies: It was a long day's walk through

wilderness country just to reach the foot of the face and, once committed to the vertical and overhanging upper wall, climbers would have no chance of rescue.

The challenge of the north face was taken up in August 1974 by two outstanding alpinists – the quiet, bold, intelligent American academic, George Lowe; and his British expat climbing partner, Chris Jones. It was a brilliant partnership, honed on numerous pioneering climbs throughout the Canadian Rockies, but both men knew that North Twin would demand a whole new level of commitment.

They chose August, when most of the winter snow would have melted from what promised to be mainly a rock climb, interspersed with sections of hard ice and 'mixed' climbing. Then, in what they hoped would be a spell of fine weather, they set off up the wall. On the fourth afternoon, nearing the top of the third band – the final overhanging 'headwall' – they found themselves at an impasse. Lowe fell off trying to force a way through overhangs. Then he tried traversing left to an ice gully they had spotted, but couldn't solve the problem. And to make matters worse, it had started to snow. With no other options left, the two men settled down for their fourth bivouac.

Chris Jones later described it in the seminal journal *Ascent*.

'We perched on ice-encrusted ropes with our feet thrust into our climbing sacks. After a cup of soup and a mouthful of cheese we settled into the bivouac sack. My mind raced. We were in a hell of a spot. We had almost no climbing gear. With our limited means the headwall appeared impossible. The ice gully seemed like madness. Retreat was out of the question; that option had been closed since the day before. The storm was now serious.'

Despite the grim outlook and the continuing storm, they managed to sleep, and in the morning George Lowe tried the traverse again. This time he managed to continue, crampons scratching on snow-sprinkled slabs. Then he found a huge lump of the last winter's snow pasted to the underside of an overhang. Pressing his knees into the snow and reaching behind it to cling to the underside of the

> '**I can still see the softball-sized foothold that I'd broken spinning out into space, accelerating and nailing Cheesmond in the right thigh 30 feet [9 metres] below.'**

overhang, he managed to shuffle tenuously sideways until, at last, he found a crack to hammer in a piton, clip in the rope, and tension the final sideways reach into the ice gully. The gully was ferociously steep, but there was just enough ice to support axes and crampons. Above it the wall finally lay back at an easier angle, and that night, after climbing all day through driving snow, they reached the summit.

For a younger generation, aspiring to bold adventures, the north face of North Twin was an inspiration. The Canadian climbing guide Barry Blanchard stated unequivocally, 'I'll suggest that, in 1974, the route that George and Chris opened on the north face of North Twin was the hardest alpine route in the world.'

Over the following years, many teams tried to repeat the route, but all were defeated by bad weather, rockfall and the sheer daunting difficulty. Climbers also wondered about a new route up the wall. Jones and Lowe had climbed up the left side of the giant triangle, but what about the prominent, bald rock pillar on the right-hand side? Lowe himself drove north to Canada in 1985 to attempt the pillar, hoping to claim a second glorious prize, but was stopped by dismal rainfall. A few days later, rising competitively to the challenge when the weather improved, Barry Blanchard arrived at the foot of the

wall with the South African immigrant, Dave Cheesmond, who had also been eyeing the pillar covetously for three years.

On 29 July they pitched their tent beside the glacial tarn beneath the face. 'The next morning we charged on to the face and sprinted up ledges of snow, scree and shale, cowering breathlessly against steep bands of rock as the sky screamed with rockfall. David gleefully stuffed his feet, adorned in the electric-pink socks that his wife, Gillian, had given him, into his rock shoes while bellowing the Monty Python song chorus: "I'm a lumberjack and I'm okay." … Then he logged his first masterful lead of the day, completely focused on the task at hand, oblivious to the roar of rockfall that was scaring the absolute crap out of me.'

Blanchard, for all his avowed terror, was probably Canada's finest exponent of mixed and ice climbing, and the plan was for him to lead the mixed, leaving the pure rock climbing for Cheesmond, who had brought a pair of rock shoes to change into. However, on Day 2, Blanchard did have a turn on the rock, borrowing Cheesmond's two-sizes-too-big shoes.

'I cranked and heard a sharp snap like a dry twig breaking. I grabbed a sling in flight and slammed to a stop. I can still see the softball-sized foothold that I'd broken spinning out into space, accelerating and nailing Cheesmond in the right thigh 30 feet [9 metres] below. He swore and rubbed his leg and swore again then caught himself, realizing that he was being self-centered – in the Cheesmond book that equated with being rude, even if you had a big, bloody contusion gaining heat with each beat of your heart. … From then on I led all the ice, and the rock that could be climbed in big boots, and he took all the steep rock.'

So on the third morning it was Blanchard who led across the second icefield, racing over 60° ice embedded with fallen rocks, relieved to reach the shelter of the vertical upper pillar before the sun loosened more rocks far above. Then Cheesmond

Barry Blanchard on another famous Canadian summit, Alberta, with North Twin's triangle brooding in the background.

put on his rock shoes for 'some of the best rock either of us had seen on limestone'. The gods were smiling on them that day and, just as the first pellets of hail began to strike the wall at dusk, the two men discovered a perfect little cave – complete with ice patch to melt for drinks – where they could shelter for a night shattered by thunder and lightning.

On Day 4 the storm passed and Cheesmond led up a stupendous overhanging 'off-width' crack, too wide for fists, so that arms and knees had to be wedged deep in the cavity. It was the sort of pitch that would scare most climbers on a weekend 30-metre (100-ft) crag. Here, 1,220 metres (4,000 ft) up North Twin, Cheesmond climbed on undaunted on terrain where he could often only clip the rope into a protecting wedge or peg every 15 metres (50 ft) or so, knowing that if he came off, he would fly 30 metres (100 ft) before being held. It was on the second pitch, when Blanchard was jumaring up the rope with camming devices, that the huge block was pulled off the main anchor, sending both men flying 9 metres (30 ft), to come up short on the backup anchor.

That night, their fourth on the wall, they slept on a narrow ledge, their feet hanging over the void. Cheesmond wrote later, 'I think we both knew how difficult, dangerous, expensive, and perhaps impossible retreat would be from here. I was hopeful the flake would go, but if it didn't, there was a distinct lack of alternatives.' Luckily the flake – a thin finger crack splitting the final wall – did give way. It was the hardest pitch of the route, and he graded it 5.10d, which means extremely difficult. And then the angle eased back, and they escaped from the great triangular maw to romp easily up gentler slabs to the summit of North Twin.

Reminiscing years later, Blanchard wrote: 'The North Pillar of North Twin was the greatest climb of my 26-year-old life; eighteen years later it remains one of my finest, partly because of the wall, but mostly because it was the last big climb that I did with Cheese. I will always remember Dave laughing and basking in the late-day sun on our final bivvy, proudly holding up the fingerless glove that he'd shredded while jamming that day. David Cheesmond died on the Hummingbird Ridge of Mount Logan in 1987 and not a week goes by that I do not think of him.'

El Capitan

Height
2,307 metres (7,569 ft)

Location
Yosemite National Park,
California

Origin of name
The first white men to
visit the valley called its
most majestic monolith

First ascent
Unrecorded. The first ascent
of The Nose (the first proper
big wall route on El Capitan)
1–12 November 1958:
Warren Harding/Wayne
Merry/George Whitmore

Other key routes
East Buttress 1953: Alan
Steck/W. Long/W. Siri/

Salathé Wall 1961: Royal
Robbins/Chuck Pratt/Tom
Frost

North America Wall 1964:
Royal Robbins/Chuck Pratt/
Yvon Chouinard/Tom Frost

Mescalito 1973: Charlie
Porter/Steve Sutton/
H. Burton/C. Nelson

Pacific Ocean Wall 1975: Jim
Bridwell/B. Westbay/J. Fiske/
F. East

Freerider 1998: Alexander
and Thomas Huber

Interesting facts
Although the first ascent took
45 days, the Nose was first
climbed in one day in 1975

The first ascent of the 915-metre (3000-ft) high Nose of El Capitan took forty-five days of climbing over eighteen months during 1957 and 1958, with 675 pegs hammered into cracks and 125 bolts into drilled holes. In 1993 Lynn Hill achieved the climbers' ultimate dream of climbing the route 'free' – reliant just on the friction of hands and feet on the vertical granite. The following year she upstaged her own coup by returning to do the entire route free in a single day.

Free on the World's Most Famous Rock Climb

Lynn Hill (1993)

Resting at the belay underneath the famous Great Roof, nearly 2,000 ft [610 metres] above the ground, I had plenty of time to contemplate the gravity of my situation. We had limited supplies of food, water and daylight left. Either I would make the first free ascent on my next try, or we would have to abandon our attempt.'

It was September 1993 in Yosemite National Park, and Lynn Hill was attempting what no one had ever achieved – a completely free ascent, without artificial aids, of the world's most famous rock climb, the 915-metre (3,000-ft)-high Nose of El Capitan. The first ascent had taken a total of forty-five days' climbing, spread over eighteen months between July 1957 and November 1958. Warren Harding and his various teammates hammered a total of 675 pitons into cracks ranging from incipient knife-blade seams to the infamous Stoveleg Crack, where they used enamelled legs sawn off an old stove from a San Diego refuse dump. In addition, they drilled 125 holes to hammer expansion bolts into the blankest sections of granite. The final push took twelve days, and on that day, Harding continued through the night, laboriously hand-drilling twenty-eight bolts by the light of his headlamp, to emerge from the abyss at 6:00 A.M. on November 12. He wrote afterwards: 'As I staggered over the rim, it was not at all clear to me who was conqueror and who was conquered. I do recall that El Cap seemed to be in much better condition than I was.'

Climbing is always evolving. In 1959 Yosemite's most celebrated pioneer, Royal Robbins, repeated the Nose in a single push from ground to summit. Finally, in 1975, it was climbed in a single day; most average candidates for the Nose still take three to five days – sleeping out in hammocks or on ledges, hauling up vast quantities of food, water, and gear – the current record stands at an incredible four and a half hours.

Traditional 'big wall' climbing tends to rely heavily on aid: Harding and his friends spent much of their time on the Nose standing in tape stirrups, called etriers, clipped into pegs and bolts. As subsequent parties repeated the route, the constant insertion and removal of chrome-molybdenum steel pitons chipped away at the cracks in the rock, in places transforming once hairline seams into pockets wide enough to take human fingers. Perhaps, one day, someone could use these to climb the route free.

By the '80s, free-climbing standards had exploded. Harder and harder moves on ever tinier holds up ever steeper walls, became possible, at least

Lynn Hill, relying just on the tenuous friction of fingers and rubber-soled slippers, free-climbs the world's most famous rock climb. The Nose is the great precipice, profiled on the left side of the valley, in the picture on page 56.

left, Harding's team had made a gigantic pendulum. The dizzy King Swing is still how most parties get across, but pendulums don't count as free climbing. However, a climber called Ray Jardine had discovered an alternative route, bypassing the Boot Flake by following a line of minuscule rugosities in the apparently blank granite. Graded 5.12a, it was the first really serious technical obstacle for Hill and Nadin, but they took it in their stride and eventually found themselves at the foot of a finger-thin crack cutting through a sea of smooth, pale granite, curving up beneath the dark triangle of an immense overhang – the Great Roof.

This is the most prominent feature on the Nose, clearly visible to the tourists who throng the meadows 610 metres (2,000 ft) below. Up until 1993, many climbers had managed to free-climb the first part of the crack, but as it curved around into the shadow of the great jutting roof, they had all been forced to clip their etriers to pitons and resort to traditional aid. Now, after a long day of false attempts and exhausted by repeated falls, Lynn Hill looked as though she was going to have to do the same. Unless she could somehow transcend mere physical tiredness.

for an elite of very dedicated people climbing all year-round, training every day: People like Lynn Hill, who by 1993 felt ready to free-climb the world's most prestigious big-wall route.

She had climbed in Yosemite ever since she was a teenager. And she had gone on to climb all around the world, progressing from talented tomboy to elegant world champion. Lithe, lightly built and not very tall, she proved yet again that there is more to climbing than brute strength. Of course, she did have the requisite finger strength that only comes from

'I had created a wild tango of smears, tenuous stems, back steps, laybacks, cross steps, arm bars, pinches and palming manoeuvres – I had unlocked the sequence.'

'Looking down across the valley to Middle Cathedral Rock I noticed a play of shadows form the shape of a heart. This heart on stone reminded me of the values that have always been most important in my life. I had a strong feeling that this ascent was part of my destiny

continual practice; lots of climbers achieve that, but only a handful develop the mental tricks – the bold, visualizing, creative determination – to pull off something really special.

For her first free attempt on the Nose, she enrolled a talented British climber named Simon Nadin. Together they worked their way up the legendary, hallowed landmarks of the route, passing Sickle Ledge, the Stoveleg Crack and Dolt Tower (named after Harding's companion, 'Dolt' Feuerer). Above that is the Boot Flake – a huge boot-shaped flake of granite weighing hundreds of tons, wedged miraculously onto the wall with no obvious means of support. To cross blank rock from the top of Boot Flake and gain the next crack line, way over to the

and that I could somehow tap into a mysterious source of energy. Even though I realized that in my exhausted state I could easily fall off, I felt liberated.'

So, yet again, Nadin paid out the rope as she launched herself rightward, slim fingers – much slimmer than a man's – reaching up into the tiniest pockets in the slender crack at the back of the roof, rubber-soled slippers smearing infinitesimal crystals on the smooth, plumb-vertical wall dropping sheer beneath her. Several times her toes skidded from the rock, but somehow her fingers clung on, and at last she reached the easy exit beyond the roof.

The next day, after bivouacking, she continued, but one section near the top of the wall completely

Hill climbing up into the shadow of the Great Roof.

stumped her. Nadin had to go back to Britain. So the next week Hill returned with another friend, Brooke Sandahl, this time rappelling in – sliding down ropes from the lip of the Nose, 915 metres (3,000 ft) above the ground – to work at the critical Changing Corners pitch. She was worried that with her limited reach she would never be able to crack it, but ironically her modest size was perfectly suited to a series of wild contortions: 'After three full days of effort in the smooth shallow corner, I was able to piece together a sequence of moves that went together like a crazy dance. I had created a wild tango of smears, tenuous stems, back steps, laybacks, cross steps, arm bars, pinches and palming manoeuvres – I had unlocked the sequence.'

Having solved the final puzzle, Lynn Hill returned to the valley floor and spent four days climbing the whole of the Nose free in one continuous ascent. It was a fantastic achievement, but it left her wanting something more. 'The following year I contemplated an even greater challenge: to free-climb the entire route in a day – 33 pitches, with the most difficult sections on the top third of the wall – a kind of marathon linkage in a class of its own.'

She trained hard all year. Then, at 10:00 P.M. on 19 September 1994, guided by the light of a full moon, she set off again up the familiar first pitches of the Nose, this time partnered by Steve Sutton. In the darkness they climbed fast – incredibly fast – reaching Jardine's teetering traverse by dawn, arriving back at the Great Roof at 8:30 A.M. It was still cool, and this time Hill made it on her first try. 'But my big disappointment came later that day when I fell on the Changing Corners pitch, not just once, but three times, leaving me completely exhausted. Desperate not to have my free attempt foiled, I realized that I needed to regroup and change my attitude.'

As she rested at the belay, she glanced across the valley. It was evening, and once again she saw the heart-shaped shadow on Middle Cathedral. As before, this image encouraged her to access an inexplicable source of energy. This time the fiendishly complex sequence worked and she didn't fall. She raced up three easier pitches. Then, riding a triumphant wave of confidence, she somehow found the strength to weave her way up the free version of Harding's final overhanging bolt ladder until, at 9:00 in the evening, twenty-three hours after setting out, she emerged on the summit.

South America

Autana
Chacaraju
Cerro Torre
Monte Sarmiento

Autana

Height
1,450 metres (4,757 ft)

Location
Southwest Venezuela, close to the Colombian border

Origin of name
In the mythology of the local Piaroa and Guahibo tribes, Autana is the remains of the Tree of Life which once fed the whole universe.

First ascent
Probably made by climbers from Caracas during the '70s. The route, which requires some rock climbing, passes through a cave that pierces the mountain.

Other key routes
Southwest Face March 2002: Hernando Arnal/Anne Arran/John Arran/Henry Gonzales/Timmy O'Neill/ Jose Luis Pereyra/Andre Vancampenhoud

Interesting facts
Autana and the other tepuis of Venezuela – the most famous is Roraima – are the isolated remnants, separated by continental drift and erosion, of a once unbroken layer of a pre-Cambrian sandstone over 300 million years old. After millions of years of isolation, the tepuis' summits harbour rich and sometimes unique ecosystems; some summits harbour plant species which exist on no other tepui, nor anywhere else on earth. Autana is pierced by a cave system 800 metres (2,625 ft) below the summit, which was once an underground river.

The huge 750-metre (2,460-ft) wall of Autana is a 'tepui' – a massive, flat-topped tower rising out of the Venezuelan jungle. José Luis Pereyra, the Argentinian extreme athlete, had already tried to ascend the wall but had been defeated by torrential rains, plagues of insects and collapsing bromeliads. In 2002 he returned with an international team, including Britons John and Anne Arran, to try again.

The Tree of Life

John and Anne Arran et al (2002)

You wake up each morning and you can't wait to climb. The wall is a beautiful canvas in red, gold and yellow, and the rock is incredibly hard, so that even the tiniest holds are solid. And when you're climbing really well, it unfolds like a perfect gymnastic sequence.' For Anne Arran and her husband, John, the southwest wall of Autana was the most enthralling adventure. But it was also a demanding one. José Luis Pereyra, the Venezuelan who made the first attempt on Autana's huge, vertical, 750-metre (2,460-ft)-high southwest face, reported 'plagues of insects, days of torrential rain, imminent starvation and prolonged suffering'. But no sooner had he returned to his home city of Caracas than he was planning another attempt. And it was just before setting out on that second expedition that he bumped into his friends the Arrans – fresh from an attempt on the fearsome Angel Falls and keen for further adventure – and invited them to join him on the Autana team.

Autana is one of the most spectacular 'tepuis' – huge tabletop sandstone mountains rising out of the Amazonian jungle. In the mythology of the local Piaroa and Guahibo tribes, Autana is the remains of the Tree of Life, which once fed the whole universe. One of its most extraordinary features is a 40-metre (130-ft)-high cave, which goes right through the mountain. This beautiful feature attracts occasional adventurous visitors from Caracas, but until 2001 no one had touched the immense wall to its left. It took Pereyra eleven days to hack through just 8 km (5 miles) of jungle leading from the local village to the foot of the wall. And that was after a long approach in a dugout 'bongo' canoe, first up the Rio Orinoco, then the Sipapo and then the Rio Autana itself, with the mountain growing steadily closer, framed between enclosing walls of jungle.

For Anne Arran, joining the second attempt in 2002, this exotic approach was a huge part of the appeal. 'I like to explore. I climb because it takes me to new places, new cultures.' Here that involved delicate negotiations to get permission from the local tribe before returning to the wall. This time, with a trail, the hike through the jungle took just five hours. And on the wall itself, fixed ropes were still hanging up to the 2001 high point. But there was still a lot of unclimbed rock above, much of it fiercely overhanging – the sort of terrain where you can spend a whole day tackling just one 50-metre (164-ft) rope length. So the team was going to have to live on the wall for many days, hauling up sleeping gear, food and water.

To share that labour, Pereyra had assembled a team of ten climbers. Most of the way, the lead

Anne Arran enjoying Autana's ancient sandstone.

> **'I had never spent more than one night on a wall. I'd never slept in a hammock before, dangling in space – terrifying, until I realized it was much more comfortable than lying on a lumpy ledge. But it was hard work.'**

climbers were going to use artificial aid – hanging from wedges, cams or minuscule steel knife-blade pegs, wedged and hammered into incipient cracks. Or, where cracks petered out, teetering on tiny steel 'sky hooks', pivoting on minute rugosities. But at the end of each 'pitch', or rope length, they would construct a 'bomb proof' anchor if necessary, drilling the rock to hammer in two expansion bolts. From these anchors. fixed ropes were suspended, allowing the whole team to move up the wall and take turns out in front.

The Arrans had a special target: Safeguarded by the anchors placed ahead of them, they planned to 'free climb' the entire route, making progress purely with their hands and with the rubber-soled slippers on their feet, using only the rock holds nature provided. For both of them it was their first multiday expedition climb. As Anne recalls, 'I had never spent more than one night on a wall. I'd never slept in a hammock before, dangling in space – terrifying, until I realized it was much more comfortable than lying on a lumpy ledge. But it was hard work. And we had to ration ourselves to drinking only about two litres of water a day, even in that humid heat.'

The reward for the Arrans was the thrill of solving intensely gymnastic problems on the rock. John led nearly every pitch 'on sight', with no previous practice, with extremely difficult sections. The compact nature of the rock meant that he could only place very occasional points of protection to clip the rope into, so he risked huge falls of up to 30 metres (100 ft), should his fingers slip. Timmy O'Neil, the American team member, marvelled at 'the British tendency to risk life and limb in pursuit of a pure ascent. Whatever the reasons, they generally have nerves of steel, and they perform well under duress. In fact, John is so tranquil I offer to check for a pulse as I jug past.'

Jugging is slang for sliding jumars – camming devices – up the fixed ropes to get to the high point. On this wall the ropes often hung free in space. But in the midst of all that verticality, Anne was delighted to arrive at Double Decker Ledge. 'It was fantastic: two perfect, flat ledges, with room to lie down comfortably, one above the other. And for another night, we found a cave, where we could crawl right inside the wall and lie down.'

As they neared the top, Timmy O'Neil led the way into a vertical jungle of bromeliads. 'I called them cabbages', recalls John Arran. 'They just seemed to cling to the tiniest ripples and crystals on the rock. But there was nothing solid for Timmy to aid on – no cracks … nothing. So I persuaded him to come down and try a different line further left.'

That searching out of a natural line through an apparently impossible vertical landscape is where the wall climber shows his real artistry. And for the Arrans, once their companions had led the way on aid, there was the added challenge of finding ways to climb the wall free. And a final sting in the tail was described later by Anne.

'There was only a short slab between the top and us. Timmy and José had just topped out and a huge storm descended. I had only climbed a few metres when a waterfall blasted down on top of me. To make things worse, one of the ropes jammed. I quickly abandoned the idea of climbing and transferred onto the jumar line. First my hands went numb, and then my wrists, and I sensed the seriousness of the situation we were now in. It was impossible to communicate with John because of the noise of the water, and passing the knot in the rope with a sack wasn't going to plan. In what felt like an eon, I succeeded in overcoming the knot. Unable to look up because of the force of the water, I tried to keep going before hypothermia set in. Jumaring in a waterfall in your bra top is not a pleasant experience. I was also conscious of Hernando and Henry the photographer getting cold on the ledge below, and the skeletal John who must be shivering violently above. Finally I reached the stance, shaking and gasping for breath, and put my waterproof on.'

Soon afterwards the rest of the team arrived on Autana's flat jungly summit. After eleven days on the wall, their journey was complete.

John Arran, by profession an international election observer, follows his true vocation, powering his way boldly up an overhanging corner 610 metres (2,000 ft) above the Venezuelan jungle.

Chacaraju

Height
Chacaraju Oeste: 6,211
metres (20, 378 ft)
Chacaraju Este 6,001 metres
(19,689 ft)

Location
Cordillera Blanca, Andes,
Peru

Origin of name
Chakra means 'arable fields'
and probably refers to the
parallel lines, like ploughed
fields, of the mountain's
snow flutings. Mataraju is
the name used by people to
the east of the mountain,
meaning 'twin summits'.

First ascent
Chacaraju Oeste
31 July 1956: Maurice
Davaille/Claude Gaudin/
Raymond Jenny/Robert
Sennelier/Pierre Souriac/
Lionel Terray by North Face/
Northeast Ridge

Chacaraju Este
5 August 1962: René
Dubost/ Paul Gendre/Guido
Magnone/Jacques Soubis/
Lionel Terray by Northeast
Ridge/East Face

Other key routes
Oeste Northwest Ridge
1964: H. Abrons/D. Doody/
Tom Frost/ L. Ortenburger

Este South Face/Southeast
Ridge 1976: Kunihiko
Kondo/Masatoshi Hoshino

Este South Face Direct 1978:
Nicholas Jaeger

Oeste North Face 1986:
Petr Hapala/Bretislav
Husicka

Peru's Andean summits are amongst the world's most spectacular: impossibly pointed and elusive, protected by dazzling ridges which sprout gravity-defying snow mushrooms, bulging terrifyingly over the void. Of all these glittering fantasy mountains, perhaps the most extraordinary is Chacaraju, first climbed by the great French climber Lionel Terray.

Crystal Confectionery

Lionel Terray (1956)

Lionel Terray seemed indestructible. He was a powerhouse of enthusiasm and energy, and whatever he turned his hand to – ski racing, farming, climbing, writing, filming – it was with total commitment. His first really great climb – the one that made people sit up and take notice – was in 1947, when he and fellow French guide, Louis Lachenal, made the second ascent of the notorious Eigerwand. Three years later, in an epic Himalayan retreat, it was Terray, along with Gaston Rébuffat, who saved the lives of Lachenal and expedition leader Maurice Herzog, both badly frostbitten as they struggled back from the summit of Annapurna, the first 8,000-metre (26,250-ft) peak to be climbed.

The trauma of Annapurna virtually finished Lachenal's climbing career. But for Terray it marked the start of an extraordinary sequence of global expeditioning, which ended in 1965 when he fell to his death in the Vercors, near Grenoble. During those fifteen years, he achieved a string of first ascents that has hardly ever been equalled. It included Makalu, the world's fifth-highest mountain, and Jannu, one of the hardest peaks in the Himalayas. In Patagonia he climbed the granite fortress of Mt Fitzroy; in Alaska he led his team to success up Mt Huntingdon. In 1962 he calculated that in the previous seven years he had taken part in seven

distinct expeditions, spent twenty-seven months overseas, completed approximately 108 ascents in the Alps, given nearly 700 lectures and driven more than 151,000 km (94,000 miles).

All that frenetic activity seems to have been driven by a thirst for new experience and a willingness to seize opportunities. After the first ascent of Fitzroy in 1952, he continued northward up the Andes, climbing the range's highest summit, Aconcagua, and then joining two regular Dutch clients who had asked him to guide them in Peru's Cordillera Blanca. These were serious, ambitious clients and with Terray's help they made the first ascent of one of the highest peaks: Huanstan.

Terray left for home enchanted by Peru: 'The old Inca empire had shown me another world, another point of view, a new kind of poetry. … As I returned to the kind soil of France I retained a heavy sense of nostalgia for that country of high relief where adventure still lurks at the roadside, and to return became one of my most constant dreams.'

The dream was fulfilled in 1956, when his Dutch friends employed him to guide them on two new ascents near the old Inca capital, Cuzco. These were fine climbs, but Terray also had his eye on greater things. He wanted to attempt one of the still unclimbed 6,000-metre (19,685-ft) peaks in the

Cordillera Blanca, in particular the double-spired peak of Chacaraju. So, after saying goodbye to his Dutch clients, Terray met a crack team of French climbers to attempt the first ascent.

From the south Chacaraju looks rather like an old-fashioned tent, with two steeply tilted walls suspended from a narrow ridge. At each end of the ridge a narrow triangle culminates in a point – the east and west summits. Luckily for the French team the highest, western summit – Chacaraju Oeste – looked slightly more reasonable than the east summit. Nevertheless, it proved a very tough climb. They approached it like a major Himalayan route, fixing ropes methodically up the lower part of the north face. On the final push, beyond the fixed ropes, Terray led much of the way, cutting steps all the way to the summit.

'It was a moment of supreme happiness. From every point of the horizon the great ice and rock peaks of the Cordillera Blanca, flaming with evening colour, seemed to salute us.' And yet that moment of fulfilment did nothing to curb his restless spirit. The hungry quest for summits continued, and living constantly on the edge, Terray had several near misses. Also, according to one of his Dutch friends, there was an increasingly desperate streak to Terray's frenetic activity. Many years after Terray's death, this friend told a younger Dutch climber, Ronald Naar, that 'he was often depressed. He climbed poorly and took a lot of medicine. He took several falls while climbing with us, including one terrifying plunge. … He seemed to be possessed by one thing alone: the ascent of the "impossible mountain". … Gradually it became clear that he was thinking of the east peak of Chacaraju.'

In 1961 he began writing his autobiography, *Conquistadors of the Useless*. The title celebrates the innocence of climbing purely for personal fulfilment, but also hints at the potentially self-destructive nature of the addiction. It seemed that Terray was always desperately seeking something more. Having completed the book, in 1962 he co-led the first ascent of Jannu, the hardest peak that had ever been climbed in the Himalayas. And then, a few weeks later, he was back in Peru, once again climbing Chacaraju. This time it was the lower east summit: 'A dream I had been cherishing for six years. From the summit of the west peak in 1956 … we had been able to pick out every detail of this apparently unclimbable arrowhead of rock and ice. So formidable did it seem that after our success on the higher summit, we abandoned the idea of attempting it.'

Now, six years later, leading a formidable team that included the brilliant Guido Magnone, he rose to the challenge, forging a route up the harrowing cornices of the northeast ridge. As the ridge reared up into a great overhanging rock wall, they teetered left, following precarious icy ledges and rock pitches, across the almost vertical wall of the east face, finishing up on the final crazy snow flutings on the edge of the south face. All this took place over many days, and on the hardest, most intricate section, they had to fix more than 2,000 metres (6,500 ft) of rope

> **'When I suddenly realized what these green specks were, I became extremely frightened – they were the hills on the other side of the mountain showing through the thin sheet of snow!'**

to safeguard just 800 metres (2,600 ft) of vertical ascent. 'Lengthy and exhausting as the task was, it brought its reward on 8 August, when five of us attained the delicate ice fretwork of the summit.'

Three years later Terray died. In the late '70s, with more sophisticated equipment, climbers began to climb these spectacular Peruvian summits in teams of two, 'alpine style', without fixing ropes. But as Ronald Naar put it in 1982, 'Chacaraju still lies at the limits of what is possible.' As Naar completed a new route up the south face he suddenly noticed green specks appearing in the ice. 'When I suddenly realized what these green specks were, I became extremely frightened – they were the hills on the other side of the mountain showing through the thin sheet of snow! Swiftly I dug a hole through the crest, and a chasm yawned before me. To my left and right was a razor-sharp ridge, impossible to climb; a little higher the summit of Chacaraju Este, an invincible

and extremely unstable bastion.' He decided it was too dangerous to climb those last 25 metres (82 ft). Other, modern climbers have been slightly luckier with the conditions and made it right to the top, but Chacaraju Este remains a nearly impossible summit to attain.

Above: Lionel Terray at home in the Alps with two famous heroes of Everest: Tenzing Norgay and his Genevan companion on the 1952 Everest attempt, Raymond Lambert.

Opposite: A distant view of Chacaraju's snow-fluted south face, with the west summit on the left, and east on the right. The photo on page 68 shows the daunting spire of the west summit from the side Terray's team climbed it in 1956.

Cerro Torre

Height
3,128 metres (10,262 ft)

Location
South Patagonian ice cap, Andes, Argentina

Origin of name
Cerro is a common generic Andean name for 'mountain'. Torre means 'tower'.

First acknowledged ascent
13 January 1974: Daniele Chiappa/Mario Conti/ Casimiro Ferrari/Pino Negri by West Face/Southwest Ridge

Other key routes
Southeast Ridge 'Compressor Route' 1971: Enzio Alimonta/Carlo Claus/Cesare Maestri

East Face 'Devil's Diretissima' 1986: Janez Jeglic/Silvo Karo/Peter Podgornik/Pavle Kozjek

South Face 'Infinito Sud' 1996: R. Manni/Ermanno Salvaterra/P. Vidi

North Face 'El Arca de los Vientos' 2006: Alessandro Beltrami/Rolando Garibotti/ Ermanno Salvaterra

Interesting facts
By drilling his bolt ladder up the Southeast Face, Cesare Maestri created a comparatively secure route up what would otherwise be an incredibly difficult peak. Nowadays the 'Compressor Route' is climbed frequently – albeit during very brief weather windows – whereas most of the mountain's other routes remain unrepeated.

When Cesare Maestri fought his way to the summit of Cerro Torre his ascent was hailed as one of the greatest climbing feats of all time. Until the doubters began to question his sketchy tale. Maestri's sole companion had been killed on the descent; and with no witness to corroborate his extraordinary tale, Maestri soon found himself defying a growing band of sceptics who were convinced that he had actually never been anywhere near the summit of Cerro Torre.

Hoaxer or Maligned Hero?

Cesare Maestri (1959 & 1971)

The wind was rising as Cesare Maestri and Toni Egger reached the summit. Blasted by stinging ice particles, they fought their way back down through the giant overhanging snow mushrooms to the ice cave they had left that morning. Here they huddled for a second night, their fourth bivouac on the mountain. Then for two days they abseiled down the smooth walls of the north face, as ice and snow avalanches crashed past them. The wind was so violent that the first man down had to be lowered on the end of the ropes, acting as a weight to stop them from being whipped away. They spent the fifth night lashed to the wall, hanging beneath a large ice bollard. By the evening of the sixth day they were close to the ropes they had fixed on the bottom section of the wall, but with darkness approaching fast, Maestri decided they should stop for a final night in the open. Egger, fearful of avalanches, insisted on continuing down to escape the mountain; as Maestri lowered him in the darkness, a huge avalanche crashed down, snapping the rope, and sweeping Egger to his death.

Frozen, shocked and exhausted, Maestri struggled down alone the next day. 'Hours go by until I get to the fixed ropes, along which I descend. The wall is hell; just a few metres above the glacier my feet slip and I don't manage to hold myself with my hands and therefore I fall … The spirit of survival takes me across the tormented glacier to a point some 300 metres (nearly 1,000 ft) from Camp 3 where Cesarino had stayed alone for six days waiting, and therefore it is he who finds me a few hours later.'

Thus, 3 February 1959, ended the astounding first ascent of Cerro Torre – the mountain many people thought unclimbable. When the news got out, Lionel Terray, the Frenchman who was probably the finest mountaineer alive in 1959, called it 'the greatest climbing feat of all time'.

Cerro Torre may not be very high, but it is the epitome of inaccessibility, the ultimate fantasy mountain; a soaring spire of smooth vertical granite, towering above the Patagonian ice cap, blasted by the malevolent westerlies that come screaming out of the Pacific Ocean. When they are cold, those winds plaster the tower with monstrous encrustations of white rime, stuck like icing to the rock. The actual summit is encased in a gigantic bulbous rime mushroom, which changes shape from day to day. And when the temperature rises, huge chunks of the mushroom collapse, crashing down on the walls below.

Lionel Terray was not exaggerating when he praised Maestri so fulsomely. Not only had the Italian made the first ascent of Cerro Torre, but he had pulled off this incredibly dangerous feat with just one companion in under a week: In terms of skill, speed

Cesare Maestri. He remains a hero in his native Trento, but most experts find hard to believe his claim to have climbed Cerro Torre in 1959. The picture on page 70 shows Mt Fitzroy in the background, with the fantastically iced summit of Cerro Torre in the right foreground. The route claimed by Maestri rises straight out of the V-shaped gash that he called the Col of Conquest.

Maestri's excessive drilling infuriated mountaineers around the world, who felt that he had desecrated a beautiful mountain. But he was unrepentant. In an interview in 1972 he insisted that he just wanted to do something new. In the same interview he talked about his tough adolescence, fighting with the Italian partisans during the Second World War, and about his early, driven climbing career, soloing some of the hardest routes in his native Dolomites. 'I followed a rigorous diet, went to bed at 8:00 P.M. and exercised the whole time, whatever I was doing. Even when I made love to a girl I did it in the press-up position to strengthen my arms.'

The same machismo pervaded his climbing partnerships: 'After my first climb I never followed another person up a route and I never will. The day I feel I want to hand over the lead to another man will be the day I give up climbing.' The interviewer, climbing journalist Ken Wilson, then mentioned the brilliant Austrian, Toni Egger, who was supposed to have led most of the first Cerro Torre climb in 1959. Maestri admitted that that had been an exception. Wilson then pressed him for precise details of the extraordinary summit climb but was fobbed off with blustering bravura.

By now more and more climbers were travelling to Patagonia to attempt the fearsome tower and its

and boldness this represented a quantum leap in climbing standards. The only problem was that not everyone believed they had actually climbed the mountain.

Carlo Mauri, another Italian climber who had attempted the Cerro Torre himself in 1958 and was to do so again in 1970, found Maestri's claim too fantastic to believe. Others began to doubt Maestri's vague account. He had no photos, and his only companion on the climb was dead; the third man – the Italo-Argentine, Cesarino Fava – had only been in a

> '**I** followed a rigorous diet, went to bed at 8:00 P.M. and exercised the whole time, whatever I was doing. Even when I made love to a girl I did it in the press-up position to strengthen my arms.**'**

support role and had not witnessed the summit attempt. Maestri's tale was simply not believable. Stung by criticism, Maestri returned in 1970 to climb a completely new route up the southeast ridge of Cerro Torre, spending seventy days hauling a diesel-powered compressor to drill holes in the granite, placing over 400 expansion bolts on the mountain. The compressor still hangs on the final headwall as proof that on this occasion Maestri got close to the summit, although by his own admission he did not surmount the final rime mushroom.

neighbouring spires. In 1976 three Americans succeeded in climbing the slightly lower Torre Egger, named after Maestri's companion, whose remains had recently been discovered on the glacier. The first half of the Torre Egger climb followed the same route claimed by Maestri in 1959, to the deep cleft between the two towers, which he had named the Col of Conquest (in egotistical contrast to Carlo Mauri's Col of Hope on the other side of the mountain). For the first 300 metres (nearly 1,000 ft) of extremely hard climbing, the Americans found copious relics of

Maestri's ropes and pitons. Then they stumbled across a huge bundle of cashed equipment, still well short of the Col of Conquest. Above that they found nothing. Not only that, but the terrain differed completely from Maestri's descriptions. Where he had romped easily, they found desperate ground; where he had described a technically demanding traverse, they found an easy ramp leading quickly to the Col.

As for the fearsome final wall of Cerro Torre, as they looked across the Col of Conquest from their own Torre Egger climb, the Americans were amazed at its vertiginous smoothness. How on earth had Maestri climbed up and down it in just four days?

Maestri claimed that in 1959 a seasonal carapace of ice, smeared over the smooth rock, had enabled his companion Egger to hack steps up the wall. For belay anchors they had drilled into the rock beneath, hammering in expansion bolts. But in any case the terrain had been surprisingly straightforward, he

said, at an angle between 45° and 60°. Years later, questioned at a conference, he stated, 'It was one of the easiest climbs of my life. It was certainly the most dangerous, and the only deadly one, but technically it was just a race, a race over a snow sheet.'

In 1974 Cerro Torre was ascended by a team of climbers from the Italian town of Lecco, led by Casimiro Ferrari. They approached from the southwest, via Carlo Mauri's Col of Hope. On this southwestern, windward side, there was indeed a solid sheet of snow and ice, stuck firmly to the tower, enabling them to claw their way up, albeit at an extreme level of difficulty, with some very hard rock pitches thrown in for good measure. As they emerged onto the mushroomed summit ridge, they were on the final section of the route that Maestri claimed to have climbed in 1959. It was extremely complex and difficult.

As for the 'easy' north face plunging down to the Col of Conquest, it looked desperate. From a

One of Garibotti's photos of the first universally accepted ascent of the North Face in 2005, looking down and across to the summit of Torre Egger, named after Maestri's companion Toni Egger, who was swept to his death in 1959.

Another of Garibotti's 2005 shots, showing the truly desperate nature of the ground that Maestri claims he climbed in 1959.

One of the team abseils down one of the very few easy sections of the route.

Translated for the layman, ED4 represents a standard of rock climbing unknown in 1959. Dry tooling is a technique on mixed rock and ice, where the angled pick of the ice axe is slotted into a thin crack or hooked over tiny wrinkles on the rock's surface. A skyhook is a tiny steel hook with an attached foot sling that can be pivoted precariously on a nubbin of rock. Burke was teetering at the very limit of possibility.

It was the same when an Italian team in 1995 attempted the northwest face, and in 1999 when two Austrians tried another line up the north face. All three attempts failed to attain the final mushroomed ridge. Between them they covered virtually all the terrain that Maestri, in his confused and varying accounts, claimed to have climbed in 1959. Not only was the wall phenomenally difficult, there was not a single trace of Maestri's passage, even on the Austrians' route, which corresponded almost exactly to one of the lines Maestri had drawn on a photo.

Some mountaineers hold to the belief that first ascents are a matter of trust, of assuming honourable behaviour. Even in the late '90s elaborate scenarios were still being created to prove that Cesare Maestri and Egger could have pulled off an astounding ascent in 1959, way ahead of its time. Others were less forgiving. One man in particular, Rolando Garibotti, was determined to prove that Maestri's ascent was a complete fabrication.

Growing up in Patagonia, Garibotti climbed from an early age, became intimately acquainted with Cerro Torre and became convinced that Maestri was a self-deluding fraudster. In 2004 he published in the *American Alpine Journal* a detailed, brilliantly researched analysis of events on the Torre since 1959. Drawing on the knowledge gleaned from all the climbers who had covered the vertical terrain claimed by Maestri – and comparing the evidence of their eyes to the garbled, inconsistent accounts given by Maestri and his only live witness, Fava – Garibotti demolished the few remaining arguments left to the romantic school-of-honour apologists for Maestri. The man had simply lied. He and Egger, supported initially by Fava, had climbed the first 300 metres (nearly 1,000 ft) to the gear dump. At some point, probably by the dump, Egger had been killed, probably by an avalanche, as Maestri stated. But they probably never

distance, seen in profile, it has an angle of 70° to 80°. Sometimes it does display a white carapace. However, by the 1980s the world's most skilled technicians were finally exploring Maestri's enigma wall and discovering that the white layer is a misleading chimera – an ephemeral fluffy skim of rime which, stuck at that steep angle, crumbles to the touch. Beneath it the rock offers few holds or cracks for protection. And the only solid ice tends to be wedged in these cracks. In 1981 two British climbers almost succeeded in getting to the top of Maestri's wall. One of them, Phil Burke, described a typical pitch: 'The grade would be modern ED3 to 4, with high standard rock pitches and particularly difficult ice pitches from 70° to overhanging, as well as dry tooling on one pitch, where I fell jumping from a skyhook for a good hold. The average angle of the wall is more than 70°.'

climbed much higher than that, they probably never reached the Col of Conquest, and it seems utterly implausibly that they ever reached the summit.

The case was closed finally in January 2006 by Rolando Garibotti himself, accompanied by two equally exceptional climbers, Ermanno Salvaterra and Alessandro Beltrami. Their aim was to climb very fast, in a single push, up the purported 1959 line to the summit. The first attempt was defeated by the weather. They retreated to the comfort of their camp in the Patagonian forest. Like all Cerro Torre veterans, they were accustomed to this frustrating game where you wait, sometimes for weeks at a time, for a brief, elusive window in the prevailing stormy weather.

This time they got their lucky break. Phenomenally fit and skillful, they raced back up their route, past the Col of Conquest and up onto the stupendous north face. As Garibotti put it, 'There are only a few natural lines – cracks, flakes and grooves leading to the top. To succeed, the alpinist must pick his way up the line of least resistance.' Like the contenders of 1981, 1995 and 1999, this team found not a single trace of the sixty-odd bolts Maestri claimed to have left. They followed a slightly different line from their predecessors so that no corner of the north face would be left unexplored. And even with their superlative technique and modern equipment, they found the climbing extremely hard. According to Salvaterra, Garibotti led with 'missile-like speed'. With his huge experience of Patagonian climbing, he managed to find a way through to the final mushrooms, and at nightfall on the second day the three men stood on Cerro Torre's summit. It was the fastest ascent ever of a new route up the tower. And it was the first ascent of the line first claimed forty-seven years earlier.

Maestri got very close to the summit when he bolted his way up the southeast ridge in 1970. We must assume that in 1959 he barely left the ground. Now, Rolando Garibotti is pleased to point out, the history books can be rewritten to give credit to the team from Lecco – Daniele Chiappa, Mario Conti, Casimiro Ferrari and Pino Negri – who on 13 January 1974, completed their route from the west. They, not Maestri and poor Egger, were the first people ever to stand on the summit of that supremely beautiful, dangerous, elusive mountain, Cerro Torre.

Monte Sarmiento

Height
2,404 metres (7,887 ft)

Location
Tierra del Fuego, Andes, Chile

Origin of name
Pedro Sarmiento de Gamboa was a Spanish sea captain who established an ill-fated colony on the Straits of Magellan in 1582.

First ascent
7 March 1956: Clemente Maffei/Carlo Mauri by South Face

(West Summit 8 December 1986: Daniele Bosiso/ Marco Della Santa/ Mario Panzeri/Paulo Vitali)

Other key routes
West Summit South Face 1995: Tim Macartney-Snape/John Roskelley/ Stephen Venables

Interesting facts
The first attempt on Monte Sarmiento was made in 1869 by Domingo Lovisato, whose name is given to the glacier and river flowing westward, on the south side of the mountain. Alberto de Agostini made several first ascents in Patagonia, the most

impressive summit he reached himself was San Lorenzo, which he climbed with two Argentinians, Alex Hemmi and Heriberto Schmoll, in 1943, aged sixty. After Agostini's death, the explorer who did most to unravel the complexities of Tierra del Fuego's mountains was Eric Shipton, who made several first ascents in the Darwin range.

Tierra del Fuego became something of a life obsession for Salesian missionary, Alberto de Agostini. For over forty years he explored the length and breadth of Patagonia, mapping, photographing and climbing. His first attempt on Sarmiento was in 1913 and the final successful one in 1956, when he was 73.

A Life's Mission in the Patagonian Wilderness

Alberto de Agostini (1913 & 1956)

When Captain Fitzroy published his account of the Voyage of the Beagle, he included a description by one of his lieutenants of a remarkable mountain at the southern tip of the Andes, in Tierra del Fuego:

> 'At the southeast channel of the Magellan channel stands Monte Sarmiento, the most conspicuous and the most splendid object in these regions. Rising abruptly from the sea to a height of about 7,000 feet [2,133 metres], it terminates in two sharp peaks, which seem absolutely in the sky, so lofty does the mountain appear when you are close to its base. …When the sun shines it is a most brilliant and magnificent sight.'

The sun does not often shine in this damp corner of Patagonia, but over the last four centuries this never deterred Europeans from exploring the region. Ferdinand Magellan was the first in 1521, followed in 1578 by Francis Drake. Then, instructed by the Spanish colonial government to try to intercept Drake on his return in 1579, came Captain Pedro Sarmiento de Gamboa, who had already made a bloodthirsty name for himself in Peru, capturing the last of the native Inca sovereigns, who was then executed in the great plaza at Cuzco.

In 1582 Sarmiento established a colony of 400 people on the Straits of Magellan, but when it was visited by a British ship in 1589, only one man remained alive. As for Sarmiento, he had meanwhile been captured at sea by Sir Walter Raleigh and imprisoned in England. His life was beset by misjudgement and misfortune, but he did at least have a beautiful mountain named after him.

Europe's progressive colonization of South America was often a cruel business, and in the far south the settlers viewed the indigenous Indians as little more than animals. Sir Martin Conway, a distinguished president of the Alpine Club who made an early attempt to climb Monte Sarmiento in 1898, commented on what a 'pestiferous nuisance' the native Indians were, hunting the domestic animals that Spanish colonizers had brought to eastern Tierra del Fuego. Further west, close to the Pacific, where dense rain forest cloaks the intricate network of sea channels guarding Sarmiento, he met a family of Yaghan Indians in their dugout canoe: 'It contained a man, two squaws and a baby, some of the most ill-looking and unclean specimens of humanity I ever saw. They were scantily clad, greasy-looking creatures, more like seals than human beings.'

Right: The base camp kitchen in the forest, on Father Agostini's first expedition to Monte Sarmiento, in 1913.

Far right: Forty-three years later, Agostini returned with another team. This time Carlo Mauri and Clemente Maffei reached Sarmiento's elusive summit.

Not all Europeans were so dismissive of the locals. Alberto de Agostini, a Salesian missionary who spent the best part of his life in Patagonia, seems to have had a great affection for the indigenous tribes of the region. He also, in his spare time, became a passionate explorer of this wild, windy land, with its immense ice caps, glaciers, mountains and, on the western Pacific side, dense temperate rain forest, surveying, photographing and climbing. His name is associated in particular with one mountain, Monte Sarmiento.

In 1869 Domingo Lovisato had explored the southwestern approaches to the mountain, which stands on a peninsula surrounded on three sides by water. Then in 1898 the British mountaineer Conway, so scornful of the natives, attempted to reach the mountain from the west. In 1913, as a

peninsula to explore a new route up the Glacier Blanca. This eventually led them back to the plateau beneath the north face. All that separated them now from the ridge linking Sarmiento's two summits was a short but very steep wall. But the snow was adhering so precariously to this wall, ripe to avalanche, that they beat a retreat. In the end, two members of the team skirted around onto the southeast ridge of the main, east summit, then finished directly up the south face. One of the men was Clemente Maffei. The other was a climber from Lecco, near Lake Como, a town that over the years would produce a succession of outstanding Patagonian pioneers. He was Carlo Mauri, and two years later he would stand with Walter Bonatti on the summit of Gasherbrum IV, one of the world's most difficult mountains.

On Sarmiento, Maffei watched in amazement as Mauri powered his way up ice of unimaginable steepness. In fact, it was not exactly ice, but a kind of rime, typical of Patagonia, plastered liberally onto the mountain by the prevailing damp and

> 'Under the influence of global warming, the Glacier Blanca had shrunk back, leaving a lake and bare rock cliffs in its place, making the approach a logistical nightmare.'

young man recently arrived in Patagonia, Agostini led an expedition to follow in Conway's steps, eventually reaching a high glacial plateau beneath the north face of the twin summits. But the attempt failed.

Over the next forty-three years Agostini continued his missionary work and his passionate exploration of Patagonia. Finally, in 1956, aged 73, he returned to Monte Sarmiento, as leader of a team of Italian climbers. This time the boat put them down in the Bahia Escandallo on the east side of Sarmiento's

stormy winds from the Pacific. Finally, on 7 March 1956, the two men climbed out onto the bulbous domed summit of Monte Sarmiento, giving Agostini the success for which he had waited for forty-three years.

Another thirty years passed before Sarmiento's western summit was also climbed. Then the mountain was deserted until 1993 when a Welsh party anchored in the Bahia Escandallo and attempted to repeat Agostini's eastern approach. But under the influence

of global warming, the Glacier Blanca had shrunk back, leaving nothing but a lake and bare rock cliffs in its place, and making the approach a logistical nightmare.

Two years later, in 1995, I had a chance to visit Monte Sarmiento with the Australian climber Tim Macartney-Snape; Spokane's county commissioner and top international mountaineer, John Roskelley; and expedition leader, Jim Wickwire, who had made the third ascent of K2 with John, back in 1978. Mindful of the Welsh experience on the east side, we anchored to the west of Sarmiento and found a new approach up the Lovisato valley. What was most striking about this mountain was its elusiveness. During two weeks in the area, we only saw the mountain two or three times; the rest of the time it lurked invisibly behind impenetrable cloud. Just to get onto the mountain, we had to hack our way through virgin forest, bridge a raging torrent, wade through muddy quagmires and trudge over endless ridges.

Once established on the mountain itself, both Jim Wickwire and our boat skipper, the highly experienced climber Charlie Porter, were injured when the wind flung them across bare ice. In the end, the remaining three of us, seizing the one really fine day we had during a whole month in Tierra del Fuego, were able to dash up a new route on the south face of the west summit to enjoy a few moments of total enchantment, gazing out over an infinity of mountains and sea, stretching as far as the eye could see in every direction.

We had hoped to snatch both summits, but it was too late to traverse the weird icy encrustations leading to the higher, east summit. As it was, we had to struggle just getting down from the west summit.

Since then, several teams have been to Monte Sarmiento, but none has reached either summit. This beautiful mountain, which so entranced that sailor on the *Beagle* and framed the extraordinary career of Alberto de Agostini, remains as elusive as ever.

Tim Macartney-Snape and John Roskelley starting the descent from Sarmiento's west summit on a glorious afternoon in 1995. Behind them rises the final part of Mauri's and Maffei's 1956 route to the east summit. The picture on page 76 shows just the west summit.

Australasia

Ball's Pyramid

Height
562 metres (1,844 ft)

Location
Next to Lord Howe Island, Tasman Sea, 642 km (400 miles) northeast of Sydney

Origin of name
The pyramid was named after an eighteenth-century British naval officer, Lieutenant Ball.

First ascent
14 February 1965: Bryden Allen/John Davis/Jack Hill/Jack Pettigrew/David Witham, by Southeast Ridge

Other key routes
North Ridge 1970: Keith Bell/Howard Bevan/Ray Lassman/Hugh Ward/Kevin Wilson/John Worral

Interesting facts
The Pyramid, along with other sea stacks in the area, is all that is left of a huge volcanic caldera that once towered above the Tasman Sea. The Pyramid is home to about 50,000 sea birds, including the wedge-tailed shearwater; it is also the last refuge of the Lord Howe Island Phasmid or Land Lobster, *Dryococelus*

australis – a large flightless insect about 15 cm (6 inches) long. Once abundant on Lord Howe Island, the phasmids were thought to be extinct after a shipwreck introduced rats in 1918. However, an expedition in 2001 found three living specimens on Ball's Pyramid; in 2002 more were found at the same spot. The pyramid is now banned to climbers.

This 'mountain' is a 562-metre (1,844-ft) rock stack rising out of the Pacific 643 km (400 miles) east of Sydney. In 1973 Australians Bell and Mortimer made a traverse of the pyramid, bivouacking twice on the route before being marooned for several days by a cyclone. Forced to swim through heavy surf to make their escape, they finally made it to the pick-up boat.

Ocean Mountain

Greg Mortimer and Keith Bell (1973)

Greg Mortimer was one of the first two Australians to climb Mt Everest. He did it without oxygen and by a new route. He has also climbed the gigantic North Ridge of K2. He has made numerous first ascents in Antarctica and now runs a highly successful polar tour company. He is a top international mountaineer. But it all started on the rock outcrops of his native Australia and his first real expedition was to an Australian mountain – a unique mountain that rises straight out of the sea.

Ball's Pyramid is the jagged remnant of what was once a huge volcanic caldera. It still towers 562 metres (1,844 ft) over the Tasman Sea, 643 km (400 miles) northeast of Sydney, and is probably the world's largest sea stack. The only way to get onto it is to approach by fishing boat from Lord Howe Island, a few miles to the north, and brave the crashing ocean swell as you leap onto abrasive rocks covered in barnacles and sea urchins.

By 1965 an estimated six parties had landed and tried unsuccessfully to climb to the top of the pyramid by its southeast ridge. That January, the seventh party got very close, reaching the foresummit known as Winklestein's Needle. (With fine Australian irreverence, one of the unsuccessful parties had spurred themselves on with repeated renditions of 'Balls to you, Mr Winklestein'.)

A month later another party landed at the foot of the southeast ridge and was finally successful, climbing beyond Winklestein's Needle to surmount the final pinnacle of Ball's Pyramid. Some of the team returned four years later to repeat the ascent, filming it for television. Then in 1970 a large party managed to climb a completely new route up the north ridge.

All these teams had laid siege to the pyramid, putting in fixed ropes to safeguard their progress on the mountain. When Keith Bell took part in the first ascent of the north ridge, the seven-man team he was with fixed ropes two thirds of the way up the route. They stripped the ropes after the ascent, but that laborious safety net did detract from the adventure. 'Why not try climbing the Pyramid "alpine style"?' thought Bell. Just two people, in a single push. And why not traverse the mountain, up the southeast ridge and down the north ridge? It was for this adventure, in 1973, that he enrolled Greg Mortimer, then aged 23.

They prepared well, getting Clive Wilson, skipper of the *Lulawai*, to land them first on the north side of the pyramid on the morning of February 26, floating ashore a 15-litre (4-gallon) drum of drinking water, another drum containing sleeping bags and a third drum holding radio, spare batteries, a copy of *The Hobbit* and other odds and ends. The drums were floated ashore and cached at the foot of the north

rock.' As they took turns to teeter over the horseback ridge, unbalanced by their 16-kg (35-lb) rucksacks, they were also buffeted by alarmingly strong winds. But they got safely across and climbed the final pillar to the summit, which they reached at 3:30 P.M.

Bell noticed 'funny clouds coming through – high cirrus clouds. However, we thought they just meant rain, which would not have bothered us much on the descent.' Nevertheless, making this first traverse of the Pyramid, they were now committing themselves to some very difficult terrain. That afternoon they abseiled 75 metres (250 ft) down the north ridge to a cave, where they spent their second night out. On the radio schedule that evening, Clive Wilson warned them that a cyclone – Cyclone Kirsty – was approaching.

'Wednesday, Feb 28. We decided to continue the descent, despite the approaching cyclone. What really worried us was the thought of a section I remembered from 1970, which had been pretty hair-raising even in good weather … a line of towers too rotten to traverse, where we had dropped 150 feet [45 metres] down the east face.' Now Bell and Mortimer, after two long abseils to the traverse, had to climb *up* those 45 metres, just as rain and violent wind swept in from the ocean.

They struggled through the towers in driving rain, at one point reaching a platform just 30 cm (1 ft) wide, with a huge drop to the raging sea on either side. They made three long abseils down the west face to a great flake of rock, where Bell tried without success to radio Wilson. So they carried on down, to a bivouac ledge he remembered from 1970. But there was no shelter here, so they carried on down for another two hours. Each time they had to pull the sodden ropes down after an abseil, they threatened to jam, and their ends were whipped away by the wind, catching on rock bollards, but eventually the pair reached a cave 60 metres (200 ft) above the sea.

ridge. They then sailed around to the south side, where they took ashore supplies and gear for the climb, and spare rations to leave at the bottom in case of retreat. Then they waved good-bye to the *Lulawai*.

Keith Bell wrote later in the *Sydney Morning Herald*: 'There was a real feeling of loneliness when the boat turned back for Lord Howe Island. There you are – just the two of you on a huge rock with 50,000 sea birds. It hits you how serious it would be if you hurt yourself.' It was daunting, but they made rapid progress that afternoon, climbing more than 300 metres (1,000 ft) up the southeast ridge and stopping to bivouac in a little cave.

They spent a comfortable night and continued on 27 February over Winklestein's Needle, and then another pillar, which led to the Cheval Ridge, so

'One of the things that worried us was that we got so used to the place, forgetting how dangerous it was. We kept having to remind ourselves that we only had to trip and it was 200 feet [60 metres] down to the sea.'

narrow that you straddle it with one leg on each side, poised over a drop of at least 450 metres (nearly 1,500 ft). At one point the blade of rock is pierced by a hole, which Sir Francis Chichester had noticed as he sailed past on one of his voyages. 'It's really narrow,' said Mortimer, 'and some of the rock is lousy – dolerites, basalts and magma… a mishmash of volcanic

reached a cave 60 metres (200 ft) above the sea.

They longed to fetch the supplies they had cached three days earlier, but they dared not descend any closer to the sea in the violent winds. Instead, they just sat and shivered in the sloping cave, rigging a rope across the entrance to stop themselves from sliding out and tumbling into the ocean.

That night was wild, and Greg Mortimer still remembers it vividly. 'It was a maelstrom, an amazing unleashing of natural forces – a great vortex of wind, water and birds, like a column, hanging in the air in front of us and seeming to blast right over the top of the Pyramid. It was frightening.' But at least the climbers were safe, unlike the birds. Bell wrote afterwards, 'They were just being plucked off the Pyramid and dashed into the sea, their wings flapping uselessly in the frenzy of whirlpools. Afterwards their bodies were floating round like debris, their black feathers showing up in the white froth.'

On 1 March the rain stopped and they managed to descend to collect food, water and dry sleeping bags, but the winds were still violent, at one stage blowing both men off their feet. That night they got through to Wilson, who said there was no chance of picking them up in the heavy seas. They would have to sit it out.

'Friday, March 2. We spent the day waiting around, reading and sleeping. We were beginning to wonder if we should have brought the whole of *The Lord of the Rings* instead of just *The Hobbit*. One of the things that worried us was that we got so used to the place, forgetting how dangerous it was. We kept having to remind ourselves that we only had to trip and it was 200 feet [60 metres] down to the sea.'

The sea was still in turmoil. That afternoon the *Lulawai* appeared offshore but was unable to clear the giant waves. On Saturday she returned. The sea was still surging 4.5 metres (15 ft) up and down, making any landing out of the question. But as Greg recalls, they were getting desperate: 'We were starving and very thirsty. We had been rationing water, and the little we had left was filthy with bird poo. We just wanted to get out of there. So we stripped off to swimming trunks, and prepared to dive in, leaving all our gear behind.'

The Tasman Sea at the tail end of a cyclone is a wild place. Mortimer was also worried about the sharks: 'Right from the top of the Pyramid we had seen these huge shapes in the water – very disconcerting. We crouched for ages on the edge, trying to time the surges, plucking up the courage to dive in. Luckily we were both strong swimmers.' Committed totally to the ocean, arms and legs fighting the huge swell, they powered clear of the lacerating rocks and forced their way out to the waiting boat, where they were hauled aboard like fish – cold, thirsty and exhausted, but immensely relieved to escape Ball's Pyramid.

Winching supplies during a filming expedition to Ball's Pyramid.

Aoraki/Mt Cook

Height
3,754 metres (12,316 ft)

Location
Southern Alps, New Zealand

Origin of name
Named after the eighteenth-century British navigator, Captain James Cook; but now prefixed with the

First ascent
25 December 1894: James Clarke/George Graham/ Tom Fyfe by the North Ridge

Other key routes
Zurbriggen's Ridge 1895: Matthias Zurbriggen

The Grand Traverse 1913: F. du Faur/P. Graham/

South Ridge 1947: Harry Ayres/Edmund Hillary/ R.Adams/M. Sullivan

East Ridge 1938: L. Bryant/ L. Mahan

Caroline Face 1970: J. Glasgow/P. Gough

Interesting facts
Lying near the ocean, right

Forties, New Zealand's highest mountain is notorious for fierce weather and heavy precipitation. In 1991, 6 million cubic tonnes of rock crashed down the mountain, leaving the summit 10 metres (33 ft) lower, with a very unstable new precipice overhanging

The east ridge of the middle peak of New Zealand's highest mountain should just have been a spring training climb for these local experts. But as they started their descent a vicious storm almost blew them off the peak, forcing them to crawl into a crevasse just beneath the summit. They remained trapped there for fourteen days as colleagues fought blasting winds to get a helicopter through to them. After the rescue both men had to have their frostbitten feet amputated.

Nightmare in the Middle Peak Hotel

Phil Doole and Mark Inglis (1982)

When Mark Inglis set off for Aoraki/Mt Cook on 15 November 1982, the expedition was intended just to be a training climb. After several years working for the National Park Board, he had finally been appointed leader of a search-and-rescue team. Keen to get to know one of his new team members, Phil Doole, before the rescue season got started, he had suggested that they climb the classic east ridge together. Both men knew New Zealand's highest mountain intimately; the east ridge was a serious climb, but not extreme, and two or three days' reasonable weather should see them safely up and down.

So on the afternoon of 15 November the two men took a ski plane to land on the glacial Grand Plateau, close to the foot of the east ridge. Before setting off, Mark had sent his wife, Anne, and 10-month-old daughter, Lucy, to spend a few days with Anne's parents in Christchurch.

At the Plateau hut, the two men cooked a meal, cutting down the amount of food they would have to carry on the climb. They left spare food and a stove at the hut, expecting to be back the following night. Then they traversed across a big snow shelf to the foot of the east ridge, where they sheltered for the

night in a crevasse, poised ready to start the ridge at dawn. Mark's tactic was deliberately lightweight: 'I climb light: always have and still do. You either carry everything for every eventuality and have to use it as the heavy loads slow you down; or you take just enough for survival, not comfort, and climb fast.' Nevertheless, he was annoyed to discover that he had forgotten his closed-cell foam mat – a standard, almost weightless pad that hugely improves insulation while sleeping on snow.

At 5:00 A.M. the next day they left their crevasse and broke through soft snow. Phil, the heavier man, broke deep through the crust, until they reached the ridge proper. Now they were on a spectacular knife edge, poised above the immense precipice of Mt Cook's Caroline Face. Soft snow gave way to hard, brittle ice, which broke off in 'dinner plates' under the blows of their ice axes and crampons. It was hard, laborious work, moving one at a time, for 700 metres (nearly 3,000 ft), 50-metre (164-ft) rope length by 50-metre rope length. And as they inched up the ridge, high-altitude mare's-tail clouds spread across the sky.

By late afternoon Mark was getting worried. The wind was increasing and the mare's tails were turning

into evil-looking lenticulars. But with the horrible
ice conditions on the ridge, he decided that their
planned descent back down would be too difficult:
better to push on to the middle of the three summits,
from where it would be a quick, easy descent down
the west side of the mountain to Empress Shelf,
and thence to the shelter of the Gardiner Hut.

That was the theory. But nothing had quite
prepared him for the full force of the southwesterly
jetstream when they crested the summit ridge at
6:00 P.M.

'Have you ever experienced a truly fierce wind?
One that beats your face until it's red raw with
your helmet strap, flaps your jacket hood, blows
your ice screws and slings around, picks you up

and moves you towards a 5,000-ft [over 1,500-
metre] drop? We had to yell – almost scream – to
be heard even close up. The one thing I knew
was that the wind was killing us.'

Unable to continue down to the Empress Shelf, the
two men just dived into the first shelter they stumbled
across – a large crevasse, called a bergschrund, about
50 metres (165 ft) below the summit. Here, in what
they called the Middle Peak Hotel, they cowered out
of the deadly wind and settled down for the night.

Mark later described it like this:

'Imagine a small home freezer – one that you
can't quite lie down in, can't sit up in, and with a
bend in the middle. Now prop the lid partly open
and have a fan blowing in ice crystals

continuously. Set the temperature to about -10° to -20°C (14° to -4°F). Put an empty climbing pack and your climbing rope on the bottom and hop in.'

Mark wore a woollen vest, cotton shirt, fibre-pile jacket and Gore-Tex anorak on his torso, with just pile and Gore-Tex protecting his legs, plus woollen socks, inner leather boots and outer plastic boots on his feet. Phil had similar clothing, but with two extra wool layers and a down duvet jacket. Both men had woollen balaclavas. For food, they had the remains of a packet of biscuits, a small tin of peaches, two packets of drink mixture and one emergency bar. Their water bottles were almost empty, and they had no stove, so the only way to melt snow and produce a trickle of liquid was to use their own precious body heat.

On the morning of 17 November they geared up to leave their icy prison. 'The wind sounded like a freight train, and 10 metres [30 ft] was enough to know it was even worse than before. So back into the alcove. Loosen the boots. Feet freezing. Sweat from the liners had soaked the dry socks, and even at the end of that first day I knew we would end up with some frostbite.'

They were trapped in their freezer. But knowing the standard Mt Cook weather patterns, they were fairly confident that things would improve after four or five days. So they settled into a survival routine.

The end of the grim ordeal, as the helicopter swings rescuer Don Bogie and climber Mark Inglis in his sleeping bag safely clear of the mountain.

catastrophic pressure imbalance. The southwesterly jet stream winds were to persist for nearly two weeks.

By 20 November Mark's frostbitten feet were so swollen that he couldn't squeeze them into plastic boot shells. He knew now that they needed outside help in order to escape.

Down in the valley, Bob Munro, the head of rescue, was getting increasingly concerned about his missing rescue team. It was only on the following evening that the winds relented slightly, allowing a helicopter to land climbers at Plateau Hut, where they confirmed that Inglis and Doole had not returned to their starting point. On 22 November a Squirrel helicopter managed to land another team on the west side, close to the Gardiner Hut, which Inglis and Doole had failed to reach. The pilot, Ron Small, reported that while stationary and facing the wind, the helicopter's forward speed indicator read 80 knots. As for the climbers, 'What was normally only a ten-minute walk up to the hut took them an hour on their hands and knees.' There was no earthly chance

> **'From the first day we rationed food. An average day was two biscuits and two or three spoonfuls of drink concentrate. Snow in the spare water bottle was melted by body heat under clothing.'**

'Every day we checked outside, and each time we were nearly blown to Kingdom Come. From the first day we rationed food. An average day was two biscuits and two or three spoonfuls of drink concentrate. Snow in the spare water bottle was melted by body heat under clothing.' What they didn't know was that the high-pressure system east of Tahiti, which normally counterbalances the Australian-Indonesian low, had collapsed that spring as a result of the recent El Niño, causing a of continuing up to the Empress Shelf and Middle Peak Hotel.

By now Mark and Phil were so weak and scrawny that they reckoned they only had another day or two to live. Phil, bigger and stronger, suffered in silence. Mark was the opposite: 'I probably pissed Phil off regularly by wanting to talk all the time; I've always looked on silence as a bit of a challenge.'

Then, that evening, they heard the helicopter approaching. Mark was too weak to move, but Phil scrambled up to the mouth of the bergschrund, perching precariously on the lip above a 300-metre (1,000-ft) drop. A bag descended from the helicopter, only to bounce down the cliff. But soon the chopper returned, 'riding an escalator of wind up towards the bergschrund' to drop three more bags. 'It was Christmas: sleeping bags, bivvy boots, thermoses of hot fluids, a primus stove, cans of food, chocolate and radios spelled survival – spelled rescue! We'd received the essentials for survival just in time.'

Survival, yes, but no rescue for the time being. The next day, the wind returned with a vengeance, ruling out all flying. With radio communication, Mark now spoke to his wife, Anne, but as so often happens in these desperate situations, their conversation was awkward and stilted, and the sound of her voice only made Mark more desperate to escape his icy coffin. For the next six days, despite the food and fuel, he drifted into an increasingly hazy blur of hallucinations and nightmares. The most vivid, recurrent nightmare was of himself stumbling along an icy pavement with his frozen feet, knocking repeatedly on the doors of unlit houses where no one replied.

By 27 November (Day 12) Mark was finding it increasingly hard to picture the faces of Anne, Lucy, and his parents. He now had a chest infection, and both men were again reduced to minimal rations. Then, the next day, they heard a helicopter. Then an almighty roar. An Iroquois chopper pilot, disorientated by blinding spindrift, had crashed onto the Empress Shelf and come to rest upside down with the tail plane hanging over a 300-metre (1,000-ft) drop. The crew and climbers inside were mercifully unhurt and were later picked up by Ron Small in his Squirrel, who had meanwhile flown up to the summit ridge and spotted what looked like two bodies but were in fact empty drop bags, left outside the cave by Phil Doole as markers.

Down in the valley, Bob Munro was under siege by an army of journalists. Rumours and counter rumours were flying through the air. Amidst increasing concern for Doole and Inglis, a doctor mentioned past cases of reviving hypothermic patients even when they had appeared clinically dead. This was overheard by a journalist who filed a report for that night's television news, stating that Doole and Inglis were clinically dead. Bob Munro reassured anxious mothers, thanked Mrs. Inglis for her offer to buy a new helicopter, wished he could find a journalist to hit, then concentrated on the weather forecast, which was at last looking more hopeful. Excitement mounted as everyone prayed that Monday, 29 November, Day 15, would be The Day.

At 4:00 A.M. there was no cloud over the Tasman Sea. The team of climbers standing by on the Empress Shelf reported clear skies above them. In the Middle Peak Hotel, Phil Doole lay, 'watching mossy threads of spindrift overhead. The light of another dawn spread into the tunnel. Waiting. Listening. Just the slightest shiver runs across the roof. Silence. Is it really calm outside?'

But down below, between the sea and the mountain, a layer of cloud lay over the Hooker Valley. By 7:20 A.M., when it was clear that the cloud was holding a ceiling of 2,700 metres (nearly 9,000 ft), the decision was made to go. And sure enough, Ron Small's Squirrel broke through the cloud into sunlight. Soon he was hovering over the Middle Summit, dropping another radio to Phil Doole, who was incredibly relieved to hear that no one had been hurt in the previous day's helicopter crash. He then reported that he could be lifted out in his harness but that Mark would need a stretcher.

So the chopper flew down to the Empress Shelf, where rescue expert Don Bogie got out and clipped himself on to a winch line, with a Bauman Bag – a large nylon stretcher that can be clipped into the line – attached to his waist. Then, as the cloud below began to bubble up and more cloud drifted in over the Caroline Face, the chopper took off again, dangling Don Bogie right over the mouth of the bergschrund. Then Bogie radioed to Ron Small to give him more slack so that he could crawl right down into the cave, where Mark was lying in his sleeping bag.

'All I can think is, "Jesus, Bogie, you look beautiful!" With Phil's help he moves me out

nearer the entrance. All the time, with the din of
the Squirrel hovering above, I am aware that
Don is still attached to the line. All I can think is,
"Awesome flying, Ron." Then it's into the icy air,
the familiar elevator-like lift and then the
unmistakable feeling of dropping rapidly,
spinning under the chopper. Cloud and snow
flying around, hands lowering the stretcher to
the snow, unclipping, seeing Don lift back up into
the freezing air. Faces crowd in, I lie strapped in
still, cocooned against the elements, the faces that
look as relieved and happy as I feel.'
A few minutes later the Squirrel returned, having
collected Phil. Both climbers were then flown down,
down, down, from icy whiteness into the greys,

browns and greens of the valley, where at last they
were safe.

Both Mark Inglis and Phil Doole knew that they
were going to lose frostbitten toes, but they hoped
that the amputations would be swift and simple,
allowing them to get back to duty in the National Park
that same summer season. So it was a grim shock to
discover that the damage from their fifteen-day ordeal
had spread further than they realized, causing
irreparable tissue damage right to the back of their feet
and up to their ankles. On Christmas Eve both men
had their legs severed below the knees. When they
next went to the mountains in 1983 – Phil Doole on
an expedition to Peru and Mark Inglis returning to
work for the park service – it was as double amputees.

Carstensz Pyramid

Height
4,884 metres (16,024 ft)

Location
Sudirman Mountains, Irian Jaya, Indonesia

Origin of name
Named after the Dutch navigator, Jan Carstensz, first European to sight the peak, in 1632. Also known by a local name – Puncak Jaya.

First ascent
1962: Heinrich Harrer/Phil Temple/Bert Huizenga/ Russell Kippax by North Face and West Ridge

Other key routes
East Ridge 1971: Reinhold Messner/S. Bigarella

American Direct (North Face) 1980: Geoff Tabin/Robert Shapiro/Samuel Moses

Interesting facts
Immediately south of Carstensz Pyramid there used to be a mountain called Ertsberg, meaning 'Ore Mountain'. This black knob of copper ore reached a height of 180 metres (585 ft) above the surrounding meadows, with another 360 metres (1,180 ft) of ore beneath the surface. It has now disappeared, providing the world with over 25 million tons of copper. The American-owned Freeport Copper Mine continues to excavate ore from beneath the surface, pumping copper slurry along a 120-km (75-mile) pipeline to the seaport of Amamapare.

Named after a Dutch navigator, the Carstensz Pyramid is the highest mountain in Australasia, towering above the jungles of Irian Jaya. When Heinrich Harrer (the Austrian famous for the first ascent of the Eigerwand and *Seven Years in Tibet*) climbed the Pyramid with New Zealander Phil Temple, the greatest adventure for him was the approach, walking for a month through remote forests, in the company of tribesmen who had not changed since the Stone Age.

Back to the Stone Age

Heinrich Harrer (1962)

In 1632, when the Dutch navigator Jan Carstensz reported dazzling snow towering high above the jungle coast of New Guinea, right on the equator, he was ridiculed. Even today the mountain that bears his name still has an exotic, almost surreal, aura of remoteness. Guarded by some of the wettest, densest jungle terrain on earth, where, until recently, local tribes were renowned for cannibalism, Carstensz Pyramid proved to be one of the world's most elusive mountains – not to climb, but just to approach. One of the neighbouring summits was climbed by a Dutch team in 1937. Then twenty-four years passed before a failed attempt by a New Zealand team. The next year one of the New Zealanders, Phil Temple, returned, this time acting as virtual guide to one of Europe's most famous mountain explorers – the Austrian who had taken part in the first ascent of the north face of the Eiger, attempted Nanga Parbat in 1939, then escaped from a British prisoner-of-war camp in northern India, to spend seven years living in Tibet. This man, Heinrich Harrer, later turned his experiences into a best-selling book and film, *Seven Years in Tibet*.

For Harrer the mountain was just an excuse – the catalyst for a great adventure. For him the greatest draw of New Guinea was its tribal people, who literally still lived in the Stone Age. In 1962 the western half of the island was still governed by Holland. The days of the Dutch colony were numbered, but Harrer was unperturbed when he arrived in January. As he wrote in his diary: 'People keep asking me doubtfully whether it isn't risky to carry on with my expedition in view of the imminent threat of an Indonesian invasion. I always give them the same answer: if you were to let your plans depend on threatening crises, and on political happenings in general, you'd never get anywhere or do anything.'

Those fine sentiments were backed by sound contingency plans. He arrived armed with maps, coastal charts, rope, thread, needles, sailing tackle and ponchos with which he could improvise sails. If necessary, he would build a boat fit to navigate the Arafura Sea and escape to the western, Australian, part of New Guinea or even to Australia itself.

From the airstrip at Merauke, on the south coast, he flew 900 km (560 miles) to Hollandia on the north coast, then 290 km (180 miles) back inland, southwest to Wamena, a Dutch settlement in the heart of the Baliem valley. From there it was a shorter hop to the airstrip at Illaga, staging post for the final trek to the mountain. A further flight was made to drop supplies close to base camp, 80 km (50 miles) to the west.

Harrer was no shrinking violet. This was his expedition, and he was leader. Phil Temple was 'chief scout'; Russell Kippax was the Australian doctor, and

Bert Huizenga was a Dutch government official in charge of porters – the local Dani tribesmen who helped the Europeans survive in the jungle.

Harrer quickly became educated in the hazards of jungle travel during an early training walk. Slipping into a rushing torrent, he was swept underwater and squeezed through a mesh of tangled tree roots. Later in the expedition he was swept down another waterfall and had to be stretchered out, trussed to a pole like a dead pig, with serious head injuries and a twisted knee.

Undeterred, he returned after three weeks' recuperation to become the first European ever to see the Stone Age quarry. Six months after his arrival in New Guinea, Harrer also completed an epic river journey – making the first descent of the Baliem river coast, all the way to the south, despite hostile tribes and difficult conditions. But his first objective was to reach and climb Carstensz Pyramid.

While Temple went ahead scouting out a base camp site, Harrer followed with Huizenga, Kippax and a small army of Dani porters, all completely naked apart from their traditional gourd sheaths and hairnets. Once they reached base camp, the climbers were aided by just fifteen men to help carry loads to higher camps, and to help with the return journey.

Heinrich Harrer, veteran of the Eigerwand first ascent and author of *Seven Years in Tibet*, was a compulsive collector of tribal art. His journeys through the jungles of Irian Jaya were the toughest of his whole career.

> **'These men had never worn a pair of trousers before in their lives, or had boots on their feet, or proper headgear. Left to themselves some of them would attempt to put the trousers over their heads, or their legs into sleeves …'**

For the Danis, these equatorial mountains were truly magical. They had never seen snow before and assumed it was a tasteless variety of what was for them a very precious commodity – salt. Thrilled by this white substance, they packed samples into tins to take back into the jungle to show friends at home, along with precious steel axe heads and cowrie shells, which the Europeans had brought for wages. To face the cold temperatures above 3,000 metres (10,000 ft), Harrer had brought a supply of clothing. 'These men had never worn a pair of trousers before in their lives, or had boots on their feet, or proper headgear. Left to themselves some of them would attempt to put the trousers over their heads, or their legs into sleeves … [then] each Dani had to be persuaded individually to abandon his sheath. There was just no room for it in an ordinary pair of trousers, because some of these pumpkin-like gourds came up to their chests.'

They continued upwards, 'through tropical moss-carpeted forest with bright flowers growing all around. … Finally we reached the edge of the forest and the tree line. A little further up we came to a pass, and there before us rose the broad north face of the Carstensz'. Harrer and his companions were the first people to see this scene, apart from the Dutch climbers who had been here in 1937 and the British explorer, Alexander Wollaston, who had tried to reach Carstensz from the south in 1913. That night Harrer wrote in his diary: 'If [Wollaston] had brought back a single photograph of this magnificent scene I am sure that the ice-covered peaks would not still be unconquered today. Such a photograph would have drawn mountaineers from all over the world.'

Before tackling the peak itself, Harrer and his companions checked the stone cairns left twenty-five years earlier by the Dutch, marking what had in 1937 been the edges of glaciers. The Carstensz Glacier had

retreated 440 metres (1,446 ft) and the Meren Glacier 726 metres (2,384 ft); today they have almost disappeared.

On 12 February Harrer recorded:

'The pattering of rain on the tent awoke me. It meant our assault on the Pyramid would have to be postponed. During the course of the morning the weather did improve, but just as on the Eiger after a storm, so it was here … there was sloppy snow everywhere on the North Face.'

The next day, the rain stopped at 3:00 A.M. At 5:00 A.M. it was still cloudy, but Harrer decided that it was pointless waiting for perfect weather. Their route lay up the right-hand side of the rocky north face. Phil Temple led; Harrer, Kippax and Huizenga followed.

'The limestone was so rough and with so many small flutings that with our rubber soles we could find a good footing even on almost vertical places. And with every foot we ascended the weather improved… there was no need for hesitation now… by nine o'clock we had reached the serrated west ridge. It consisted of innumerable sharp, almost black, limestone needles that looked like a relief map of some ghostly landscape. The fine points crackled and broke underfoot. You could have got hold of them only with those thick leather gloves iron puddlers used.'

Razor-sharp rocks alternated with snowy gullies. The clouds descended again, and the four men found themselves negotiating awkward 'mist towers' and sudden chasms, where they had to lower themselves on the rope. They got soaked and chilled to the bone and at one point sheltered beneath an overhang from violent snow flurries. They traversed from the south face back onto the north face. 'It was dangerous now, like a winter climb in the Alps. Once again we had to go through a gully. Carefully secured, we ascended laboriously, making our way around a pillar of rock and balancing along a snow peak. And suddenly it was all over. We were on the peak itself.'

They were the first people to stand on top of Carstenz Pyramid, the highest point, as Harrer put it, between the Himalayas and the Andes. Late that evening, fourteen hours after setting out, they returned to their tent, where they celebrated with half a bottle of Dutch gin and a 'fresh' cucumber, which Harrer had been saving lovingly in his knapsack for the last three weeks. During the next fortnight he and Temple, the other most enthusiastic mountaineer, climbed all the summits surrounding the Pyramid.

Harrer and his companions were humbled by the Dani tribesmen's mastery of their environment, beside which their own stumbling progress through the jungle seemed positively incompetent. Today Dani continue to help foreigners reach the Carstensz Pyramid, but they have become more familiar with western clothing.

Africa

Mt Kenya
Margherita
Blouberg

Mt Kenya

Height
Batian: 5,199 metres
(17,057 ft)
Nelion: 5,188 metres
(17,021 ft)

Location
Kenya, East Africa

Origin of name
'Kiinya' is a Wakamba name
meaning 'Hill of the Cock
Ostrich', referring to the
pattern of white snow on
dark rock. Batian and Nelion
were the names given to the
two highest summits by
Sir Halford Mackinder, after
Masai chiefs.

First ascent
Batian 29 August 1899: Sir
Halford Mackinder/Joseph
Brocherel/César Ollier by
Southeast Face & Diamond
Glacier

Nelion 6 January 1929: Eric
Shipton/Percy Wyn Harris
by Southeast Face

Other key routes
West Ridge (Batian) 1930:
Eric Shipton/Bill Tilman

Diamond Couloir 1973: Phil
Snyder/T. Mathenge

Ice Window 1973: Phil
Snyder/Y. Laulan/B. Le Dain

Diamond Buttress 'Equator'
1979: Ian Howell/Iain Allen

Interesting facts
The present summits of
Mt Kenya are all that remain
of a volcano, once probably
8,000 metres (26,250 ft) high.
The glaciers are receding
very fast: The famous ice
routes of 1973, the Diamond
Couloir and Ice Window,
have all but disappeared.

Ian Howell spent all his working life in Kenya, devoting his spare time to exploring the mountains of East Africa. Perhaps his most remarkable adventure was the first serious attempt to climb the ribbon of ice descending from the Gate of Mists between the two summits – the Diamond Couloir. Despite a gripping attempt, he was unable quite to reach the summit.

Ice on the Equator

Ian Howell (1971)

For a man who has pioneered bold new climbs throughout the wild mountains of East Africa, Ian Howell seems remarkably modest. And engagingly sane. 'After my first season in the European Alps, when we climbed twenty-five big routes, I realized that we had been lucky and that in the Alps people often got caught in storms. I thought, "I want to climb, but I don't want to die in a storm." I heard that on Mt Kenya there was wonderful climbing but no serious storms; with nothing worse than some afternoon snow, I would survive.'

So in 1967 this Englishman emigrated to take a job with a radio telecommunications company in Kenya. With Iain Allen and other local climbers, he began to explore the hills and cliffs of that magnificent country, in particular the mountain that gave the modern state its name. 'Kiinya', meaning Hill of the Cock Ostrich, is how the Wakamba tribe, 200 km (125 miles) to the southeast, describe the mountain's pattern of white snow on dark rock. Like Africa's highest mountain, Kilimanjaro, Mt Kenya is an extinct volcano; unlike Kili, most of Mt Kenya's dome has eroded, leaving a spectacular central 'plug' of hard rock. This vertiginous tower culminates in two summits named after old Masai chieftains, Batian and Nelion. The gap between them is known poetically as the Gate of the Mists. And plastered onto the south side of this gap, right on the Equator, is the snow-covered ice of the Diamond Glacier.

When Sir Halford Mackinder made the first ascent of Mt Kenya in 1899, after a long, hazardous bushwhack all the way from the Indian Ocean, he and his Italian alpine guides cut steps across this glacier to reach the final rocks of the highest peak: Batian. Thirty years passed before another ascent was made, this time by a colonial district commissioner named Percy Wyn Harris and a coffee planter called Eric Shipton, both of whom would later climb to more than 8,500 metres (27,888 ft) on Mt Everest. Failing to follow Mackinder's original route, they inadvertently made the first ascent of the second peak, Nelion, before crossing the Gate of the Mists to Batian.

For present-day climbers the Shipton Route is now the 'normal' way up the mountain – a fine rock climb, with sections of moderately hard climbing. But there are much harder routes to the summit, many of them pioneered in the '60s and '70s by Iain Allen, along with Ian Howell. 'My favorite,' Howell enthuses today, 'was the Equator – *beautiful* climbing on perfect rock up the Diamond Buttress.'

The rough red rock *is* beautiful. The approach to it is also beautiful, for Mt Kenya's summit tower sits atop an immense gently rising dome cloaked in

Ian Howell, who made thirteen journeys up and down Nelion's south face (see page 98) to build his famous bivouac hut right on the summit.

his ice axes popped, and his weight fell onto the peg. Snyder lowered him to the ground and took a turn himself, 'cutting elephant holes in the ice.' He succeeded in reaching the top lip of the initial 50-metre (165-ft)-high ice wall, but it was now ten in the morning – too late to reach the top that day.

So they abseiled down and returned early the next morning to climb back up the rope before continuing up the main couloir, following pale icy undulations between dark walls of rock. Near the top, fearful of a great vertical barrier festooned with giant icicles, they veered left up a subsidiary ramp, and it was right at the top of this ramp – when they were about to turn back right onto the upper, easier slopes of the Diamond Glacier – that they suddenly decided to pack it in. Mist, tiredness, a feeling that they had cracked the main difficulties – and Ian Howell's firm belief that climbing is about enjoyment, not summits – made them turn round. Two years later Snyder returned with one of his wardens, Mathenge, to complete the route all the way to the Gate of the Mists.

Ian Howell subsequently made the second ascent and later climbed the direct route up the final vertical

successive zones of vegetation, ranging from dense tropical forest to an alpine zone studded with the fantastic candelabra shapes of giant groundsels and giant lobelias and scoured by spectacular gorges. But perhaps the greatest fascination is to find snow and ice at the heart of Africa. And the single most dramatic feature is the pale, vertical sliver of ice that dropped from the Diamond Glacier – the Diamond Couloir.

Ian Howell hoped to avoid this equatorial ice challenge. 'I liked climbing on nice warm rock, but Phil Snyder, the Mt Kenya National Park

'I liked climbing on nice warm rock, but Phil Snyder, the Mt Kenya National Park warden, was very keen on ice climbing and he talked me into attempting the couloir.'

warden, was very keen on ice climbing and he talked me into attempting the couloir.'

And so, in the grey light of one early June morning in 1971, Ian found himself gasping at a height of 4,000 metres (over 13,000 ft), hacking with the hooked alloy picks of his pterodactyl axes at the near vertical ice that guards the base of the couloir. June was chosen because this is the winter season on Mt Kenya's south face. (At Christmas it is summer on the south face, and the couloir is melted down to hideous remnants of black ice and bare rock, with no comforting firm white snow to ease the climber's progress.) After a while he hammered in an ice peg and clipped the rope to it with a carabiner. Then at about 15 metres (50 ft) his cramponed boots slipped,

wall, claiming, 'I didn't really like ice climbing, but I felt I had to do it.' For him mountains are about pleasure, and on Mt Kenya the greatest pleasure is to be unhurried, free to sleep out on the summit and enjoy one of the greatest views on earth in the clear light of evening and dawn. Carrying heavy bivouac equipment cancels the pleasure, so in 1969 Howell decided to build a hut on the summit of Nelion, 5,188 metres (17,021 ft) above sea level. 'I designed it myself and built it in the garden in Nairobi, before taking it to pieces and breaking it down into pack-sized sections of aluminium panels on an alloy dexion frame. Then, on Boxing Day 1970, the Kenya Air Force parachuted it in five loads onto the Lewis Glacier at the foot of the Shipton Route. Over three

Ian Howell photographed by John Cleare during one of the 1972 attempts on Africa's most celebrated ice climb – the Diamond Couloir. The first complete ascent fell to Phil Snyder and Mathenge the following year. Today, global warming has reduced the Couloir to a meagre, patchy streak of dirty, black ice that is likely to soon disappear completely.

weekends I then made thirteen ascents of the Shipton route, soloing up and down, putting fixed ropes to safeguard the hardest sections. By the end I could descend from the summit of Nelion to the foot of the route in just twenty-nine minutes.'

The hut is still standing on the summit. Its floor is 1.8 metres (6 ft) by 2 metres (6½ ft); the back wall is 1.2 metres (4 ft) high, with the roof sloping down to

0.6 metres (2 ft) high at the front. It is said to have space for four people, but I have spent a night there with six other companions; we were cramped but cozy. Now that global warming has ravaged Mt Kenya to the point that the Diamond Couloir barely exists anymore, this improbable residence, right on the summit of Nelion, is perhaps the most enduring monument to one of the mountain's great climbing pioneers.

Margherita

Height
16,762 feet (5,109 m)

Location
Rwenzori mountains,
Uganda-Congo border

Origin of name
Because the mountain had
no local name, Abruzzi
named it Margherita after
his aunt, the Queen Mother
of Italy. In honor of the

British explorers who had
preceded him, he named
the second-highest summit
after the British Queen,
Alexandra.

First ascent
18 June 1906: Duke of
Abruzzi/Joseph Brocherel/
César Ollier/Joseph Petigax
by Stanley Plateau

Other key routes
East Ridge Integrale 1939:
T. Bernardzikiewicz/
T. Pawlowski

West Face Integrale 1960:
B. Ferrario/P. Ghiglione/
Carlo Mauri

Interesting facts
The Rwenzori range has a
rich and unique ecology,
with several endemic species
such as the local tree hyrax,

*Dendrohyrax aboreus
rwenzorii*. Most prolific of all
are the plants, with several
endemic species, such as
the Rwenzori blackberry,
Rwenzori sedum and
Rwenzori thunbergia. Wild-
life in the Rwenzori was
decimated by the troops of
Milton Obote in 1979 when
he returned from exile to
oust the dictator Idi Amin.

When the Duke of Abruzzi set sail from Naples on April 16, 1906, almost nothing was known of his goal. For centuries geographers had speculated about mysterious snowy peaks, shrouded in almost perpetual mist, rising at the heart of Africa, but as yet, no one had managed to set foot on the highest summits of the Mountains of the Moon. He succeeded in climbing them.

Mountains of the Moon

The Duke of Abruzzi (1906)

Although Henry Morton Stanley was not actually the first European to see the high snows of the Rwenzori mountains, he was the first to publicize them, and in 1901 he announced to the Royal Geographical Society: 'I wish that some person devoted to his work, some lover of Alpine climbing, would take the Rwenzori in hand and make a thorough work of it, explore it from top to bottom, through all those enormous defiles and those deep gorges.' Three years later, when the celebrated Victorian explorer died, those words were printed in his obituary. They immediately attracted the attention of another explorer, the Duke of Abruzzi.

Luigi Amedeo Giuseppe Maria Ferdinando Francesco di Savoia-Aosta was born in 1873 in Madrid. His grandfather was King Vittoria Emanuelle II of Italy; his father was briefly king of Spain, before assassination threats forced him to take his family home to Italy, where the young Luigi was brought up in Turin. From an early age he hunted and climbed in the Alps, developing a love of wild mountain country; at sixteen he was sent to naval college, and he rose through the ranks to eventually become an admiral of the Italian fleet. When his father died, he was given the title Duke of Abruzzi.

The navy gave Abruzzi a love of travel and a tradition of disciplined efficiency, which he applied to his own meticulously organized expeditions. He was an ambitious man with huge vision, determined to reach for some of the greatest prizes of exploration. It was his 1909 expedition to the Karakoram that first attempted the ridge on K2 that now bears his name. But his first great enterprise, in 1897, was the first ascent of one of Alaska's highest summits, Mt Saint Elias. Building on that experience, he then led an attempt from Spitzbergen to reach the North Pole. Unlike British polar explorers, he recognized the value of using dogs to haul sledges, and his team established a new record for reaching the farthest northern point on the frozen wastes of the Arctic Ocean. Then, in 1904, he spotted the Stanley obituary, with its provocative quote about the Rwenzori mountains. The gauntlet had been thrown down.

It was actually an Italian, Romolo Gessi, who was the first European to sight snow on the equator, on the border of British East Africa and the Congo. Ever since the fifth century B.C., when Aeschelus mentioned 'Egypt nurtured by snows that melt into the waters of the Nile,' writers and geographers had speculated about snowy mountains at the heart of Africa. In the second century A.D., the Alexandrian geographer Ptolemy declared that in Africa, 'There rises the Mountain of the Moon, whose snows feed the lakes, sources of the Nile.'

The Mountains of the Moon sobriquet has stuck, because it encapsulates the fantastical nature of these peaks, but their proper name is Rwenzori, which means, very appropriately, rainmaker. They are almost perpetually shrouded in cloud, and when Abruzzi's expedition set sail from Naples on 16 April 1906, the range of mountains that awaited him was still virtually unknown. One or two British explorers had attempted to reach the highest summits but had been defeated by thick fog and rain. The Rwenzori was still, to all intents and purposes, unexplored.

From the port of Mombasa the team of eleven Italians travelled for two days by rail to Lake Victoria. Then they took a paddle steamer to Entebbe. This was still the age of grand imperial exploration. When the expedition set off from Entebbe on 9 May, carrying food for two months, the eleven Italians were supported by 200 porters, plus their caravan leaders and the leaders' servants, the animal herders, and an additional escort of twenty-seven soldiers, with their own sixty-seven porters. This lumbering army marched nearly 482 km (300 miles) across alternating savannah and forest to reach Fort Portal, at the eastern foot of the Rwenzori, on 29 May. It was on a hill near here, during a brief clearing of the clouds, that the celebrated photographer Vittoria Sella took the first-ever photograph of the Mountains of the Moon.

From Fort Portal local Bakonzo tribesmen took over, portering for Abruzzi and his companions, showing them the route up the Mubuku valley, where, forty-five days after leaving Naples, Abruzzi established base camp under a huge overhang called Bujongolo. Here, at 3,798 metres (12,461 ft) above sea

'In this forest trunks and boughs are entirely smothered in a thick layer of mosses which hang like waving beards from every spray, cushion and englobe every knot, curl and swell around each twig, deform every outline and obliterate every feature, till the trees are a mere mass of grotesque contortions, monstrous tumefactions of the discolored leprous growth. … No forest can be grimmer and stranger than this.'

These things are all a matter of perception. It is a bizarre landscape but in the right mood, it can also seem utterly enchanting, gorgeously luxuriant. The vegetation in this primeval Eden is similar to that on Kilimanjaro and Mt Kenya, but on an even more grand and extravagant scale and with an even richer variety, sustained by the almost relentless dampness wafting up from the Congo and settling over the giant sponge that is the Rwenzori.

'When it was possible to light a fire, the Bakonzo men would cook themselves great pots of a glutinous kasava flour porridge flavoured with the stinking dried fish they carried up from the valley lakes.'

level, he found himself in an extraordinary landscape. Later, when his diary was written up for the official account, this is how the author Filippo de Filippi described the high-altitude forest of giant tree heathers:

Ever forceful, efficient and fearful of competition from potential British rivals, Abruzzi pressed on, following his predecessors to their high point and beyond, reaching the top of a mountain they had called Edward Peak and continuing to another summit, Semper. From this ridge Abruzzi, unlike his predecessors, was granted a brief clearing of the clouds. Suddenly he saw what no one else had realized – that the Rwenzori was not a single line of peaks, but a complex tangle of massifs, separated by deep valleys and the remnants of once huge glaciers. And there, on the far side of a deep valley to his west, was the highest massif of all.

That evening, Sella set up his huge tripod and plate camera to record a magnificent sunset over the entire Rwenzori range. Then the mountains disappeared for a week, as rain fell nonstop, and the expedition retreated to Bujongolo. Firewood became too sodden to burn, and the team kept warm by constantly digging squelching mud from around the tents. When it was possible to light a fire, the Bakonzo men would cook themselves great pots of a glutinous kasava flour porridge flavoured with the stinking dried fish they carried up from the valley lakes, or perhaps with the fresh flesh of a newly killed tree hyrax – a little furry animal related taxonomically to the elephant.

On 16 May, the weather improved slightly, and they set off once more. Sella took a wonderful portrait of the Duke flanked by his two mountain guides from the Val d'Aosta, César Ollier and Joseph Petigax. The two guides – ibex hunters turned mountaineers – have the bearded, furrowed visages of men exposed constantly to wind, snow and sun. Between them the Duke has just a skim of stubble on his clean jaw, and he looks rather debonair, with a jaunty flower in his hat. All three have puttees wound around their calves and over the tops of their sturdy nailed boots, and they rest their hands on the picks of long ice axes held in front of them.

With their alpine assistant guide, Brocherel, and a team of Bakonzo men they headed up a slope of squelching bog and over a saddle, which they named Freshfield Pass in honour of their distinguished

Bakonzo tribesmen helping modern expeditions approach the Mountains of the Moon still use the same rock shelters as the Abruzzi expedition.

Giant mushrooms of frozen rime encrust the final ridge of Margherita.

predecessor. Then they descended again into dense forest to the enchanted lakes of Kitandara, nestling in a deep hollow, fringed by giant groundsels and the pearly globes of helichrysums, which, during rare moments of sunshine, open up into the radiant blooms of Everlastings. Then onward, upward again, slogging through the mud, fighting their way up a near-vertical jungle of tangled vegetation, emerging eventually onto bare rocks coated in a lethal slick of jade-colored lichen.

Most of the Bakonzo, fearful of hostile tribes as they got closer to the mountain border with the Congo, fled back to base camp, but the mountaineers pressed on. At daybreak on 18 May they emerged from the forest on to a snowy ridge, which led to a high summit. But then, as the mist lifted, they saw a slightly higher summit to their north. They descended to a saddle and then started climbing again. Petigax, veteran of countless alpine climbs and holder of the world's furthest-north record, led the way up a steep ice wall, heading into a fantasy world of huge snowy encrustations festooned with giant icicles. Eventually Petigax had to start chopping with his axe, hacking a tunnel through an overhang, until suddenly he emerged right onto the highest summit.

By the time the others had joined Petigax, the sun was shining amidst a blue sky, and they all stood above a sea of cloud. They unfurled the Italian tricolor and Abruzzi named this highest summit Margherita, in honour of the Queen Mother of Italy, who also happened to be his aunt and was herself a keen mountaineer.

By the time the four men had returned to their camp that evening, they were all half blind and moaning with pain: Despite their huge experience, they had not bothered to wear sunglasses, because of the mainly misty weather. Now they suffered the gritty agony of temporary snow-blindness, which they treated with poultices of wet tea leaves.

Margherita was the highlight of Abruzzi's expedition, but not the end. During the next few weeks the expedition climbed no less than fourteen major peaks and made a comprehensive survey of the range. They also discovered that the Bujuku valley, not the Mubuku, was actually the quickest and most direct route to Margherita. Today that route – up a riverbed and over the bizarre plain of Bigo Bog to Lake Bujuku and Groundsel Gully – remains the standard approach to the highest summit in the Mountains of the Moon.

Abruzzi's ghost writer described 'monstrous tumefactions of the discoloured leprous growths', but on a bright dewy morning like this the giant heather forest can be quite enchanting.

Blouberg

Height
2,051 metres (6,729 ft)

Location
Northern Transvaal, South Africa

Origin of name
Afrikaans for Blue (blou) Mountain (berg)

First ascent

Other key routes
Left Face 1952: Bob Davies et al

Last Moon 1978: Paul Fatti/Art McGarr

Hey Jude 1981: Romey and Eckhardt Druschke/ J. Linke/H. Zangerl

Wall of White Light 1985:

Eight Miles High 1988: George Mallory/Stewart Middlemiss/Kevin Smith

Interesting facts
Like most South African peaks and escarpments, the Blouberg monolith is made of ancient sandstone which originated, like that of Australia, in the continent of

Blouberg is part of the Waterberg series. The slopes of the Blouberg have been inhabited since early Stone Age times. Pottery dating from the ninth century has been found on ledges at the foot of the north escarpment.

The Blouberg, with its turrets called the 'Donjons', rises like a great castle above the huge plain of the northern Transvaal. Perhaps the most famous feat was the climbing of five 300-metre (1,000-ft routes in a single day by South African George Mallory, grandson of the George Mallory who died near the summit of Everest in 1924.

Blue Mountain of the Transvaal

George Mallory and Kevin Smith (1989)

George Mallory was hardly aware of the significance of his name until, while doing compulsory military service in the South African army at age nineteen, he read his grandfather's biography and learned all about the man who had died near the summit of Everest in 1924. Grandson George eventually climbed Everest himself, reaching the summit in 1995, but long before that – even before reading that biography – he had discovered rock climbing for himself. 'My best friend at high school in Pretoria persuaded me to join the school mountain club, and halfway up my first rock climb, I was addicted. I was fifteen.'

That first climb was in one of the canyons that cut through the Magaliesberg – a range of ancient sandstone mountains just north of Johannesburg. Here George Mallory honed his skills and came to know other climbers, who told him about the great north face of Blouberg, in the far northern Transvaal, near the borders of Mozambique, Zimbabwe and Botswana. The Afrikaans name means Blue Mountain, perhaps alluding to the abundant forest cloaking its lower slopes. But Blouberg's great northern escarpment is actually a shimmering rock curtain of silvers, yellows and rich reds.

George Mallory's first visit to Blouberg was in 1983. 'I was in my third year at university and when

I arrived after the long drive and three-hour walk, it was extraordinary. A thousand feet high! I felt intimidated and anxious about completing our route in a day, so I insisted on starting before dawn.'

So after camping beside a cave, he and his climbing partner crossed the Glade by torchlight and descended the Ramp, before reaching the start of Last Moon – a route pioneered in the '60s by another leading Johannesburg climber, Paul Fatti. All day they climbed, following vertical cracks and corners, interspersed with spectacular horizontal rails typical of South African sandstone. On the upper wall the rock was deep russet, speckled with brilliant yellow lichen and knobbled with fantastic corrugations – huge jughandles that seemed to be created specially for climbers. The forest was now 300 metres (1,000 ft) below them, but they could still hear the dry bark of the baboons and the twittering of a thousand songbirds.

They finished at dusk and nearly got lost descending from the summit through the Maze, which leads back to the camping spot, but George's brother Stephen, who had climbed a different route that day and had packed a torch, helped them regain the path. Both brothers were hooked and returned many, many times over the next few years, adding their own new routes to Blouberg's north wall. One of the finest was Stephen Mallory's Lost Tribe, where

George Mallory (left) and Kevin Smith happy after completing another route on the north wall of Blouberg. This great escarpment, pictured on page 108, is over 300 metres (1,000 ft) high.

he found old shards of pottery on a ledge at the start of the climb. George later upstaged his brother by doing the route completely 'free' – using just the natural rock holds and pulling on no equipment.

'That was the same weekend I soloed Last Moon: I was young, confident and incredibly competitive.'

That sheer physical, tactile exuberance was equally evident in George's regular Blouberg partner, Kevin Smith. Both men revelled in the crazy Friday night 380-km (236-mile) drive from their Johannesburg offices to Frans' kraal, where the village elder guarded the car in his stockade, while the climbers raced up through the yellowwood forest,

dispensing with torches if there was a moon. Then Saturday and Sunday would be spent climbing, often two routes in a weekend, something which very few other climbers had achieved. On one occasion, with

'Over a bottle of wine one evening he said, ''Why not *five* routes in a 24-hour day?'' I replied that that was ridiculous. Then Kevin explained that if we learned to climb in the dark and practised the routes, we would stand a chance.'

another partner, George left Johannesburg at midnight on Friday, climbed two 300-metre (1,000-ft) routes on Blouberg and was back at a party in the city by 10:30 P.M. on Saturday.

It was Kevin who talked George into managing 900-metre (3,000-ft)-high routes in a single day. And then he suggested something preposterous: 'Over a bottle of wine one evening he said, "Why not *five* routes in a 24-hour day?" I replied that that was ridiculous. Then Kevin explained that if we learned to climb in the dark and practised the routes, we would stand a chance.'

They did their first torch-lit climb, a ten-pitch route called Hey Jude, in July 1987 – the first of many weekends preparing for the Big Push. Then Kevin was knocked out by hepatitis, and it was only in March 1989 that they were finally ready to tackle their adventure.

They chose a full-moon weekend and spent Saturday with Kevin's wife, Michele, stashing water bottles and chocolate bars at the top of each of the five selected routes. Then, at exactly midnight, they set off from their cave for the first route, Hey Jude. 'My anxiety melted as we cruised up the pitches by torchlight, reaching the top just after 3:00 A.M. before walking back down to the bottom to start our second route, Half Moon. Soon after midday they had completed the third climb, Last Moon, which six years earlier had taken George a whole day to climb.

Near the top of the fourth route, Big Corner, George began to flag. 'My arms, weary from 1,200 metres [4,000 ft] of climbing, felt too weak to cope. Suddenly the momentum vanished and was replaced by a strong urge to retreat. I managed to will myself on, but on the final pitch, I was composing my resignation speech. However, when I joined Kevin on top, I couldn't deliver the speech: We had invested far too much to bail out now.'

So they started their fifth route, Malaboch, soon after nightfall. It was a bizarre experience: 'While actually climbing, movement provided enough stimulus to keep me awake, but I dozed off repeatedly while belaying Kevin at the stances. Being a chimney route, there was no danger of getting lost, but despite the full moon, it was pitch dark inside and it was hard to pinpoint the holds with our headtorches.' They managed to spur each other on and at 11:30 reached the top. A few minutes before midnight they made it back to the cave where Michele was waiting: Mission accomplished.

Summing up those 1,500 metres (5,000 ft) of climbing (and descent) on Blouberg, George Mallory likes to quote his grandfather: 'What we get from this adventure is just sheer joy. And joy is, after all, the end of life. We do not live to eat and make money; we eat and make money to be able to enjoy life. This is what life means and what life is for.'

Kevin Smith, photographed by George Mallory, on the first ascent of their new Blouberg route, Razor's Edge.

Mt Carse
Mt Erebus
Kubbestolen
Peak 4111

Mt Carse

Height
2,300 metres (7,546 ft)

Location
Salvesen Range, South Georgia, Southern Ocean

Origin of name
The mountain is named after Duncan Carse, leader of the four South Georgia Survey expeditions of the 1950s.

First ascent
21 January 1990: Brian Davison/Stephen Venables, by Northwest Ridge

Interesting facts
South Georgia, in the southern hemisphere, is at an equivalent latitude to Glasgow in the northern hemisphere, yet it has extensive glaciation right down to sea level. This is because of the cooling effect of Antarctica on the surrounding Southern Ocean. There are no trees on the island, but ice-free beaches and hillsides of tussock grass provide breeding grounds for some of the world's largest populations of penguins, seals and albatrosses. The glaciers, like those in most of the world's mountainous regions, are currently retreating at a drastic rate. The first known landing on South Georgia was made in 1775 by Captain James Cook, who named the island after King George III; it has remained British sovereign territory ever since but was briefly occupied by Argentine troops during the Falklands War of 1982.

Carse, explorer, photographer, broadcaster and actor, made South Georgia his life's work, leading four expeditions to explore and map its 152 glaciers and record the final days of the whaling industry. He never managed to climb the mountain named after him, but gave his blessing to the successful ascent made by Stephen Venables and Brian Davison in 1990.

Island at the Edge of the World

Duncan Carse (1950's)

The white dome of Mt Carse is not a particularly remarkable mountain. At just 2,300 metres (7,546 ft) above sea level, its only statistical boast is that it is the highest mountain in an obscure massif called the Salvesen Range. But more importantly, Mt Carse is special because of *where* it is – rising out of the Southern Ocean on one of the most remote islands on the planet, on the fringes of Antarctica. And for all its rugged remoteness, it is also special because of its rich human associations.

Duncan Carse was born in 1913, and after being educated in Dorset and Lausanne, he joined the Merchant Navy. His first big adventure was sailing south with the research vessel *Discovery II* in 1933. In the Falkland Islands the ship encountered the schooner *Penola*, carrying the British Grahamland Expedition to Antarctica. Hearing that they were shorthanded, Carse managed to arrange a transfer, then joined the expedition and found himself on the Antarctic Peninsula, laying depots for the shore party.

It was only in 1937 that he finally returned to Britain to take up a new career as an actor and broadcaster with the BBC. After the Second World War, he took on the role of Dick Barton Special Agent in the popular, long-running radio series, and his sonorous baritone became familiar to millions throughout the country.

But he was still entranced by the Antarctic, and when his proposal for a crossing of the continent was turned down in favour of Vivian Fuchs's trans-Antarctic project, he decided to find his own exploratory niche: the sub-Antarctic island of South Georgia.

The island was famous for two things. It was the centre of the southern whaling industry, now in terminal decline as whale stocks dwindled to unviable levels. And it was the island where Ernest Shackleton and five companions had arrived in 1916, having crossed the Southern Ocean in a 6.7-metre (22-ft) open boat, after the sinking of their expedition ship *Endurance*. Their subsequent crossing of South Georgia's mountains to reach Stromness whaling station and organize a rescue ship for the rest of the expedition, stranded 1,300 km (800 miles) away on Elephant Island, was one of the great legends of exploration. Apart from that desperate mountain crossing and a subsequent expedition by the German-Norwegian Kohl-Larsens, the interior of this island was completely unknown – a mountain range 160 km (100 miles) long rising from a network of 152 glaciers, still unexplored and unmapped.

Duncan Carse sailed south with his first survey expedition in 1951. For the next four austral summers he and his various companions worked their way up and down the length of South Georgia. Nowadays

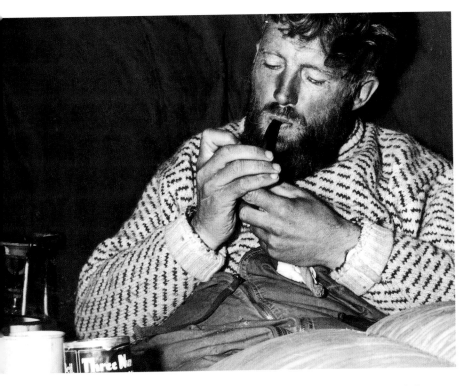

Duncan Carse, the classic polar explorer, snug in his sleeping bag with his pipe and a primus stove standing by to cook the next meal. But the calm is deceptive – several tents were destroyed by South Georgia's notorious winds during Carse's survey expeditions.

aerial and satellite photography has dissolved that thrill of the unknown, where the only way to unravel the intricacies of remote mountain country was to work your way physically over the landscape, on foot.

The expeditions were not without mishap. In 1952 a geologist fell unroped into a crevasse, badly twisting his knee. On another occasion, during a typical South Georgia blizzard, the famous Scottish mountaineer John Cunningham fell into a crevasse and, during the subsequent confusion, was left to fight his own way out with no ice axe, pressing his stockinged feet repeatedly to the vertical walls of the crevasse until they melted the ice sufficiently to stick and allow him to chimney another foot higher. Tents were frequently demolished by the Filthy Fifties – the frenzied winds that sweep across the Southern Ocean from Cape Horn.

It was in 1956 that Carse finally got the chance to explore the Salvesen Range, at the southern end of the island. On 28 January a sealing vessel put his team ashore in Royal Bay (named by Captain Cook in 1775), leaving them to relay heavy stores up onto the Ross Glacier. Then, manhauling all the supplies on sledges in the tradition of Captain Scott, they worked their way up over the Ross Pass, surveying as they

went, and making their way around onto the western side of the range.

On 8 February they started heading southeast up a glacier subsequently named after one of the team, George Spenceley. Four days later, blessed with rare, perfect weather, four members of the team, including Cunningham, made the first ascent of Mt Patersen. Then they all pressed on, linking a series of previously untrodden glaciers and, whenever they got a break in the cloud, setting up plane tables and theodolites to survey the landmarks, gradually filling in the blanks on the map. Then on 22 February, just a few miles short of their planned rendezvous with another sealing vessel on the southern tip of the island, another blizzard struck. This time they were pinned down for a whole week, fearful that the screaming ice particles would rip the worn fabric of their much abused tents.

The highest peak that they sledged past – Mt Carse – remained unclimbed. Carse himself led one final survey expedition the next year. Then in 1961 he returned to South Georgia, hoping to live completely alone for eighteen months in a hut he built on the southwest coast. After only a few weeks it was smashed by a freak wave, leaving him to struggle on with dwindling rations in a bleak tent. He had been alone for seven months when a passing sealer spotted him and rescued him.

> **'You will love South Georgia, and once you have been there, you will always want to go back.'**

When I met Duncan Carse at his home in Sussex in October 1989, he was an old man who knew that he would now not get the chance to climb his own mountain. Earlier that day, we had loaded supplies for three months onto *H.M.S. Endurance*. A month later we would meet the ship in the Falklands and sail the remaining 1,300 km (800 miles) to South Georgia, taking with us Duncan Carse's 1:50,000 map of the island. As we talked about the island he knew so well, he pulled out sheaves of photos: images of glittering mountains, immense glaciers, seals, penguins and albatrosses. And images of the tough whalers and sealers who had still been working on the island during the '50s. He bade us good luck and warned us about the screaming winds at the Ross Pass. Then he said, 'You will love South Georgia, and once you have been there, you will always want to go back.'

Two months later, on New Year's Day 1990, having already seen one tent ripped to shreds by the screaming winds, we began digging a large ice cave at the Ross Pass. After three days' work we had a luxurious but gloomy subterranean shelter, with two large bedrooms and kitchen for the five expedition members. From this haven we escaped only occasionally to scurry up various minor peaks before being beaten back by the next blizzard. Then, after three weeks, just as our supplies were running out, the wind veered to the east and died away. Julian Freeman-Attwood, Lindsay Griffin and our cameraman Kees 't Hooft set off to make the first ascent of Mt Kling. Brian Davison and I headed south on a mad dash to take Mt Carse by storm.

I think that only one other party since 1956 had followed Carse's route up the Spenceley Glacier. It was thrilling to ski up that great ice highway and see our mountain framed in the V of the pass at its head. Then to glide on, past Mt Patersen and Mt Baume, named after another of Carse's companions. Then over another pass, to arrive at the foot of Mt Carse itself. Thirteen miles from the ice cave, with just a light tent and one day's supplies, mindful of Carse's seven-day incarceration near here in 1956, we felt very vulnerable. Speed was of the essence, so after pitching our tent and eating a snack, at 5:00 P.M. we zipped up the tent and started up the northwest ridge of the mountain.

As we cramponed up icy slopes, the shadows lengthened beneath us on the Novosilski Glacier. Out to the west the evening sunlight glinted on stray icebergs. Further we could see the offshore Annenkov Island, where Shackleton and his five companions came within a whisker of being shipwrecked in 1916. As we approached the summit, we found ourselves crunching across a tilted field of crystal snowflowers glowing orange, then violet, as the sun set over the Southern Ocean. On the final ridge we wove a route between great bulbous encrustations of rime, reminiscent of similar features that adorn Africa's Rwenzori Mountains, caused by the same freezing of damp air on crenellated ridges.

The sun had already sunk beneath the horizon as we stepped out onto a broad snow ridge, the first

human beings ever to reach this place. In the words of the great explorer Bill Tilman, 'We so far forget ourselves as to shake hands on it.' After skiing 21 km (13 miles) and then climbing 1,200 metres (4,000 ft) from the tent, we were tired, so we shared a pound of marzipan to reboost blood sugar levels before starting back down through the darkness, eventually getting to bed at midnight. At dawn we packed up the tent and left, skiing back over to the Spenceley Glacier. I took one look back to Duncan Carse's snowy dome, where we had stood the previous evening, then cursed angrily as a vicious squall swept across the glacier, enveloping me in swirling spindrift and flinging me to the ground. South Georgia had reverted to type, and it was two numb, breathless, ice-encrusted mountaineers who stumbled back into the ice cave an hour later. We had escaped just in time.

Brian Davison nearing the summit of Mt Carse as the sun sets on a rare day of fine weather, January 1990. The picture on page 114 shows him skiing home from the mountain the following morning.

Mt Erebus

Height
3,794 metres (12,448 ft)

Location
Ross Island, Antarctica

Origin of name
The mountain was named after one of the ships of James Clarke Ross's Antarctic expedition of 1839, H.M.S. *Erebus*. Another mountain nearby was named after the other ship, H.M.S. *Terror*.

First ascent
13 February 1908: Jameson Adams/Edgar Davis/ Alistair Forbes Mackay/Eric Marshall/Douglas Mawson

Other key routes
Various variations on the original route from Cape Royds.

Interesting facts
Mt Erebus is the most prominent landmark on Ross Island, which appears linked to the main Antarctic landmass by the Ross Ice Shelf, Antarctica's largest floating ice shelf, varying in thickness from 200 to 1,000 metres (650 to 3,300 ft) and covering an area about the size of France. The cliffs on

60 metres (200 ft) high and were referred to by the early expeditions of Scott, Shackleton and Amundsen as the Great Ice Barrier. In 1979 an Air New Zealand flight crashed into the pass between Erebus and Terror, killing all passengers, including guide Peter Mulgrew, whose friend Sir Edmund Hillary was to have been

The 1911 Australasian Antarctic Expedition was leader Mawson's second visit to the white continent. His first had been with Shackleton, on the 'Nimrod' expedition of 1907 to 1909, when Mawson and four others made the first ascent of the volcano, Mt Erebus. The climbers struggled with heavy sledges, crawled on their hands and knees and braved a 36-hour blizzard to reach the summit plateau where they found red hot magma boiling beneath the ice.

Boiling Ice

Douglas Mawson (1908)

Erebus is not a particularly high, steep, or difficult mountain. It is not even very beautiful. But there is a special fascination about this snow-sheathed volcano, steaming and spluttering above Ross Island on the edge of the white immensity of the Ross Ice Shelf. A fascination derived from human association – from the layered memories, almost legendary, of the heroic age of Antarctic exploration. This mountain is redolent with the names of Shackleton, Scott, Cherry-Garrard, Wilson, Wild, Crean, Oates … and with the name of Australia's most revered polar explorer, Douglas Mawson.

Mawson intended to go into the mining industry, but it was his professor at Sydney University, Edgworth David, who persuaded him to become an academic geologist. It was also through David's influence that Mawson got himself invited on Ernest Shackleton's Nimrod expedition and found himself setting sail for Antarctica at the end of 1907. Shackleton was building on the experience he had gained five years earlier, on Captain Scott's first expedition – the first expedition to penetrate the interior of the still completely unknown southern continent.

Like Scott before him, Shackleton made his base on Ross Island, discovered more than sixty years earlier by James Clark Ross. Like Scott, he brought a prefabricated hut to enable his team to survive the darkness of the Antarctic winter. The hut was built at Cape Royds, close to the foot of Mt Erebus, in February 1908, towards the end of the austral summer.

For the following summer Shackleton planned ambitious sledging journeys, including an attempt to reach the South Pole. In the meantime, the remaining weeks of the present summer were a chance to try out men and equipment. It was decided almost immediately that Erebus would make a good objective for one of these training exercises.

Edgworth David clearly *did* find Erebus beautiful, describing it thus:

'If Ross Island be likened to a castle, flanking that wall at the World's End, the Great Ice Barrier, Erebus is the castle keep. Its flanks and foothills clothed with spotless snow, patched with the pale blue of glacier ice, its active crater crowned with a spreading smoke cloud … Erebus not only commands a view of incomparable grandeur and interest, but is in itself one of the fairest and most majestic sights that Earth can show.'

David was well respected by Shackleton, who asked him to lead a party up the mountain. The 50-year-old professor chose the Scotsman Dr Alistair Forbes Mackay and his Australian former student, 26-year-old Douglas Mawson. There was also a support team to carry additional stores – Philip Brocklehurst, Eric Marshall and Jameson Adams – with permission to attempt the summit if Adams thought they were up to the task.

In those naive days when British and Commonwealth pioneers were making up polar exploration as they went along, with little knowledge – particularly of glaciated mountains – their progress was a lumbering, haphazard affair. They set off on 5 March, hauling a monstrous sledge weighing 254 kilos (560 lb), struggling when they had to cross ridges of exposed moraine rocks or Antarctica's famous sastrugi – contorted waves and blades of wind-blown snow frozen to iron-hard consistency.

They spent the night in two tents, sleeping in reindeer-skin sleeping bags. The next day, the terrain became too steep and awkward for their unwieldy sledge, so they continued on foot, as David later described: 'We filed off in a procession more bizarre than beautiful. Some of us with our sleeping bags hanging straight down our backs, with the foot of the bag curled upward and outward, resembled the scorpion men of the Assyrian sculptures.'

Although the crampon was already familiar equipment in the Alps, Shackleton's men had to make do with homemade spikes riveted to leather strips that they lashed to their boot soles. And some of the men did not even have these. Since Mawson was carrying the heavy plate camera, he was one of the most heavily laden.

On 7 and 8 March the whole party was pinned down by a blizzard. Separated in their own tent now far from the sledge, the support party had to make do with just one biscuit and chocolate bar in thirty-six hours. They should really have stayed put or descended, but on 9 March they struggled on with the lead team. At one point Mackay fainted with exhaustion after cutting a line of steps in the ice, overcome by altitude sickness. Brocklehurst was also stricken by the altitude, and his feet were getting frostbite, so the following day he was left alone in his tent, on the rim of the ancient extinct crater, while the rest

of the party continued to make their way to Erebus's central, active crater.

Douglas Mawson measured the depth of the steaming, booming crater as 270 metres (885 ft) but never described the experience in his diary, which he had neglected since arriving at Cape Royds and only resumed later that year. For a really vivid description, we have to jump forward nearly seventy-six years, to 1984, when Roger Mear climbed Erebus alone in

'We filed off in a procession more bizarre than beautiful. Some of us with our sleeping bags hanging straight down our backs, with the foot of the bag curled upward and outward, resembled the scorpion men of the Assyrian sculptures.'

winter – the first-ever winter ascent of an Antarctic peak, in temperatures ranging from -30°C (-22°F) at sea level to about -60°C (-76°F) on the summit. Crossing the outer crater, where Mawson and his companions had made their last camp, Mear

described 'several ghostly towers, scattered indiscriminately across the plateau. These polymorphous growths, some of which were 6 metres (20 ft) in height, were the ice-encrusted vents of fumerals, and clouds of vapour billowed from their tops like organic chimneys.' And on the lip of the inner crater, 'foetid, sulphurous fumes grabbed the breath. Enormous silvery boils of cloud filled the chasm and drifted in majestically slow rises over my head. … Nine hundred feet below in that mist-obscured cauldron glowed an iron-red heart, and when for a moment the air cleared, I saw rents of soft orange heat.'

By 1984 ascents of this extraordinary ice-bound volcano were becoming almost commonplace. But for Douglas Mawson and his companions in 1908 the ascent was a first ascent – not just of Erebus, but of any noteworthy Antarctic summit. And a day after their success, after sliding, slithering and stumbling back down to Cape Royds, they were welcomed

home by Shackleton with champagne, porridge, ham, bread and butter.

By modern standards it had been a rather shambolic affair: to use a modern cliché, the British and Australian explorers had experienced a very steep learning curve. That experience was put to good use the following summer. While Shackleton and two companions made their epic attempt to attain the Geographic South Pole, claiming to have reached within 160 km (100 miles) of that holy grail, three of the Erebus veterans – David, Mackay and Mawson – claimed the first successful journey to the Magnetic South Pole. In recent years doubts have been raised over whether they did reach the exact location of the magnetic pole, where it was in January 1909 (it moves from year to year); but no one has ever doubted the magnitude of David's, Mackay's and Mawson's journey of exploration – a round-trip of 1,265 km (790 miles), which for eighty-four years would remain the longest, unsupported sledging journey achieved.

Shackleton's hut still stands exactly as he left it at Cape Royds, beneath the active volcanic cone of Mt Erebus.

Kubbestolen

Height
2,070 metres (6,791 ft)

Location
Hotedahlfjella, Queen Maud Land, Antarctica

Origin of name
The Norwegian name means 'carved log chair'.

First ascent
January 2000: Cestmir Lukes/Irene Oehninger

Interesting facts
Queen Maud Land is a triangular 2,500,000 sq-kilometre (1,553,500 sq-mile) wedge of Antarctica. The inner apex of the triangle is the South Pole; the outer edge is bound by the coastal terminus of the Stanscomb-Wills Glacier at 20°W and the Shinnan Glacier at 44°38'E. Most of the significant mountains which are really nunataks – large rocks piercing the ice sheet – lie between 160 and 320 km (100–200 miles) from the coast. Inland from the mountains there is nothing but featureless snow-covered ice cap all the way to the Pole. Norway, Germany, Russia, South Africa and Japan each have a manned research station in Queen Maud Land.

Several climbing teams have now visited the spectacular granite towers of the Hotedahlfjella, including a National Geographic-sponsored expedition in 1999, when Conrad Anker, Jon Krakauer and Alex Lowe made the first ascent of Rakekniven.

The Czech climber 'Mirek' and his Swiss partner Irene spend their lives chasing dreams. The most challenging dream of all was to find the money to travel over 16, 000 km (10,000 miles) using three planes to reach the incredibly remote spires of Queen Maud Land at the South Pole. Here they explored glaciers never trodden before and made first ascents of five peaks – some of the most fantastic and isolated mountains on the face of the earth.

The First Humans

Cestmir Lukes and Irene Oehninger (1999)

The Czech climber Cestmir Lukes – or Mirek, as he is universally known – was in the hospital, receiving treatment for frostbitten toes when he met his life partner, Swiss-born Irene Oehninger. They live on the south side of the Alps, near Bellinzona. He works as a writer, photographer and lecturer; she is a physiotherapist with a sufficiently flexible timetable to allow her frequent extended trips abroad. Together they have made many journeys roaming, exploring and making first ascents in the remote regions of Pakistan, Tibet and Chad.

Their expeditions are usually lightweight minimalist affairs, self-financed, with no publicity. But Mirek lives to fulfil dreams, and his most urgent dream was to visit the fairy-tale granite castles of Queen Maud Land in Antarctica – a dream that he knew could never be financed from the personal savings of a freelance climbing writer and a part-time physiotherapist. From Punta Arenas at the southern tip of Chile, they would have to fly 5,000 km (3,000 miles) to Patriot Hills, a camp in the Ellsworth Mountains, Antarctica, run by Adventure Network. From Patriot Hills there would be another flight of nearly 5,000 km (3,000 miles) over the ice, with one refuelling stop before they reached Queen Maud Land. Adventure Network's standard charge was $20,000 – each. And they first had to fly halfway around the world to Punta Arenas.

As soon as Adventure Network started running flights to Queen Maud Land in 1998, Mirek knew that he would have to go there. Remembering the polar explorer Fridtjof Nansen's famous dictum, 'Nothing is impossible; the impossible just takes a little longer', he drew up plans and started looking for a sponsor. After six months of meetings and letter-writing, he finally stumbled upon an interested party: the Swiss life insurance company, Elvia. The following austral summer, on 10 December 1999, Mirek and Irene found themselves skidding to a halt on the ice runway at Patriot Hills.

At first they were thrilled to reach Adventure Network's semi-permanent tented Antarctic village. Then frustration set in as 130-km (80-miles) per hour winds smothered the ice runway in 0.5 m (20 inches) of swirling snow. They had to wait two full weeks before taking off again, on Christmas Eve. Then there was more frustration as, after traveling 800 km (500 miles), news of bad weather at their destination forced them to land on Berkner Island in the middle of Antarctica's second-largest floating iceshelf: the Filchner.

'During the following two days, for the first time we start to feel the immeasurable vastness of the polar landscape: flat, no elevation, white and vast to the horizon. Then we succeed in reaching the next fuel depot and continue to the South African research station, Sanae, situated about 120 miles [193 km] from the coast and said to be the best-equipped base in Antarctica. We are condemned to wait here until December 30, but that gives us a chance to have a look around. The main function of the station is geophysical and meteorological research. We notice the total absence of garbage. For decades mountains of garbage were part of the sad picture of human presence in the Antarctic. Now everything has to be removed. The South Africans do this with the help of two helicopters that fly the garbage to ships waiting on the coast. Liquid waste goes to a special sewage plant.'

No one could argue with the long overdue regulations on waste disposal. More controversial is the decision of the Antarctic Treaty nations to ban all non-indigenous animals (apart from man). The days of dog-sledging are now over, and the only way to travel long distances over the ice is to travel on foot or use motor skidoos. Or fly.

On the penultimate day of the millennium, they took off from Sanae, but even on this final short hop inland, they were delayed and had to touch down on the coast before taking off again. And then, at last, staring out of the fuselage window, they saw the vast granite towers rising out of endless whiteness. If it were not for their dark colour, they could have been

giant icebergs, apparently floating in an infinite frozen sea. This landscape seemed quite unlike anywhere else on earth, and it occurred to Mirek that hardly any more people had been here than had visited the moon.

'Our plane dives into the white surface, skims over the snow-covered ground and comes to a halt. We unload, and our belongings are barely stashed before the DC-3 has vanished from sight. We find ourselves alone in the midst of granite cathedrals and organ pipes, surrounded by an indescribable mystical silence. There is no question of sleep. Not because of the sun high over the horizon at midnight or because of the altitude, which is only 1,900 metres [6,233 ft]. No, it is this void, this silence, this whiteness that doesn't let us rest – this seeming nothingness that has become all-encompassing.'

Intoxicated by this dazzling landscape, the next day they set off on skis to explore it. The plane had left them on the Fenristunga Glacier, a slightly raised white plateau, rimmed on either side by russet granite monoliths. They skied all the way around one of these towers, Holtana, assessing its potential but deciding that the brittle rock and paucity of obvious belay anchors made it too risky for a two-person party with no support team.

That night, by the light of the midnight sun, they celebrated the arrival of the new millennium with

Cestmir Lukes, photographed by his partner Irene Oehninger, amongst the granite spires of Queen Maud Land. The pair climbed several previously untouched summits, including Kubbestolen, seen on the previous page, framed by a fantastically eroded granite boulder.

champagne. Then, for the first five days of 2000, they continued exploring the area around their camp, making the first ascent of one peak. However, they were most tempted by a parallel line of peaks several miles to the east, so they packed everything into their pulks – fibreglass sledges – skied down 200 metres (650 ft) off the plateau and headed across the Sigynbreen Glacier, towing their food and gear behind them.

'It takes three long days and a maximum of concentration to cross the Sigynbreen Glacier. With full extended ski poles I sound out every step of our traverse and discover insidiously covered crevasses. In our isolation a fall might have fatal consequences.'

The history of Antarctic exploration is rife with cautionary tales of gigantic snow-concealed crevasses capable of swallowing entire snow tractors, let alone two isolated humans on skis, so Mirek's caution was justified. They made it safely across the glacier to the edge of the parallel range, which Norwegian mapmakers had named Holtedahlfjella. With just ten days left before their air pickup, they now focused on a cluster of peaks within this range, forming a horseshoe around a glacier that they named Swiss Glacier, a little alpine-scale corner hidden among the immensity of Antarctica.

For Irene it was totally magical: 'Of all our travels, this was the journey which brought us closest to Nature. It was just incredible to be alone in such a special place, which had never been touched by another human being.' They climbed six peaks in all. One they named Byrd, after the famous American polar explorer; another Soglio, after a famously beautiful village in the Bregaglia valley near their home in Switzerland; another Elvia, after the sponsor who had made this journey possible. But the finest summit – the one they had earmarked as they flew in two weeks earlier – was a peak marked Kubbestolen on the Norwegian map. Its knife-edge summit ridge formed a ring, almost like the rim of a volcanic crater or the top of a castle keep, with smooth rock walls falling away all around it, except for one weakness, where

'It is this void, this silence, this whiteness that doesn't let us rest – this seeming nothingness that has become all-encompassing.'

the ring was breached by an ice-filled gap – a great slanting ramp, coated white with wind-packed snow. Up this weakness they kicked steps with their crampons, glad to find a steep ice wall near the top, then a sharply serrated ridge, providing just enough tension to make this their most memorable climb in Queen Maud Land.

Finally, it was time to pack up their camp and ski back out onto the open expanse of the Sigynbreen Glacier and wait for the drone of the DC-3 engine. Back at Patriot Hills they were again delayed, prisoners of the weather. Jostling among all the other climbers returning from the popular Vinson Massif, their white adventure faded back into dreams, and they grew impatient to return to all the obligations waiting back in Switzerland. But they knew that the real reward of their adventure was still to come. As Mirek put it, 'These two weeks would grow to a treasure of incalculable worth, which could never be lost.'

Peak 4111

Height
4,111 metres (13,487 ft)

Location
Sentinel Range, Antarctica

Origin of name
Spot height on map.

First ascent
13 January 1996: Erik
Decamp and Catherine
Destivelle, by South Face

Interesting facts
The Sentinel Range is also
known as the Ellsworth
Mountains, after Lincoln
Ellsworth who was the first
to discover them, with
Herbert Hollick-Kenyon,
when they flew over the
range during the first aerial
crossing of Antarctica in
1935. The range is so remote
it has only ever been
approached by plane.

Vinson was first climbed
in 1966, along with several
other summits, during
a National Geographic
sponsored expedition
led by Nicholas Clinch.
Probably the most
audacious climb ever
achieved here was Mugs
Stump's 1989 solo ascent
of the 2,500-metre
(8,200-ft)-high west face of
Mt Tyree. 'Probably the

hardest climb done by man,'
was how he described it.
He was joking. But he was
also serious. Catherine
Destivelle's record-breaking
climbs include the first
female solo ascent of the
Eigerwand in winter. She
was also the first person to
repeat Walter Bonatti's
famous solo climb of a
direct route up the North
Face of the Matterhorn

France's most famous climber, Catherine Destivelle, and her husband Erik Decamp spent two days skiing to a remote unclimbed mountain in the Vinson Massif range. Posing for a summit photograph, Destivelle slipped on crumbly snow and shot down an ice slope, badly fracturing her leg. Her devoted husband lowered her 1,500 metres (5,000 ft) down the face, then dragged her for miles across crevassed glaciers to their tent to wait for a rescue plane.

Marital Bonding in the Great White South

Catherine Destivelle and Erik Decamp (1996)

For nine hours they worked in perfect partnership – husband and wife – climbing a previously unknown mountain face 1,500 metres (5,000 ft) high. As they traversed backward and forward, seeking out the twisting line of weakness, Erik Decamp noted that this face would be hard to reverse: Thank goodness they had spotted an alternative descent on the other side of the mountain.

They emerged onto the summit snow ridge – a precarious knife-edge that they would have to cross to reach that descent route. First Erik asked his wife, Catherine, to move a bit farther left, across a snow slope, into his camera frame for the perfect summit photograph. It was not particularly difficult, so she left her ice axes where they were, and with gloved hands punching the snow and cramponed boots kicking steps, she moved up to the very tip of the summit. Erik clicked a couple of frames. Then 'suddenly the snow gave way beneath her right foot, and she toppled backward down the slope, unable to self-arrest.'

Tumbling head first, Catherine had a lot of time to think. 'I was terrified that I was going to pull him off – miserable that he was going to die because of my stupid mistake.' Erik was anchored just to his ice axes, thrust into the snow, but there was enough slack in the rope for him to brace himself before bringing Catherine to a halt.

As she struggled to pull herself upright again, one leg wobbled, its foot hanging at a strange angle. 'I pulled up the trouser leg and saw the bone sticking through the skin. There wasn't much pain, until I tried to put weight on it. Then it really hurt.'

Erik called to Catherine to ask if she was all right, and she responded that she had an open fracture. '*Merde*', he muttered. They were utterly alone on the summit of an unknown, unnamed mountain, deep in the interior of the world's highest, driest, coldest continent. The nearest other human beings were climbers 60 km (37 miles) away, on Mt Vinson. Patriot Hills, Adventure Network's Antarctic air base, was an hour's flight away; their radio was 2,000 metres (6,500 ft) beneath them in the camp they had left the previous day. For these world-class mountaineers, coming down alive was going to be the biggest test of their careers so far.

Erik Decamp grew up in Paris and only started climbing when he was nineteen. Hugely talented, he quickly became a highly competent mountaineer,

But he, too, remained a superb climber, keen to share adventures with his new wife. So in January 1996, midsummer in Antarctica, the two of them arrived at Patriot Hills camp, staging post for the Sentinel Range. Ninety percent of climbers flying here are bound for the highest point in the range – and in Antarctica: the summit of Vinson Massif. But Catherine and Erik planned something more exploratory, flying on past Vinson, to be dropped at the far end of the range. From there they planned to spend twenty-one days working back towards Vinson, on skis, towing their mobile camp on sledges, picking off previously unclimbed mountains as they went.

On 10 January they waved good-bye to the twin otter plane and settled into the dazzling silence of their new environment. The next day, they made an easy 1,200-metre (3,937-ft) ascent of Mt Viets. They found it easy, but 'everything was about twice as big as we had imagined, and we were surprised by the heat and by our dehydration. This first taste also allowed us to observe the large south face of a peak called 4111 on the USGS map from a better vantage point. It was immense, and quite sobering, but we could see a line of ascent.'

Having spotted their line of ascent up the huge south face of Peak 4111 – and a potential descent route down the easier, west face – they set off on 12 January, leaving main supplies and radio at their base and skiing up with a light tent to camp just beneath the towering wall of Peak 4111. From there it was about a two hours' walk to the foot of the route,

Catherine Destivelle at the final camp below Peak 4111. After the accident at the summit, it took seventeen hours for her husband Erik to lower her down the huge, 1,500 metre (5,000 ft) north face in the background. The pair then had to wait two days before a plane was able to come and fly them out to the ice runway at Patriot Hills (pictured on page 126).

embarking on a parallel career of mountain guide and academic. Catherine Destivelle also grew up in Paris; she learned to rockclimb on the famous Fontainebleau boulders just south of the city and by her early twenties was climbing some of the world's hardest routes. In 1991, after soloing a new route on the mirror-smooth wall of the Dru, above Chamonix, a public poll revealed that she was better known to the French public than the prime minister. She was a star, and when Erik married her, friends remarked that he had a full-time job just being the husband of Catherine Destivelle.

'I was terrified of getting frostbite – *very* worried. I kept wiggling my toes. But the good thing is that at 'nighttime' the sun was shining on the south face, so we had a little warmth.'

which they started at about 10:00 A.M. the next day.

The face was 1,500 metres (5,000 ft) high – nearly as big as the Eigerwand – but they quickly dispatched the initial 900-metre (2,952-ft)-high 50° snow gully. Then they started on the 600-metre (1,968-ft)-high headwall. 'It was awkward without being really difficult. Long upward-ascending traverses allowed us to find the weaknesses of the face, which proved to be truly grandiose. A route that would be very hard to downclimb … We rejoiced in the magic of exploration.'

By about 7:00 P.M. they had emerged from the wall. To continue to the summit, the easiest line involved crossing over onto the snowy north face. It was here that Erik anchored himself while Catherine sidestepped across for the summit photo. Still unsure of what exactly happened, Catherine believes her foot slipped on some rotten snow and that, as she began to slide, her legs broke through into a powdery hollow, flipping her upside down and snapping one leg.

Now battered and bruised, with one shoulder damaged, a mangled elbow and one leg unusable, she somehow had to get down. The intended descent route, involving an initial knife-edge ridge, was out of the question. She would have to be lowered, with the rope directly above her, so the only viable option was to go back down the way they had come up – the south face.

But right now she was sprawled 20 metres (65 ft) down the north face. And she was off to the side from Erik, so she was going to have to climb across before he could pull her up to him. He clipped ice axes onto the rope and swung them across to her, terrified of hitting her in the face. But she managed to grab hold of them and, wincing with the pain, do a crampon hop across the slope and up to her husband. 'I could use both arms, and one leg was working. But with all my weight coming on the other foot, I was terrified of getting frostbite – *very* worried. I kept wiggling my toes. But the good thing is that at "nighttime" the sun was shining on the south face, so we had a little warmth.'

Having regained the crest of the summit ridge, she now started down that face, lowered over the shattered rocks by Erik. On this steep upper section, he often had to follow by abseiling on a double rope, as they had brought only one 50-metre (164-ft) rope, which limited them to descending just 25 metres (82 ft) at a time on a wall 1,500 metres (5,000 ft) high.

'It was a long, long descent. There were several sections where we had traversed on the way up, so I couldn't lower her. I had to traverse a short way, get a belay, then hold the rope while Catherine pendulumed across beneath me. Then she would try and find an anchor, while I abseiled down to her – or downclimbed, hooking the rope over spikes of rock to protect myself. It was very laborious.'

Pitch after pitch they lowered themselves down and across, zigzagging painfully back toward the big snow gully. Then at last they could move more quickly. 'We became a very good team. I lowered Catherine 50 metres [164 ft]. When the rope was nearly finished, I signalled with a thumbs-down. Then she got in her axes for an anchor, and the minute she gave me the thumbs-up, I started down. But once, she was too eager and gave the thumbs-up too soon; luckily she managed to save herself.'

Seventeen hours after leaving the summit, Erik lowered Catherine down the last rope length to the flat glacier. They were safe!

Except that they still had to get back to Patriot Hills. And first get back to the tent. Catherine was eager to keep moving: 'I thought that Erik would drag me across the snow, but no, he insisted on going down to fetch the sledge. So I had to wait for two…three…four hours? And now it was midday and I was in shade again, just sitting in the snow. It was *freezing*. I did some breathing exercises to relax, and eventually he came back. With the sledge and medicine and food and *warm clothes*.'

Once Erik had brought her down to the tent, he continued skiing down to their base camp, desperate to make a radio call to Patriot Hills. Unfortunately, he couldn't get through, so he skied back up to the high camp, taking the radio with him. Then everything started to go wrong. 'On the sixteenth we were hit by a storm. The wind was terrible, and I was terrified it would snap the wire antenna, strung between skis outside the tent.' Catherine was in a lot of pain and wondering what would happen if they could not get through. 'We realized that Erik would have to leave me and ski alone, 60 km (37 miles), to the Vinson base camp. That would take maybe three days.'

But they were lucky. That evening Erik finally made contact with Patriot Hills and explained that he did not have any strong painkillers. 'Don't worry,' the doctor assured him, 'just double her dose of antibiotics to be safe. We'll come and get you as soon as we can.'

The twin otter finally got through at 4:00 P.M. on 16 January. An hour later they were airborne, passing swiftly over the route they had intended to ski, skimming past peaks they had hoped to climb. But they had at least climbed a fantastic route up Peak 4111 and survived a potentially disastrous accident.

Asia

Mt Everest

Height
8,850 metres (29,035 ft)

Location
Himalayas, on the frontier of Nepal and Tibet

Origin of name
Named in honour of Sir George Everest, a retired director of the Survey of India. The mountain is known to Nepalese Hindus as Sagamartha. Tibetan and Sherpa Buddhists call it Chomolungma.

First ascent
29 May 1953: Edmund Hillary/Tenzing Norgay by South Col/Southeast Ridge

Other key routes
North Col/Northeast Ridge 1960: Wang Fu-zhou/Chu Yin-hua/Konbu

West Ridge/Hornbein Couloir 1963: Tom Hornbein/Willi Unsoeld

Southwest Face 1975: Doug Scott/Dougal Haston

West Ridge Direct 1979: Andrej Stremfelj/Nejc Zaplotnik

Kangshung Face 1983: Carlos Buhler/Jay Cassell/George Lowe

Great Couloir 1984: Tim Macartney-Snape/Greg Mortimer

Interesting facts
The granite rocks near the base of Everest are geologically extremely young, formed only about 20 million years ago. The summit is still rising at a rate of 2.5–5 cm (1–2 in) per year.

Tenzing Norgay was born a few miles from Everest (known to Tibetan Buddhists as Chomolungma). He became a professional Sherpa, travelling all over the Himalayas with British and Swiss expeditions. In 1953, with New Zealander Edmund Hillary, he finally achieved his life-long ambition to climb to the summit of the world's highest mountain.

A Life's Pilgrimage to Chomolungma

Tenzing Norgay and Edmund Hillary (1953)

The two men were squeezed into a tiny tent, pitched askew on two sloping ledges, 8,424 metres (27,639 ft) above sea level – higher than any human being had ever camped before. At 4:00 A.M. the lean, tall New Zealander, Ed Hillary, lit the stove and held over the blue flame his size twelve boots, which had become frozen during the night. The other, shorter man, Sherpa Tenzing Norgay, had kept his boots on all night, inside his sleeping bag, so was spared this chore. Looking out through the tent flap, he gazed down into the misty blue valley and spotted a thin curl of smoke rising from Thyangboche monastery, almost 5,000 metres (16,400 ft) below him. God is good to us, he thought. Chomolungma is good to us.

Tenzing had been born within sight of the sacred mountain a few years before the first Englishmen arrived in 1921 to try to find a route up what they called Mt Everest. As a boy, he had looked after his father's yaks in the high meadows of the Kama valley in Tibet, immediately beneath the mountain's immense eastern face. Later the family had crossed one of the high passes and come to Nepal, on the south side of Everest, to live among the Sherpas, who had also migrated originally from Tibet. Like many

Sherpas, Tenzing travelled to the Indian hill station of Darjeeling to find work with the European expeditions, which in those days were forbidden entry to Nepal.

His big break came in 1935 when he was taken by his landlord, Angtharkay, to meet a British expedition heading for the north side of Everest. The leader, Eric Shipton, wrote afterwards: 'From a hundred applicants, we chose fifteen Sherpas to accompany the expedition from Darjeeling. Nearly all of them were old friends, including, of course, Angtharkay, Pasang and Kusang; but there was one Tibetan lad of nineteen, a newcomer with an infectious smile. His name was Tenzing Norgay.' Norgay means 'fortunate one', and his winning smile endeared him to Shipton. Tenzing did well on the 1935 expedition and joined subsequent British attempts on the north side of Everest. But load-carrying for foreigners was a precarious career, with long spells of impoverished unemployment, made harder when Tenzing's first wife died, leaving him to bring up two daughters alone until he found them a foster mother.

Tenzing's expeditioning continued through the '40s, when he became friendly with the leading Swiss climbers of the day. By now he had become a

Above: On 28 May 1953, Hillary and Tenzing, carrying loads of over 23 kilos (50 lb), climb up the Southeast Ridge on the way to their final camp.

Right: The two men, relaxed and ecstatic four days later, safely down from their historic climb.

competent mountaineer in his own right, with several first ascents under his belt. And in 1952 he was overjoyed to be asked by the Swiss to be sirdar – headman of the Sherpas – on the first attempt at Everest from the newly opened kingdom of Nepal: 'They might as well have asked if I would eat or breathe. The way I behaved about the house for a

few days, Ang Lhamu and the girls must have thought I was possessed by devils', Tenzing told his biographer.

As sirdar, Tenzing had to provide the lead and motivate the Sherpas, on whom the Swiss depended for carrying equipment and supplies up an almost completely unknown route – the chaotic jumble of the Khumbu Icefall; the immense white Valley of Silence, which Mallory, thirty years earlier, had called the Western Cwm; then the relentless 1,200-metre (nearly 4,000-ft) -high ice wall of the Lhotse Face; and then the utterly bleak, inhospitable, wind-scoured shelf of the South Col, almost 8,000 metres (26,250 ft) above sea level. It was from this godforsaken campsite that the Genevan mountaineer Raymond Lambert and Tenzing set off on a desperate summit attempt. With help from their companions, they placed a higher camp – a single tent – at 8,310 metres (27,265 ft). But the expedition had run out of steam. Despite Tenzing's fantastic energy and drive, his fellow Sherpas had not managed to stockpile enough gear high on the mountain. Now, shivering in the tiny tent, he and Lambert found themselves without stove or sleeping bags. Tenzing melted some snow with the flame of a candle to produce a dribble of water. But, as Lambert recalled afterwards, 'We were overtaken by a consuming thirst, which we could not appease.'

Despite the horrific night, the two men continued in the morning. However, their oxygen sets did not work, and although they probably climbed higher than any previous human being, gasping in the exceptionally thin air, they had to admit defeat.

Tenzing returned with a second Swiss expedition that autumn but was defeated by the arrival of the freezing winter winds. By now he was utterly exhausted, but he knew with total clarity that for him Chomolungma, the goddess mountain, was not just a job of work; he wanted desperately to climb to her summit himself. And, despite fears about his health, he knew he would have to return with the British in 1953.

So at 6:30 on the morning of 29 May 1953, Tenzing Norgay found himself roped to the tall, powerful New Zealander Ed Hillary, kicking steps into dazzling white snow, on the final steepening of

'From a hundred applicants, we chose fifteen Sherpas to accompany the expedition from Darjeeling ... there was one Tibetan lad of nineteen, a newcomer with an infectious smile. His name was Tenzing Norgay.'

Everest's southeast ridge, heading for the bump of the south summit, which they reached at about 9:00 A.M. Tom Bourdillon and Charles Evans had reached this point three days earlier, too late in the day to continue. Tenzing and Hillary, starting from a higher camp, had a much better chance. Building on Swiss experience, the British and their Sherpa supporters, inspired by Tenzing, had managed to build up sufficient support – and properly functioning oxygen sets – to put the summit team in a very strong position. Now all they had to do was tackle the final sting-in-the-tail.

Hillary led the way across a knife-edge ridge – a slender ribbon hanging in the sky over a 3,000-metre (10,000-ft) -high precipice, leading to an abrupt cliff 20 metres (65 ft) high. Then Tenzing paid out the rope as Hillary wrestled his way up a narrow chimney between snow and rock, bringing in the rope as Tenzing followed him. Above what is now known as the Hillary Step, the ridge continued for approximately 300 metres (nearly 1,000 ft), almost flat, over a series of tantalizing undulations. Then, at about 11:30 A.M., the two men emerged on top of the final, highest mound of snow.

Tenzing posed for one of the twentieth century's most enduring images, as Hillary photographed him holding aloft his ice axe, flying the flags of Britain, India, Nepal and the United Nations. Then Hillary buried in the snow the small crucifix the expedition leader, John Hunt, had given him, while Tenzing laid down his offerings of some sweets and a blue-and-red pencil given to him by his daughter Nima, then added the flags from his ice axe. Hillary held out his hand in a gesture of Anglo-Saxon reserve, but Tenzing, the Tibetan who had become a revered Sherpa, flung his arms around the New Zealander's neck as he whispered, 'Tuji Chey, Chomolongma' – I am grateful.

The 1988 American-Canadian-British Everest Expedition was the smallest team ever to climb an extreme new route up the world's highest mountain – just four climbers, no high-altitude Sherpas and no oxygen. The experts said they were crazy, but they ignored the experts and climbed a succession of terrifying walls, gullies and overhanging ice cliffs. On the final push Venables reached the summit alone, without oxygen equipment, at 3:40 P.M.

Four on the Kangshung Face

Robert Anderson, Paul Teare, Stephen Venables and Ed Webster (1988)

It might seem a bit presumptuous to include my own climb here, but it was a new route up the biggest wall of the world's highest mountain, and it was achieved by a very special team – the smallest group ever to pull off anything quite so hard on Everest. And like most of the best adventures, it happened almost by accident.

Robert Anderson grew up in Denver, started climbing, went to live for a while in Norway, returned to Colorado and, in 1985, found himself joining a large team of fellow Colorado climbers attempting Everest's gigantic West Ridge Direct. He came very close to the top and vowed to return. Two years later, when he applied for permission to the Chinese Mountaineering Association hoping to attempt the north face, they told him the north side was booked up for years but that he could have the east face in 1988.

Given that choice, most people would have waited a few years for the more conventional option. The east face – the Kangshung Face – was the biggest and probably most dangerous on the mountain, and no one had set foot on it since the one ascent in 1983, which had involved climbing of unprecedented difficulty. But Anderson was a bold entrepreneur (in his spare time he ran an advertising agency) and decided to give it a go. In Beijing he bumped into one of his Colorado companions from the west ridge attempt, Ed Webster, and persuaded him to come along. Back in America, Anderson tried to enthuse several other leading climbers, but they all declined politely, apart from a Canadian ex-pat named Paul Teare. By the end of 1987 Anderson had just three climbers. But he was successfully raising sponsorship money and upping the expedition's profile. When he asked John Hunt, the man who had led the first ascent of Everest in 1953, to be 'honorary leader', Lord Hunt – to use his official title – said he would be delighted, provided that Anderson invited a British climber to join the team. Which was how I got involved.

So on 1 March 1988, the American-Canadian-British Everest East Face Expedition assembled in Tibet – four climbers, who would be supported at base camp by Dr. Mimi Zieman, photographer Joseph Blackburn, Sherpa Pasang Norbu (cook) and Kasang Tsering (cookboy). Right from the start I knew that our chances of getting up the mountain were slim, but that uncertainty just added to the sense of adventure. Even though I had been to the Himalayas ten times before, everything about this trip, from the team to the mountain, was completely new.

That sense of heightened anticipation was intensified by the long approach, slogging through

Ed Webster took this picture at sunrise on 12 May, looking down onto the bleak expanse of the South Col. The eastern horizon is dominated by the world's fifth highest mountain, Makalu. Many, many hours later, caught out by darkness on the way back down, Webster and Anderson would spend a miserable night huddled without sleeping bags in the abandoned orange tent, at about 8,300 metres (27,000 ft), while Venables shivered 300 metres (1,000 ft) higher up.

The 1988 Kangshung team, from left to right: Venables, Anderson, Webster and Teare.

One of the highlights of their new route up the Kangshung Face was Webster's rope bridge over a crevasse at about 6,840 metres (22,500 ft).

snowdrifts, as we coaxed a hundred local Tibetan porters to carry all the baggage over an 5,500-metre (18,000-ft) pass leading to the Kama valley, one of the most beautiful valleys on earth. It was only at the end of March that we finally paid off all the porters and settled into the base camp that would be our home for the next two months.

When Everest was first climbed in 1953, the British expedition approached from Nepal, climbing up the Khumbu Icefall and Western Cwm to a bleak, high pass called the South Col, which is already higher than most other mountains in the world. Our plan, proposed by Webster, was to make a completely new route to the South Col from Tibet – up the Kangshung Face. If we ever got to the Col – and that seemed improbable – we would try to continue up the final part of the original route, the southeast ridge, to the summit. Because we were such a small team, with no Sherpas carrying loads for us, it didn't seem practical to carry heavy oxygen equipment. Like Peter Habeler and Reinhold Messner, who had proved it possible ten years earlier, we would just have to manage without.

We started climbing on 3 April 1988, and that first day set the tone. At dawn gigantic avalanches crashed down either side of our proposed route, falling thousands of feet in a few seconds. Nervous but confident that our line largely avoided the danger zone, we started work. It was thrilling to go where no one had ever been before, weaving a line up a series of ramps and chimneys, pausing to tackle a 60-metre (200-ft) wall of steep rock draped with icicles, then getting established in a huge snow gully.

The vertical landscape was stupendous, with great turrets and gargoyles hanging above our heads, gleaming against a dark sapphire sky. And for the next five days we continued to explore this landscape, taking turns to run out 100-metre (328-ft) lengths of rope, pushing the line ever higher, into ever more improbable terrain. On Day 4, Teare and Anderson led up an immense wall of marbled ice. On Day 5, Webster and I emerged onto the crest of some gigantic towers, where Webster climbed a wall of overhanging ice. On Day 6, after coming all the way back up the ropes from Advance Base, I led the next section, only to be stopped dead by an immense chasm spanning the whole of what we had come to call the Neverest Buttress.

A big climb like this is a psychological game, where you have to contend with a whole series of highs and lows, reasserting your belief in the project after each setback. Once we had had a few days at base camp, we returned to work, carrying up supplies for a 'Camp One' and dealing with the Crevasse, which meant sending our star climber, Webster, down into the bowels of the ice to engineer his way up the overhanging far wall of the Crevasse until he could pull a rope across to create a bridge. We called it the Highest Bridge in the World.

Bad weather confined us to base camp for a week. Then we returned to work, pushing the route out to 7,500 metres (24,600 ft). Then, in this infernal game of snakes and ladders, the weather sent us back to base. We had several abortive starts. Nerves grew frayed. Finally, on 8 May, we set off on what we hoped was our push to the summit.

Up to this point, despite occasional moments of terror – particularly when the avalanches crashed down in the darkness – we had enjoyed ourselves. The climbing had been utterly spectacular, and everyone had seen a share of the action. It had been fun. Now, though, we were going to have to notch up commitment levels as we pushed our bodies higher and higher into the thin air, fighting our own weakness with little prospect of actual pleasure.

But even on that final masochistic push, there were moments of pure enchantment. Like waking up on 10 May at our Camp 2, having slogged for fourteen hours through knee-deep snow to get there the previous day, to be greeted by a vista of peaks stretching eastward all the way to Bhutan, dazzling under a sky of deepest Prussian blue. That day it took us eleven hours to climb the remaining 400 metres (1,310 ft) or so to the top of our route: the South Col. And even then, despite the desperate panting and the malevolent, numbing wind, it was thrilling to know that we were the first people ever to reach this bleak spot from Tibet.

For Paul Teare the South Col was the end of the road. He felt ill, feared the high-altitude killer – cerebral oedema – and decided courageously the next morning to descend. Three of us remained at almost 8,000 metres (26,250 ft) above sea level, hoping that

Stephen Venables, still with his headtorch on his forehead, trying to force a smile through frozen lips, after his night out in the open at about 8,500 metres (28,000 ft).

the flat surface began to rise up into the first big snow gully leading towards the southeast ridge. There was no moon that night. Higher than any other human beings on earth, we felt utterly alone. That loneliness was intensified by climbing unroped, each of us choosing his own speed and rhythm, seeing how far he could push his puny body.

We had already crossed so many barriers on this climb, surprising ourselves as we discovered that our presumptuous plan was actually working. Now, on this final leg of the journey – 900 metres (2,950 ft) of ascent from the South Col to the summit – we had to cross even bigger barriers. Several times that day, I thought that I had reached a wall, only to find that I could pass through it and push my body further. And even here, struggling just to exist, it was possible through the numbing fog of hypoxia to feel little bursts of pleasure: the visceral, animal joy of sunrise, bringing warmth and hope; the excited recognition of the Western Cwm far, far below; then, much later, the nervous thrill of reaching the south summit and staring across a scarily exposed ridge at the famous Hillary Step.

It was now about 1:30 P.M.. Anderson and Webster were some way behind, and it seemed unlikely that they would reach the summit before nightfall. I figured I had just enough time to reach the top, so I continued along that knife edge, gasping and kicking up Hillary's famous cliff, plodding along the final ridge, easy but interminable, racing the clouds that were now swirling around the summit.

I reached the top at 3:40 P.M. and allowed myself just ten minutes sitting there, alone in the swirling mist, trying to soak up the experience and store it away to be treasured later. As soon as I began my descent, I knew that this was going to be a supreme struggle. We might have crossed several barriers that day, but there were still even bigger ones awaiting us on the way down.

Ed and Robert were both forced by driving snow and cloud to turn around at the south summit, at about the same time that I was fighting my way down from the main summit, stumbling, hyperventilating, groping myopically through the stinging snow and starting to shiver. I had always wondered what it would be like to have to really fight for survival, and now I was finding out.

By the time darkness fell, the other two had taken shelter in an abandoned Japanese tent at about 8,400

the battering wind would subside and give us a chance at the summit.

That night we got our chance. We prepared meticulously, forcing our oxygen-starved brains to concentrate on all the vital tasks – melting snow and ice to make drinks; forcing down a meal; warming inner boots, outer boots and overboots inside sleeping bags before putting them on, lacing them loosely in an attempt to preserve circulation through our sluggish veins; checking that we each had spare headlamp bulb, spare mittens, bar of chocolate, bottle of fruit juice stuffed deep in a pocket beneath five layers of carefully selected clothing.

Then at 11:00 P.M. we zipped shut the two tiny dome tents and set off, crunching across the icy wasteland of the South Col, soon panting harder as metres (27,500 ft). I was still out in the open, 250 metres (820 ft) higher up, unwilling to risk descending in the dark. With my ice axe I cut a ledge in the steep snow slope, then lay down on my side to shiver through the long night. Occasionally I sat up and reached inside my down jacket to pull out my water bottle and sip the last remains of ice-encrusted fruit juice. Desperate for calories, I also forced myself to chew a frozen Hershey bar, which tasted disappointingly of cardboard. Then I lay down again, wishing that there were someone here to take off my boots and massage my frozen feet.

There was no wind that night, and I survived. At sunrise I stood stiffly and wobbled down the mountain to the Japanese tent, where I was delighted to discover Anderson and Webster – human company at last. Together we continued down to the South Col, where we collapsed inside our own tents, sprawling luxuriously in down-filled sleeping bags as the gas stove purred, melting snow for our chronically dehydrated bodies.

The struggle was by no means over. By the time we set off down from the South Col the next day, 14 May, we had been above 7,900 metres (25,920 ft) for nearly four days. We had overstayed our welcome in the 'death zone', and we were running on reserve. The descent back down the east face, which Paul had accomplished in just seven hours, was to take us nearly three days, one whole day completely wasted as we languished in our sleeping bags at Camp 2, enervated by the heat of the sun bouncing off dazzling snow, too weak, physically and mentally, to stir ourselves to action.

In the end it was Webster who encouraged us to continue. Taking photos on the summit day, he had accidentally frostbitten his fingers when he kept his mittens off a few seconds too long. Now his fingers were purple and blistered, and he was desperate to get off the mountain. So after our final cup of tepid dirty water, we set off on the morning of 16 May, ditching most of our survival gear to save weight. We had now hardly eaten for four days, and we were desperately weak. Time after time we stopped, slumped in the deep heavy snow, until someone found the energy to wade on a bit further. Even with gravity on our side, it seemed monumentally difficult.

I think the moment I really knew that everything was going to be all right was when we reached the top of our fixed ropes. Our intention all along had been to strip the ropes from the mountain in the course of an orderly retreat. Now there was no chance of fulfilling those fine notions, and we knew we would barely get ourselves down. Even with the ropes in place, it took all night for Webster and me to abseil our way down to the foot of the Buttress, and Anderson didn't come down until the following afternoon. There was still no moon and, just to make matters worse, our final torch bulb blew, leaving us to grope our way down in the darkness, remembering by feel every detail of the vertical landscape we had first explored seven weeks earlier. Every section of rope,

> **'Desperate for calories, I also forced myself to chew a frozen Hershey bar, which tasted disappointingly of cardboard. Then I lay down again, wishing that there were someone here to take off my boots and massage my frozen feet.'**

every anchor, every rock and icicle was redolent with memories of a great adventure, so that I almost felt a sense of sadness, of regret that this extraordinary journey was coming to an end.

However, I also felt a surge of excitement as we trudged the last mile across the glacier to advance base, approaching the haven of the tents, nine days after setting out for the summit, knowing that we really had returned safely. For Webster the return was more painful as he realized that his frozen fingers had become shredded during the long struggle down the ropes. He later had to have the tips of one thumb and seven fingers amputated. Anderson and I also suffered some damage, losing toes to frostbite. Paul Teare, the man who had been forced to descend early, was unscathed. For all of us, though, to have climbed a new route, without oxygen or Sherpas' support, up Everest's biggest and possibly most dangerous face was a great adventure – the kind of adventure that provides retrospective satisfaction to last a lifetime.

Ogre

Height
7,285 metres (23,902 ft)

Location
Karakoram Range, Baltistan,
Pakistan-occupied-Kashmir

Origin of name
The Ogre epithet was given
by Sir Martin Conway,
leader of the first modern
climbing expedition to the
Karakoram in 1892. The

local Balti name is
Baintha Brakk.

First ascent
13 July 1977: Chris
Bonington/Doug Scott by
West Face and West Summit

Other key route
South Pillar 2001: Thomas
Huber/Urs Stöcker/Iwan
Wolf – first complete ascent
of pillar to summit

Interesting facts
The Ogre rises in the heart
of one of the most extensively
glaciated regions of Asia.
The combined length of the
Biafo and Hispar glaciers is
over 96.5 km (60 miles).
The Biafo is fed additionally
by Snow Lake and the
Sim Gang Glacier. Echo
soundings to the bedrock
have measured an ice

thickness of nearly
1,500 metres (5,000 ft).
The first European to see
Ogre was probably Sir
Martin Conway, in 1892.

Over the last thirty years nearly thirty expeditions have attempted the Ogre; only two have reached its summit. On the first ascent Bonington and Scott reached the summit at sunset. On the first abseil down Scott skidded on ice, took a huge swing and broke both ankles. It was nightfall, the two men were some 7,300 metres (23,000 ft) above sea level and 3,000 metres (10,000 ft) of fiendishly difficult terrain lay between them and the safety of base camp.

Crawling Back to Earth
Chris Bonington and Doug Scott (1977)

The Karakoram is the grandest, mightiest, most savage mountain range on earth, and of all its myriad peaks, perhaps the most impressive of all is the Ogre. It towers above some of the greatest glaciers on the planet outside the polar regions – the giant corner block around which the ice of the Sim Gang Glacier, 1,500 metres (5,000 ft) thick, flows into the Biafo Glacier. Legend has it that local Balti people used to raid and trade across the great icy passes nearby, but nowadays the only visitors are the foreigners who come to gaze at the incomparable scenery. And to attempt some of the most elusive summits in the world.

The Ogre has proved the most elusive of them all. It has been climbed only twice, and the two ascents were separated by nearly twenty unsuccessful attempts by some of the world's best climbers, spread over twenty-five years. Some mountains are like cathedrals; they lend themselves to the language of soaring vaults and spires and elegant flying buttresses, but with the Ogre it is military architecture that springs to mind – ramparts, battlements and castellations. This particular castle is elongated, with three towers studding a long ridge bristling with subsidiary turrets. The central, highest tower is like an impregnable bastion with walls of smooth vertical granite, stuck unceremoniously atop a precipice 2,500 metres (8,200 ft) high.

Doug Scott, standing immediately beneath this grossly foreshortened south face in 1977, used more blunt language. 'It was not a beautiful mountain from down here, being squat and having three small cones, like misplaced nipples, defining the summit, with the centre cone the highest.' However, he and his five companions were entranced by the mountain above them. The plan was for Doug Scott and Paul Braithwaite to attempt 'the one elegant feature' – a soaring rock buttress up the south face – while Mo Anthoine, Chris Bonington, Nick Estcourt and Clive Rowland attempted a more devious flanking manoeuvre farther left, hoping to reach the triangular west face of the mountain.

This was a loose-knit team of highly talented, hugely experienced ambitious individuals, not averse to a bit of gamesmanship and opportunistic regrouping to suit circumstances. But disaster struck early, in the form of a large rock hitting Braithwaite's leg, ending the south pillar attempt prematurely. Mo Anthoine, court jester to the team, announced: 'Mountain one; climbers nil.'

Round 2 had already begun on the icy ribs farther left, leading to the west col. From here Bonington and Estcourt traversed rightward onto the upper south face, above Scott's Pillar. Feeling as though they were literally hanging out on a limb, with very little

Chris Bonington looking pensive in the snow cave as the storm rages outside. He, Anthoine and Rowland still have to descend nearly 3,000 metres (10,000 ft) and the fourth man, Doug Scott, has two broken legs.

food or gear, they veered left, away from the impregnable central summit and won themselves the consolation prize of the west summit. Mountain one; climbers one.

Meanwhile, the others had been working on the west face. Bonington and Estcourt returned to base. Estcourt had a bad cough and was due to return to his job in Britain. But Bonington was now keen to attempt the real prize: the highest summit. 'Although I was tired, I still had a driving urge to reach the top of the Ogre. It was a combination of a feeling of failure that I hadn't at least had a try at the summit block, and the very human, if somewhat childish, fear of being left out of a successful party.' So back he went, up the ropes, to the west col to join Anthoine, Rowland and Scott, who were pushing out a new route up the west face. 'I had been worried about my reception but they seemed glad to see me and I almost immediately felt part of the team. That night, as there was only one tent, I slept outside, using the Gore-Tex cover over my sleeping bag. It was chilly but also satisfying, the sky a brilliant black, studded with stars that had a clarity that only altitude can give. I decided it wasn't just ego that brought me back. It was good to be part of this mountain, part of a team with the simple, all-consuming objective of reaching the top of that great citadel of rock that had defeated Nick and me only a few days before.'

The next day, Anthoine and Rowland completed the route up a 300-metre (nearly 1,000-ft)-high rock band. Then on 11 July, the whole team set off, carrying just one lightweight bivouac tent, plus food and cooking gas, intent on crossing the west summit and continuing to the still untrodden central summit.

There was more hard ground that day, climbing diagonally across smooth rock and ice slabs, and they hadn't made the west summit by nightfall. It was only on the next day, 12 July, that they crossed the west summit and descended the far side to the huge ice face where Bonington and Estcourt had bivouacked a week earlier. It was an incredible spot for their final bivouac – an immense sweep of ice, tilted at 50°, a dizzy roof suspended over great ramparts plunging into the chaos of a fractured glacier 2,500 metres (8,200 ft) beneath them. Plastered precariously to this ice sheet was a thick layer of snow, into which they dug, excavating a cave with room for all four climbers to sleep, sheltered from whatever the weather might fling at them.

For the moment the weather remained immaculate. On 13 July, Bonington and Scott set out first, at 5:00 A.M., traversing rightward across the great tilted roof. They had a long way to go, and it was only in the afternoon that they began their ascent towards the final tower. Bonington belayed while Scott worked above him on the wall. Bonington was disappointed that his companion had bagged the best lead of the climb, but he managed to lose himself in the majesty of their surroundings. Looking west, he could see Anthoine and Rowland at work on the crenellated ridge. Beyond them a single dotted line of footprints led back across the tilted snowfield to the faint impression of the snow cave. From there the line continued *up* to the west summit. Hidden on the far side lay the convoluted complexities of the west face. To get off this mountain, they were going to have to reverse the whole of that route.

There was a shout from above, the slack was pulled in, and Bonington climbed up to join Scott. 'Doug was on a small ledge at the foot of a sheer rock wall split by a thin crack. I didn't volunteer to lead it. This was obviously going to be hard. Doug took off his crampons and started climbing the crack. Then he shouted, 'The crack's blind. Let me down.' He lowered himself about 15 metres [50 ft] from his top runner, a wired nut. Then he started running from side to side to gain some momentum, trying to reach the crack to the right with a skyhook. It took several tries, but at last he managed to lodge a skyhook, haul himself across, and jam his fingers into the crack. He tried to get a foothold, but his boot, big and clumsy against the finger-width crack, slipped and suddenly he was swinging back away from his objective. He tried again. This time he found a toehold and began finger-jamming up the crack until he was level with and then above his wire runner. It would have been strenuous at sea level. Here, at over 7,000 metres [23,000 ft], it was incredible. I lost all sense of resentment in wonder at what Doug had managed to do, at his strength, ingenuity and determination.'

Bonington followed by jumaring up the rope. It was now late, and Anthoine and Rowland had returned to the cave. Up on the tower, Bonington at last had a turn in the lead, but he was confronted by an overhang. Scott joined him and stood on his shoulder to reach holds above the overhang. Scott continued in the lead again, 'his own driving force sweeping everything else aside'. Bonington followed, and twenty minutes later he joined his companion on a tiny block of rock. The Ogre was climbed.

> 'He tried to get a foothold, but his boot, big and clumsy against the finger-width crack, slipped and suddenly he was swinging back away from his objective. He tried again.'

There was just enough time to snap a quick photo of Scott shivering against a stupendous backdrop of endless peaks and glaciers fading to grey, summits silhouetted against the purple darkening sky. Then they set off down into the night.

Scott went first, abseiling on double ropes suspended from a block, tensioning sideways to reach the peg crack he had climbed that afternoon.

'I leaned across to fix myself onto a peg, pressing myself over with my feet. I stepped my right foot up against the wall but, in the gathering darkness, unwittingly placed it on a veneer of water ice. Suddenly my foot shot off and I found myself

Bonington follows one of the very hard rock pitches on the final summit tower. In the picture on page 143 this is the right hand tower: the left one is the West Summit, which the team had to cross before they could start the long descent.

swinging away into the gloom, clutching the end of the rope. And all the time I was swinging, a little exclamation of awe, surprise and fear was coming out from inside me, audible to Mo some 600 metres (2,000 ft) away at the cave. And then the swing and the cry ended as I slammed into the opposite side of the gully. *Splat*! Glasses gone and every bone shaken. A quick examination revealed head and trunk okay, femurs and knees okay, but – Oh, oh! – my ankles cracked whenever I moved them. So that was how it was going to be: a whole new game, with new restrictions on winning.'

Bonington abseiled down to join Scott, telling him cheerily, 'Don't worry, you're a long way from death', before continuing down to a snow patch where he hacked out a large ledge for the night. As Scott joined him on the ledge, he tried walking across. 'I put my body weight on my legs and ankles. They both collapsed, the right leg cracking horribly. So I got on my knees, with my lower legs stuck out behind, and kneed across the ledge with no trouble at all. So that's how it's done, I thought.'

Calm words from a man crippled with two broken legs at over 7,000 metres (23,000 ft) just beneath one of the hardest summits in the world. But that phlegmatic calm was the product of years of experience in the high mountains, in particular his bivouac two years earlier, close to the summit of Everest, without oxygen, sleeping bag or even a down jacket. Ever since then, he had known that he could survive just about anywhere. And both men knew *how* to go about that survival, rubbing each other's toes to stave off frostbite through the long, freezing night.

On the morning of 14 July, they continued abseiling to the snowfield; then Anthoine came across from the cave to kick bucket steps for Scott's knees. That night, they ate their last freeze-dried meal, leaving just soup and tea.

Ever British and understated, Doug noted the next morning 'with some concern' that a blizzard was raging outside the snow cave. Anthoine and Rowland went out to try and climb the 100 metres (330 ft) to the west summit but returned, defeated by driving snow and white-out conditions.

The next day, the blizzard relented slightly, but it took all day to kick bucket steps up and over the west summit to a miserably cramped snow cave that they had dug three days earlier.

'Next morning Mo stuck his head out and announced that the storm was now, if anything, worse.' But they had to get down, all the way to the highest camp, where they had left a pound of sugar, in order to sustain themselves for the rest of the descent. 'It was a nightmare descent. Whenever there was a ridge of level ground, I found crawling painful, seeming always to be catching my legs on protruding rocks. Only on steep snowed-up rocks did I feel comfortable, for then Mo would have fixed up the abseil ropes and I could slide down with my body, whilst my feet stuck out, out of the way of obstacles.'

'My legs were very swollen from knocking them countless times. I stopped to examine them and was horrified to find that I had worn right through four layers of clothing and that my knees were numb, bloody and swollen.'

Abseiling down one doubled rope, exhausted and blinded by driving spindrift, Bonington failed to notice that one rope was longer than the other. As his weight came onto the long end, the shorter end whipped skyward and he found himself hurtling down the mountain. Luckily Rowland had tied off the long end, and after tumbling about 6 metres (20 ft) Bonington was brought to a halt. But he had damaged his hand painfully and smashed two ribs.

Now Anthoine and Rowland had *two* injured men to look after. And they still had a long way to go.

Late that afternoon they reached the tents, flattened under 1 metre (3 ft) of new snow. Anthoine and Rowland laboured selflessly to re-erect the tents and make the other two men comfortable, but it was nearly impossible to ease their pain.

On 17 July they stayed put, licking their wounds. Bonington now had pneumonia, and every cough racked his damaged torso. Anthoine's fingers had been numb for a week; Rowland couldn't feel his toes.

Scott remained a tower of strength as they made their way down the following day. 'I found that being on hands and knees was actually an advantage in particularly deep snow, and I did a bit of trail-breaking. At the former west col campsite, we dug around and found some boiled sweets mixed with cigarette ash, which we ate.'

They continued wading down on 19 July, Scott now crawling arms first through the snow, carrying his share of luggage in a rucksack and helping to set up the evening's camp. 'Chris came in very slowly, coughing up a rich yellow fluid from his lungs.'

At last, on July 20, the sixth day since the summit, they neared Advance Base. Anthoine and Bonington went first, chopping big steps at key points on the route. Rowland followed later with Scott, who made quick work of abseiling 800 metres (2,600 ft) down the fixed ropes. 'Crawling over soft snow down to 5,000 metres [16,400 ft] was also relatively easy, but after that I had to crawl over hard glacier ice.'

Once there, they were horrified to find nothing at Advance Base. With no alternative, they had to continue down to the base camp. According to Scott, those last 7 km (4.5 miles) of crawling were the most painful. 'My legs were very swollen from knocking them countless times. I stopped to examine them and was horrified to find that I had worn right through four layers of clothing and that my knees were numb, bloody and swollen.' At 10:30 that night he finally crawled onto the sweet, soft grass of the base camp, one week after breaking his legs on the summit.

They found a note from Nick Estcourt, who had hung on heroically, agonizing over what to do for his friends, saying, 'If you get as far as reading this then it presumably means that at least one of you is alive.' The note then explained that he had gone down to the nearest village to fetch Paul Braithwaite to try to organize a search party. Anthoine rushed off in pursuit, and five days later he and Estcourt returned with twelve Balti porters. As the Balti men carried Scott in a homemade stretcher for three days over horribly rough ground down to the village, he was overwhelmed with admiration. 'Never once did they look like they were going to drop me and I seldom felt a jolt. It was good to lie out, listening and waiting as they made decisions as to route-finding, choice of camping place, who should fetch wood and water, who should take the heavier part of the stretcher. They knew just what to do.'

He was then bundled into a helicopter, which crashed on arrival in the town of Skardu, amazingly without causing any injuries. After a week's delay for repairs, the chopper flew back to collect Bonington; then the two men were flown to the capital, Islamabad. Battered, broken, with lank, matted hair and still dressed in the same filthy thermal underwear they had worn on top of the Ogre, the two men were dumped unceremoniously on the immaculate manicured grass of the British embassy golf course.

Buffeted by wind and snow, Scott crawls over the West Summit, at the start of the long painful descent.

Nanga Parbat

Height
8,125 metres (26,658 ft)

Location
Himalayas, Pakistan-occupied Kashmir

Origin of name
The Urdu name Nanga Parbat means 'Naked Mountain.' Also known on its west side as Diamir – 'King of Mountains'.

First ascent
3 July 1953: Hermann Buhl, by Rakhiot Face and Silbersattel

Other key routes:
Diamir Face 'Kinshofer Route' 1962: Austrian-German

Rupal Face 1970: Reinhold and Gunther Messner

Rupal Flank 'Schell Route' 1976: Hanns Schell/Robert Schauer/Siegfried Gimpel/Hilmar Sturm

Rupal Face Direct 2005: Steve House/Vince Anderson

Interesting facts
Nanga Parbat marks the western end of the main Himalayan chain, where the Indus river cuts a gigantic bend towards the plains.

The elevation from river to summit is over 7,285 metres (23,000 ft), in one of the most seismologically active areas on earth. Some of the granites on the mountain, now over 6,000 metres (19,685 ft) above sea level, were formed only 800,000 years ago, about 32 km (20 miles) beneath the earth's surface.

In 1970 Reinhold Messner and his younger brother Günther reached the summit of the Naked Mountain via the Rupal Face. Unable to retrace their steps, they set off on a desperate descent of the mountain's unknown Diamir Face. Somewhere along the way, Günther was lost. After a desperate search for his brother, Reinhold – starving, frostbitten, hallucinating – was found by local shepherds and helped down to the Indus Valley.

Destiny and Obsession on the Naked Mountain

Reinhold Messner (1970)

I focused my eyes on the last sharp peak, the summit ridge dead ahead, with only the sky above. Suddenly I found myself standing on a final dome of snow – the summit of Nanga Parbat. It was the best day of my life, especially as Günther was there to share it.'

It was 5:00 in the afternoon of 27 June 1970, and Reinhold Messner had just completed a new route up the greatest precipice in the world: the summit of Nanga Parbat. It was a moment of supreme elation. And extreme danger. Messner had never intended his younger brother to follow his dangerous solo dash to the summit. Now he realized that without a rope, Günther could not reverse the precarious traverse they had taken earlier that day. The two men were completely alone, without bivouac equipment, 8,125 metres (26,658 ft) above sea level. Soon it would be dark and the temperature would plummet to at least -30°C (-22°F). They had climbed into a desperate trap – a horrific nightmare from which only one brother would escape alive.

Reinhold Messner was born in 1944, in the German-speaking part of the South Tirol, which had ceded to Italy after the First World War. Here, in the heart of the Dolomite mountains, he and his seven brothers grew up. With Günther he formed an incredibly strong climbing partnership, and during the '60s the two brothers climbed virtually all the great limestone faces of the Dolomites, in summer and in winter. Reinhold also travelled to the Western Alps, where his 1969 solo ascent of the icy northeast face of the Droites – then considered the hardest ice climb in the Alps – in just eight hours stunned the whole mountaineering world. He was a star, driven by bold vision and voracious ambition. And with his phenomenal alpine record, he was waiting for a chance to test himself in the world's greatest mountain range, the Himalayas. His chance came when Dr. Karl Herrligkoffer invited him to join the 1970 expedition to the south face of Nanga Parbat. It was only at the last moment, when another member had to drop out, that, at Reinhold's father's urging, Günther joined the team.

Nanga Parbat is a mountain of extremes. Its gigantic bulk rises 7,285 metres (23,000 ft) in just a few miles from the hot desert gorge of the Indus river, the greatest elevation on earth. It is a vast, sprawling mass, with tier after tier of immense ice cliffs stacked murderously on the ramparts of its three main faces. It is notorious for avalanches.

Reinhold Messner's thumb survived the injuries of Nanga Parbat, but he lost parts of several toes, frostbitten during the epic traverse of 1970. The Rupal Face, pictured on page 148, is more than 4,000 metres (13,124 ft) high – possibly the greatest precipice on earth.

And buttressing the western end of the main Himalayan chain, it is famous for its storms. But its notoriety stems from more than mere physical extremes, because Nanga Parbat is steeped in history – a history of triumph, tragedy and struggle on an epic scale.

That epic struggle has been a predominantly German, or German-speaking, affair. In the '30s, while the British laid siege to Everest, it was German and Austrian climbers who set their hearts on Nanga Parbat, organizing five expeditions in all. During the 1934 expedition several climbers were trapped high on the mountain by a ferocious storm and froze to death, their companions unable to get to them through chest-deep snow; in 1937 sixteen climbers were killed instantly when their tents were struck by a massive avalanche; by 1939 eleven Germans and fifteen Nepalese Sherpas lay dead on the slopes of Nanga Parbat.

The long, arduous pre-war route, crossing several tantalizing foresummits, was finally completed in 1953. Only one climber, Hermann Buhl, reached the summit, travelling completely alone from the top

camp and reaching the summit at 7.00 P.M. When darkness fell, he was forced to spend the night in the open, wearing just two layers of light clothing (he had left his rucksack with spare clothes lower down), standing upright on a precarious ledge. There was no wind that night, and he survived his torture, eventually regaining camp the next day, about forty hours after setting out. It was one of the most extraordinary survival feats in the annals of mountaineering.

That epic legacy was the background to Reinhold Messner's 1970 climb. Nanga Parbat was more than just a mountain. And as if to reinforce that sense of history, the 1970 expedition was led by Dr. Karl Herrligkoffer, nephew of Willy Merkl, who had perished in the great storm of 1934. Herrligkoffer, although not much of a climber himself, had organized three previous Nanga Parbat projects, including the 1953 first ascent; he had criticized Buhl for going alone to the top and, even though he was a doctor, virtually refused to help with Buhl's subsequent frostbite injuries. His expeditions were famous for their controversy, and 1970 would be no exception.

It was a large team, which fixed ropes steadily up the gigantic, 4,000 metre- (13,125-ft)-high, south or 'Rupal' face. Apart from the south face of Annapurna, climbed earlier that year by a British team, nothing this vast and steep had ever before been attempted in the Himalayas. The Messner

> **'As we approached the summit, maybe at midday, we should have realised that it was too late.'**

brothers did their share of the work and performed well. Reinhold, in particular, discovered that he was a natural at high altitude. Sturdy and broad-chested, he had a fantastic capacity for work in the enervating thin, dry air. Add to that physiological adaptability his phenomenal technical climbing skill and his sheer will, and there was the perfect candidate for a bold summit attempt.

After weeks of toil, supplies were running low, bad weather was threatening, and time was running out. Messner persuaded Herrligkoffer that, if the

weather forecast was bad on 26 June, the team leader should let off a red signal rocket from base camp. That would be the signal for Messner, poised at the top camp, to make a solo dash to the summit and back, relying on his speed to beat the storm. If the forecast was good, a blue rocket would signal a more conservative team effort.

For some reason, although the forecast was good, Herrligkoffer set off a red rocket, so Messner set off alone before dawn on 27 June, intending to climb 900 metres (nearly 3,000 ft) of unknown steep terrain to the summit and back in a single day. He took no food, no tent, no rope – nothing, apart from a tiny Minox camera and, for emergencies, a flimsy space blanket.

At first he followed a gully that had been named the Merkl Gully. When it became too difficult, he traversed out to the right. 'Again and again I stopped, ramming my ice axe into the snow and leaning hard on it, often looking down to make sure I had memorized the route for my descent. Suddenly I stopped short. Was that someone following me up? There, a short way below, was a climber. Who could it be? It was Günther!' At first he was angry, but soon he felt glad that he was to share this great day – which was proving to have perfect weather – with his brother.

They continued, stopping frequently to gasp and pant, tortured by the savage heat of the sun's rays burning through the thin air. 'As we approached the summit, maybe at midday, we should have realized that it was too late.' But they continued, traversing diagonally across the top of the biggest wall in the Himalayas, riding a wave of euphoria.

In 1978 Messner returned to Nanga Parbat, this time completely alone, soloing an audacious new route up the Diamir Face, culminating in this self-portrait on the summit of 'The Naked Mountain'.

virtually no wind that night. Still alive in the morning, Messner looked down and saw two team-mates, Scholz and Kuen, climbing up his route of the previous day, heading for the summit. According to Messner, he shouted across to them to deviate from the traverse and climb up with a rope; according to them, he shouted that he and Günther were okay.

Whatever actually happened, they were far from okay. Unable, without a rope, to get back down the Merkl Gully, they had to take desperate measures. 'If we couldn't get on to the Rupal Face, there was only one way down – the other side. It was very dangerous. But it was the only choice; with no food, or stove or bivouac gear apart from a space blanket, we had to get down.'

So they embarked on the first unsupported traverse of a big Himalayan peak, heading into the unknown, down the Diamir Face. Messner knew that a British pioneer named Alfred Mummery had managed to retreat from quite high on the centre of this face, when he had attempted a rocky rib on this side, way back in 1895. Surely Messner could do the same? But first he had to lead Günther down to the start of the Mummery Rib.

'At the top you can see nothing – just a big convex slope falling away – so it was very hard to find the way through ice cliffs.' But he succeeded miraculously in finding the top of the rib, and by nightfall the two brothers were halfway down. They stopped for a second bivouac – another shivering night without food, water or shelter – then continued descending at dawn. Just one and half days after leaving the summit ridge, they had descended the entire gigantic Diamir Face.

And so the two brothers shared this moment of exquisite triumph. Then they began their descent into nightmare.

Thirty years later I questioned Reinhold Messner about Nanga Parbat and he confessed: 'I still don't know exactly what happened that day.' What he did remember was the absolute conviction that, exhausted and not safeguarded by a rope, his brother could not descend the awkward traverse. Instead, they set off down the ridge to spend a miserable night huddled in a little hollow directly above the Merkl Gully. Like Buhl, they were lucky that there was

'When I saw the shepherds, I did not know if they were real or just another hallucination. I had not eaten for days, my toes were black from frostbite, and my brother was lost in the avalanche.'

It was while walking down the glacier that Günther was lost. It was the kind of mistake that one can so easily understand. Reinhold, frostbitten, hallucinating and chronically dehydrated after three days without water, pressed on ahead, desperate to find a meltwater

pool, hoping Günther would follow. The younger brother, even more wrecked, took a different route and never emerged on the lower glacier. Reinhold dredged up even deeper reserves to climb back up the glacier. He found a massive pile of fresh avalanche debris but continued searching, shouting himself delirious for another two days before abandoning hope and using the last shreds of his strength to drag his emaciated body down to the meadows of the Diamir Valley.

'When I saw the shepherds, I did not know if they were real or just another hallucination. I had not eaten for days, my toes were black from frostbite, and my brother was lost in the avalanche. I hardly knew if I was alive myself.' The shepherds helped him down to their village. On the other side of the mountain, Herrligkoffer had given Messner up for dead and was amazed to meet him, a few days later, in the hill town of Gilgit.

Back in Munich, Messner had several frostbitten toes amputated, but neither that injury nor the tragic loss of a brother dented his ambition. Over the next sixteen years he proceeded to climb all the world's fourteen 'eight-thousanders,' some of them twice, including Everest, all without oxygen equipment. And he returned several times to Nanga Parbat, his mountain of destiny, revisiting the Diamir glacier, searching for his lost brother.

Nanga Parbat became an obsession, and in 1978, a few weeks after making the first oxygen-less ascent of Everest, he made the first-ever solo ascent of a 26,248-ft (8,000-metre) peak, spending three days climbing up and down the Diamir face of Nanga Parbat – the same face down which he had made the desperate retreat in 1970. But even after that he kept returning to the mountain. Perhaps as an act of atonement, but also as thanks for saving his life in 1970, he donated money to build a school for the subsistence farmers of Diamir. But real peace came only in 2005, when the remains of Günther finally emerged from the glacier ice.

The Diamir Face – scene of Reinhold and Gunther Messner's desperate descent in 1970. The summit is in the centre. From there the two brothers descended to a gap (1) where they bivouacked in the open. The following day they began to descend the Mummery Rib (2) bivouacking again, before continuing down to the main glacier (3), where Gunther is believed to have been buried by an avalanche.

K2

Height
8,611 metres (28,252 ft)

Location
Karakoram range,
Baltistan–Sinkiang border

Origin of name
K2 was a nineteenth-century
label given by the Survey of
India during the initial
measuring of the Karakoram
peaks (the less remote

was labeled K1). On the
northern, Sinkiang, side
it is sometimes called
Chogori.

First ascent
31 July 1954: Achille
Campagnoni/Lino Lacedelli
by Abruzzi Spur

Other key routes
Northeast Ridge/Abruzzi
finish 1978: Lou Reichardt/

West Ridge1981: Eiho
Otani/Nazir Sabir

North Ridge 1982: Naoé
Sakashita/Yukihiro
Yanagisawa/Hiroshi Yoshino

South-Southwest Ridge 1986:
Peter Bozik/ Przemyslaw
Piasecki/Wojciech Wröz

South Face 1986: Jerzy
Kukuczka/Tadeusz Piotrowsk

Interesting facts
K2 is regarded as the most
difficult of the big Himalayan
peaks. Steep on every side,
all the way to the summit,
it is very unforgiving and
the expense of portering
supplies to its base prohibits
all but the richest expeditions
from using oxygen.

Since the first American attempt in 1938, the world's second highest summit was the ultimate goal for American climbers. Jim Wickwire, a Seattle lawyer, helped organize an expedition in 1975, then returned in 1978 to attempt the unclimbed East Ridge. Wickwire stayed so long on the summit that he was caught out by darkness, and forced to bivouac, alone, in the open, without shelter, at over 8,230 metres (27,000 ft). Suffering pneumonia, pleurisy and frostbite as a result, he nevertheless managed to descend to safety with the aid of his companions.

The Final Step

Jim Wickwire (1978)

For Jim Wickwire the big dream was always K2. Everest might be 239 lung-bursting metres (784 ft) higher, but K2 was the real mountaineer's mountain. It was partly the austere remoteness of the peak, on the wild frontier of Baltistan and Sinkiang; partly the uncompromising aesthetic purity of the towering pyramid; and partly a matter of history. K2 was woven deep into the psyche of American mountaineers.

That sense of American destiny dated from 1938 when Dr. Charles Houston led his first attempt on the southeast ridge, known as the Abruzzi Spur. The following year Fritz Wiessner led a woefully inexperienced team on the same route; his climb to within 250 metres (820 ft) of the summit was an astonishing performance, but during the ensuing chaos one American and three Nepalese Sherpas perished. In noble contrast to that sad affair, Houston's second attempt in 1953 culminated in a heroic attempt by six men to evacuate their seventh companion, stricken by a thrombosis high on the ridge. During the evacuation five men and the man taken ill, Art Gilkey, slipped on steep ice and were held on tangled ropes by the seventh man's ice-axe anchor, only to see Gilkey swept to his death by an avalanche later that afternoon. Without that intervention by nature, it is doubtful whether *anyone* would have descended alive;

as it was, even without a casualty to lower, the remaining six climbers were pushed to the limit to reach the bottom of K2 safely.

K2 was finally climbed the following year, 1954, by an Italian expedition. Then political turmoil and two Indo-Pakistani wars led to the closure of the Karakoram Range to foreign mountaineers, and it was only in 1975 that K2 could be attempted again. Americans headed the queue, with the first American to climb Everest, Jim Whittaker, leading a large team attempting a new route up the northwest ridge. Unlike Houston's expeditions, this was a contentious affair, with an acrimonious gulf between the bulk of the team and the perceived elite, whom they called the Big Four. The Big Four included a Seattle lawyer and veteran of many Alaskan climbs, Jim Wickwire.

Wickwire reached a new personal altitude record of about 6,700 metres (nearly 22,000 ft), the expedition's disappointing high point. Three years later he returned, intending to go higher, again with Jim Whittaker as leader. The 1978 attempt was another lavish, high-profile expedition, on this occasion made possible by Senator Ted Kennedy, who appeased the Pakistan government's concern that the team was sponsored by the CIA (a not entirely unreasonable assumption, as some members of the team had in the '60s taken part in a clandestine CIA

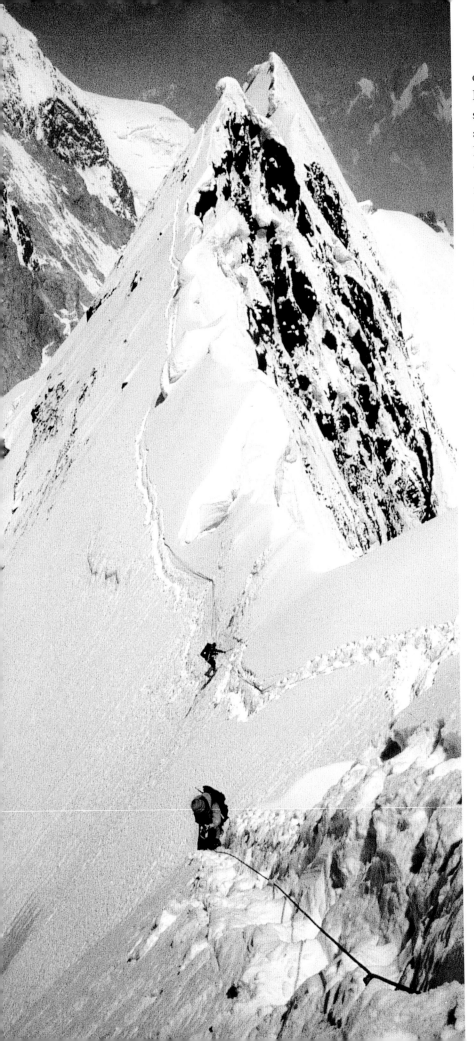

operation to place a nuclear spying device on Nanda Devi in the Indian Himalayas). Again, despite strenuous diplomatic efforts by the leader, there was a divisive 'them and us' split between perceived A and B teams. (According to the B teamers, B stood for 'best' and A stood for 'assholes'.) And just to make matters more complicated, a love triangle involving one of the three women members of the fourteen-person expedition further disrupted the team spirit.

Right from the start in 1978, the A team was virtually self-selecting. Lou Reichardt; academic mathematician, Rick Ridgeway; professional photographer and adventurer, John Roskelley, full-time mountaineer; and Jim Wickwire, the lawyer from Seattle, were all highly experienced climbers who could perform well at altitude. More important, they were also highly motivated: They were playing to win.

For Jim Wickwire that determination came at a price. He had recently witnessed a friend falling to his death from an Alaskan summit – one of several tragedies to blight his career. A master at juggling work, family and mountains, supported by a strong wife, he nevertheless had to face a huge wrench: 'Just to go there, I had to put my family in second place, and I had five young children at the time. That's a lot of family to leave behind, so I went off to K2 packing a lot of guilt.'

Perhaps it was a need to justify that wrench that made him so determined to be in the first American party to reach the top of what many regarded as the hardest mountain in the world. Since his previous attempt, K2 had finally had its second ascent – by a Japanese team in 1977 – but via the original Abruzzi Spur. The Americans in 1978 were attempting the still incomplete northeast ridge, which a Polish team had tried two years earlier.

It was a dizzily spectacular route following a jagged knife edge, spiked with huge snow cornices. Most spectacular of all was the section between camps 3 and 4, where the climbers crabwalked sideways, clipped into a safety line of ropes strung across a 60° ice slope on the Chinese side of the ridge.

As the weeks passed in hard labour, building a chain of supplies along the knife edge, the A team agonized over how they would cope when the big day came. Earlier that summer two outstanding Tyrolean climbers, Peter Habeler and Reinhold Messner, had succeeded for the first time in climbing Everest without supplementary oxygen. For Wickwire and his companions the gauntlet had been thrown down.

'We knew at least *some* human beings could survive that high. Inspired by the challenge, Lou and John said they wanted to try going without. Unlike them, I had never been above 22,000 feet [6,700 metres] so I did not know *how* I'd perform. I didn't want to risk blowing my one chance to make the summit. On the other hand, I had so far handled the altitude extremely well. Maybe I *should* go all the way without the aid of oxygen. I couldn't make up my mind. Rick Ridgeway doubted whether he could make it up and back the last 700 feet [215 metres] unassisted, so he said he would probably take oxygen.'

They also agonized about exactly which route to take. As the long, convoluted knife edge finally emerged onto a huge glacier shelf beneath the final pyramid, Roskelley and Ridgeway were determined to try to continue directly up the very steep logical conclusion to the northeast ridge. Reichardt and Wickwire were more pragmatic and traversed southward to place their final 'Camp 6' on the huge whaleback known as The Shoulder, just beneath the final section of the standard Abruzzi Ridge.

There comes a point where no amount of thought and planning can entirely combat the mind-

Rick Ridgeway photographed on K2's summit by John Roskelley. The two men reached the top the day after Reichardt and Wickwire, and were the first people ever to climb K2 completely without supplementary oxygen.

'For a few minutes we were the highest people on earth. As one of the first two Americans to climb K2, I'd fulfilled my childhood dream.'

numbing effects of extreme altitude. At this top camp, a pan of precious melted snow spilled over Wickwire's down parka and waist-length sleeping bag. So when he set off for the summit just before dawn the next day, he only wore a light down vest on his torso, with a lightweight cotton wind parka, and down trousers. 'Not expecting to travel at night and eager to keep my load light, I left my headlamp behind as well. To keep my water bottle from freezing, I put it under my jacket against my chest, but just as we prepared to leave camp, it slipped out and skittered down the slope. … I figured that with my stove and Reichardt's pot, we could melt snow.'

He also had a flimsy emergency bivouac sack. And after much agonizing, he had decided to carry an oxygen set, which he switched on once he saw that Reichardt was drawing ahead. They climbed ever steeping snow, up a gully narrowing to the infamous Bottleneck. Here, 'traversing around the base of a huge ice cliff along a narrow catwalk, we encountered snow so deep I sank up to my thighs.'

Later, Reichardt had trouble with his oxygen. Wickwire overtook, then looked down and saw that Reichardt had stopped to dump his malfunctioning oxygen pack. Reichardt shouted up that he would try the summit without it. Then added, 'If I begin to talk fuzzy, Wick, let me know and I'll head down.' Reichardt followed on the rope, then untied himself and traversed across to a spur of harder snow, where he made better progress and overtook Wickwire, who traversed across to join him. 'Try as I might, I could not close the distance between us – and I was the one on oxygen!' Finally Wickwire took over the lead again.

'Then, at 5:15 P.M. I told him, "We've come this far, let's go the rest of the way together." Lou

The Northeast Ridge of K2 gave the Americans long sections of spectacular traversing over huge drops. This ridge is out of sight in the classic view on page 154, but the summit team finished up the final section of the Abruzzi Spur, on the right skyline of that picture.

Reichardt and I walked arm-in-arm the last few steps up the tilted snow ramp to the summit. There, on top of the world, we watched the setting sun bathe the surrounding mountains in a soft, orange light. For a few minutes we were the highest people on earth. As one of the first two Americans to climb K2, I'd fulfilled my childhood dream.'

Reichardt started back down almost immediately. Wickwire lingered, savouring this transcendental moment, watching a sea of mountains turn orange, then purple in the light of the setting sun, before setting off after Reichardt. Very soon it became dark, and with no headlamp, rather than risk falling, he decided to stop and bivouac at about 8,400 metres (27,560 ft) above sea level. 'On an exposed, open slope with nothing but a thin nylon bivouac sack to protect me from the cold, I spent the longest night of my life. Without food or a pot in which to melt snow, I hovered over my stove, desperately trying to keep warm. The stove's fuel quickly ran out … then, with dawn still hours away, my oxygen ran out.'

The temperature dropped to at least -35°C (-31°F). Shivering violently, he forced himself to flex hands and feet, fingers and toes, trying to forestall frostbite and hypothermia. Then he started sliding and had to press his boot heels hard through the nylon fabric, digging into the snow beneath. Four times he nearly slid off the mountain. Then he forced himself to look out of the nylon sack.

'To my dismay, just a few feet below me the slope steepened abruptly. Though I could not see beyond the curve, I knew one more slide and I would have fallen 10,000 ft [3,000 metres] to the glacier below. Badly shaken, I climbed out of the sack and, with my teeth chattering from the excruciating cold, crawled 30 ft [10 metres] back up to the platform. There I pinned the bottom corners of the bivouac sack into the snow with my hammer and axe to prevent myself sliding down again.'

Morning finally arrived. And with it the bemused self-deception of a mind struggling to fight oxygen starvation. 'Oh, look, that's the summit up there. How nice! Maybe I'll just stay here. No, if I want to get home to my family, I must go down.' He ordered himself to put on his crampons, struggling feebly, fumbling with the straps, frequently giving up and reverting to giggling inertia, then forcing himself to focus on his wife and children, using their images as motivation to begin his descent. 'Think of Mary Lou, Annie, Susie, Cathy, Bob and David at home in Seattle. You cannot die. You must survive for them. You must return to them.'

At last the vital spikes were strapped securely to his boots and he staggered back down to the Bottleneck, where he met Ridgeway and Roskelley. They had been defeated by the direct eastern finish the previous day and had traversed around to the Abruzzi, where they had guided Reichardt back to Camp 6 by their torch lights long after nightfall. When they had set out that morning, they had not known if they were going to find a body, conduct a rescue, or climb the mountain. Wickwire assured them that he was okay, and they continued to the summit, both climbing without oxygen, despite Ridgeway's former fears. But before they continued

> 'Badly shaken, I climbed out of the sack and, with my teeth chattering from the excruciating cold, crawled 30 feet [10 metres] back up to the platform. There I pinned the bottom corners of the bivouac sack into the snow with my hammer and axe to prevent myself sliding down again.'

on their way, John Roskelley, an ambitious man renowned for his direct, even abrasive, straight talking, turned around and, in a gesture that spoke volumes of compassion, patted Wickwire gently on the head.

That evening all four climbers were reunited in the two tiny tents at Camp 6 when an exploding gas canister set fire to the Ridgeway-Roskelley tent and Ridgeway's sleeping bag. Rising groggily to a sense of

duty, the other two invited them into their tent for a horribly cramped night, Ridgeway cramming his legs with Wickwire's into the frozen half sleeping bag. In the morning it was a resolutely bonded team that headed back to the northeast ridge. Wickwire had a sharp pain in his chest, but Ridgeway seemed the weakest.

'As we crossed the last small rise into Camp 5, Rick dropped to the ground and crawled on his hands and knees, desperate for oxygen. We gave him what little remained. After another difficult night we continued our descent. Fearful but determined, we crossed the knife-edge ridge between Camps 4 and 3. Storms kept us at the lower camp for forty-eight hours. … The pain in my chest got steadily worse, but Rick seemed weaker.'

In fact, when Dr Rob Schaller met them at Camp 1 two days later, he told them that it was Wickwire who was in the most danger – not from the frostbite on two toes, but from the pneumonia and pleurisy ravaging his lungs. At the start of the 160-km (100-mile) walkout from base camp, Balti porters carried him on a stretcher.

'But the jostling became so uncomfortable I decided to walk the rest of the way with the help of Honar Baig and Ghohar Shah, the strongest of the high-altitude porters. When I started coughing up gobs of blood, Rob explained that I had developed pulmonary emboli – blood clots in my lungs – another painful legacy of my bivouac beneath the summit. When I turned back to look at K2 for the last time, I felt nothing. Hungry, weak and breathless, my pace slowed. I seemed to be in my own private world. Ten steps, fifty, a hundred, a rock to rest on, then repeat. At night I coughed incessantly, the pain in my chest cutting through me like a razor.'

The doctor grew so worried that he urged Jim Whittaker to radio the Pakistan army for a helicopter to hurry Wickwire to hospital. A few days later his family greeted him at Seattle airport, a shrivelled husk in a wheelchair. A couple of operations and a few weeks' convalescence quickly healed the physical damage. With recovery also came relief from that weary sense of emptiness, a feeling soon replaced by the lifelong glow of retrospective satisfaction from his extraordinary summit journey.

Balti porters carrying expedition supplies across a typical glacial torrent, thick with rocky sediment.

Gasherbrum IV

Height
7,925 metres (26,001 ft)

Location
Karakoram range,
Baltistan–Sinkiang border

Origin of name
In the local Balti language,
rgasha translates as
'beautiful' and brum means
'mountain'. The highest
summit in the group,

Gasherbrum I, is one of the
world's fourteen 8,000-metre
(26,250-ft) peaks, also
known as Hidden Peak.

First ascent
6 August 1958: Walter
Bonatti/Carlo Mauri by
Northeast Ridge

Other key routes
West Face 1985: Voytek
Kurtyka/Robert Schauer –
to North Summit only

Northwest Ridge 1986: Greg
Child/Tom Hargis/ Tim
Macartney-Snape

West Face Central Spur
1997: Y. Hak-Jae/B. Jung-Ho/
K. Tong-Kwan

Interesting facts
The first ascent of the
mountain was led by one
of Italy's greatest mountaineers, Ricardo Cassin, and
recorded in a marvellous

book by historian Fosco
Maraini. The final climb up
the northeast ridge was led
almost entirely by Walter
Bonatti, making one of the
hardest Himalayan first
ascents of all time, with Carlo
Mauri, who later crossed the
Atlantic in a reed boat with
Thor Heyerdahl.

The gigantic, glowing marble West Face of Gasherbrum IV had defeated at least five big expeditions. Then two climbers succeeded in a lightning raid, knowing that once they were committed there could be no escape back down the wall – the only way off was over the summit.

The Shining Wall

Voytek Kurtyka and Robert Schauer (1985)

In the heart of Switzerland there is a great glacial crossroads where three rivers of ice converge to form the biggest glacier in the Alps. This crossroads is called Concordia. Over a hundred years ago, when the first European explorers penetrated the mighty Karakoram Range, they discovered a similar convergence, which they also named Concordia. But this Concordia, at the head of the Baltoro Glacier, is on a totally different scale, far grander than anything in Europe. And dominating this Asian Concordia, glowing with an intense, saturated luminosity as its western face absorbs the evening light, stands the Shining Wall.

Its official title is Gasherbrum IV. Its highest point doesn't quite make the 8,000-metre (26,250-ft) mark so beloved by trophy hunters, but it *does* just scrape 7,925 metres (26,000 ft) above sea level and is indisputably one of the most beautiful and elusive of the world's highest summits. The first ascent in 1958 stretched the legendary Bonatti and his companion Carlo Mauri to the limit and was regarded for many years as the hardest climb to have been achieved in the Himalayas. And that was by the 'easy' route, around the back. It was only twenty years later that mountaineers began to contemplate the monstrous challenge looming over Concordia – the 2,400-metre (7,875-ft)-high west face: the Shining Wall.

As so often happens in the mountains, the reality close-up was a mean travesty of the beautiful vision. Successive teams laid siege to the obvious central spur, only to grind to a halt on the crumbling, tottering chaos of the Black Towers. Then in 1984 one of the world's boldest, most brilliant and inventive mountaineers, Voytek Kurtyka from Warsaw, made an exploratory snoop, climbing partway up the northwest ridge on the left, assessing it as a potential escape route from the Shining Wall. The following year he returned to Concordia to put his plan into action.

He brought just one climbing partner: Robert Schauer. The tall, genial Austrian film-maker was a veteran of several 8,000-metre (26,250-ft) peaks, including Everest. He was used to big team efforts, but he also had the talent and ability to adapt to the completely different approach of the charismatic Polish Himalayan guru: For Voytek, 'style' was everything; for him the 'small is beautiful' ethos applied to climbing, even on the biggest, highest, hardest walls on the planet.

So it was just two men who set off with two ropes, a handful of pegs and carabiners, a flimsy bivouac tent, a stove, a few gas cylinders and subsistence rations for four days. Ever canny and creative, Kurtyka decided to avoid the laborious

Grade V difficulty. The real nuisance was the very deep snow on the mixed ground, through which we tunnelled vertically, demanding tortuous work.'

Night-time brought no relief. 'The second and third nights we sat almost sleepless and separated from each other, very uncomfortably, on spiky pinnacles. Sleeping bags were the only shelter. All the following nights were troubled by furious winds and impetuous spindrift. Even together in the bivouac sack, we had little sleep, buried on ledges hacked into the ice.'

Despite all that, on the sixth day they had almost reached the top of the Shining Wall. But there, close

> **'The sound of beautiful and passionate women singing, something between Barbra Streisand and Santana, came from the rubbing of the rope sliding over the rough snow surface punctuated by our steps.'**

to 8,000 metres (26,250 ft) above sea level, they were pinned down for two nights. 'Masses of snow constantly buried, squeezed and suffocated us. The whirling, blinding wind so oppressed us that we could fend off the snow only by crawling on all fours.' At one point, almost hallucinating from sleep

Voytek Kurtyka, one of the greatest postwar Himalayan climbers, grapples with the immense tilted wasteland of shattered marble known as the Shining Wall.

Black Towers. He chose instead to carve a diagonal slash up the face, starting on the right up a huge ice gully, which allowed the pair to make rapid progress on the first day. Then things became steadily more difficult.

'The rock (the pale golden stone that gives the wall its name) was either completely rotten or of completely compact marble. Due to the total lack of belays, we had often to extend pitches from 40 to 80 metres [130 to 260 ft], even though some were deprivation, hunger, thirst and hypoxia, Robert Schauer became one of the Karakoram's ubiquitous ravens, hovering in the air, looking down on his own shivering, emaciated body. Later he confessed that for him, a father of three, the Shining Wall had been a step too far. Kurtyka, on the other hand, seemed almost to relish his altered state: 'For long periods I heard strange sounds like music, the twittering of birds or whispered talk. Sometimes it was easy to discover them as transformed real sounds. For instance, the sound of beautiful and passionate women singing, something between Barbra Streisand and Santana, came from the rubbing of the rope sliding over the rough snow surface punctuated by our steps.'

It was now the eighth day, and the storm had cleared – 'thank you, angry sky, you cleared on the second night' – and the two men continued in near delirium to the north summit. 'Uncommonly intense was our ability to associate rocks, snow or clouds with human figures and shapes. Who made you, lovely and quiet figures? But particularly painful was repeatedly falling asleep suddenly and unchecked at the belay stances, followed by an equally sudden awakening with a sense of terror. Equally unpleasant were the tormenting visions of food and drink: we carried food for four bivouacs, fuel and drink for five, but the complete climb lasted eleven days.'

Staggering onto the north summit, they had just two options: Turn right and follow the final ridge to the main summit, climbed by Bonatti and Mauri twenty-seven years earlier, then return – at least another day's climbing – or turn immediately left down the northwest ridge. In their condition, Kurtyka and Schauer had no choice, really; survival was all that mattered.

On the descent, they fell ravenously on the food cache they had left earlier, during a reconnaissance partway up the northwest ridge. That gave them strength to continue descending safely back to the base. But for Voytek, despite surviving one of the most remarkable Himalayan climbs of all time, there was a lingering sense of regret. 'Though it was the most beautiful and mysterious climb I have ever done, I feel miserable for having failed to reach the summit. I can't resist the conviction that this beautiful mountain and its Shining Wall are too splendid and too perfect to consider any ascent of it without its most essential point – the summit – as really completed.'

Yamandaka

Height
6,218 metres (20,401 ft)

Location
Arganglas valley, East Karakoram, Ladakh

Origin of name
Named by the 2001 Kapadia expedition. Stanzin Tsewan, an elder from the village of Tigur, suggested Yamandaka –

the name of a Buddhist protective deity.

First ascent
13 September 2001: Mark Richey/Mark Wilford, by North Face

Interesting facts
Yamandaka lies at the extreme eastern end of the mighty Karakoram Range, in northern Ladakh, which is

administered by India. This end of the range is enclosed on three sides by a great bend in the Shyok River, a major tributary of the Indus. Higher up, the river has often been blocked by an advancing glacier, which caused the water to rise by up to 125 metres (410 ft) and form a huge lake. When the glacier then retreated, the

dam collapsed and millions of cubic metres of water crashed downstream, causing death and destruction, on one occasion as far as 1,200 km (745 miles) downstream into the Indus valley. Major dam bursts occurred in 1760, 1826, 1835 and 1839. Shyok means 'river of death'.

Indian explorer Harish Kapadia led this expedition in which two Americans –
Richey and Wilford – found themselves descending from a previously unclimbed
summit into a precipitous gorge, trapped by a huge overhang. In the most
terrifying pitch of his life, Richey found an escape across a crumbling wall,
and they eventually descended safely to a monastery, where the monks
had been praying for their safe return.

The Tightening Noose

Mark Richey and Mark Wilford (2001)

It all started with Harish Kapadia, the man from Mumbai who knew more about every nook and cranny of the mountains thronging his country's northern frontier than anyone else alive. In the far north of India's quasi-Tibetan province, Ladakh, lay a group of unexplored mountains clustered around a single name on the map – Arganglas. Kapadia invited along two of his regular partners from Mumbai, Divyesh Muni and Cyrus Shroff. Then he contacted his British friend, the renowned mountaineer, Chris Bonington, who invited his local Lake District landowner friend, Jim Lowther. And then, to complete the team, they invited from America the two Marks: Mark Richey and Mark Wilford.

From the start it was an unusually happy expedition. Kapadia regaled the teams with countless tales of travels throughout the Himalayas; Bonington astounded everyone with his passion for technology, beaming news and photos back to his website; Lowther tried to explain the rules of cricket to the Americans. From Ladakh's capital, Leh, they took an army lorry over the Kardung La – at 5,600 metres (18,500 ft), the highest motorable road in the world – then descended 3,000 metres (10,000 ft) to the hot bed of the Shyok valley. Then, in the village of Tigur, they hired mules to carry all their baggage on the three-day walk to base camp in the Arganglas valley.

It proved to be a journey of enchantment. For a mountaineer, there is nothing more thrilling than to head up a secret valley where you have no idea what the peaks are going to look like. Around each corner new mountains appeared – snowy domes, sharp-chiselled ice ridges and great needles of russet granite. All untouched. The two Americans were particularly thrilled. Both outstanding mountaineers, they wanted to get their teeth into something steep and elegant, where they could be absorbed totally by the technicalities of the climbing. One mountain in particular, marked on the map at 6,218 metres (20,401 ft), fitted the bill. Its north wall of snow-smeared granite was bisected by a perfect plumb line, a well-defined spur falling more than 1,000 metres (3,280 ft) directly from the summit. It seemed the perfect line.

So while the British and Indian climbers and two Sherpa assistants split into groups to explore the upper glaciers, the two Marks packed food for five days, fuel for seven, a tiny bivouac tent, sleeping bags, two ropes and a basic rack of climbing hardware and headed off for what promised to be a delightful adventure.

As they approached the foot of the face, it started to snow, so they stopped to camp on the glacier. The following morning, 9 September 2001, it was still snowing, but at 11:00 A.M. the clouds lifted, so they set off up the face, making about 350 metres (1,150 ft) that afternoon before pitching their tent on a little ledge. Snow was falling again the next morning. The lovely rocks they had expected to climb were now plastered with new powder. Everything was more awkward than planned, and they were also feeling the altitude, having had little time to acclimatize.

The great challenge on a big-face climb like this – particularly when the weather is poor – is finding somewhere to spend the night: get a good night's sleep and anything seems possible. That second night on the face, they managed to find room to pitch the tent on the top of a huge bank of windblown snow and ice stuck to the base of a rock overhang. As Mark Richey put it: 'We hacked and flattened the mushroom until it was large enough for our perch. With part of the tent hanging over the void, it was not hard to imagine the horrifying scenario should the ice mushroom collapse during the night, sending us instantly to the end of our tethers, trapped in our sleeping bags in a tent filled with all manner of paraphernalia. We tied our boots securely to the belay, and fortunately the night passed uneventfully.'

Day 3 brought blue skies and some very hard climbing, at one stage tensioning sideways from blade-thin pegs hammered into incipient cracks. Late that night, by the light of their headlamps, they found themselves slaving for two hours to hack pathetic ledges from a 50° slope of iron-hard ice. During the night, avalanches of spindrift hissed down the face, repeatedly pushing the climbers off their 0.6-metre (2-ft)-wide ledge. To add to the misery, Richey had developed a dry, hacking cough. The cumulative effect of the climb was wearing them down, and on Day 4 they were bitterly disappointed to discover that the final slope, which had looked like soft, white snow from base camp, was in fact bullet-hard ice. Late that evening, utterly spent, they tunnelled through a final overhanging snow cornice onto the summit ridge, hacked out a ledge, and collapsed in their tent, just beneath the summit. Again Richey suffered, recalling, 'It snowed all night and into the morning, dumping over a foot of snow as my coughing fits intensified, keeping me and Mark from any sleep.'

The snow let up at noon the next day, allowing them to trudge the remaining few feet to the summit and a glorious view of limitless mountains. Less glorious was the view down their proposed descent route, the northeast ridge, which proved to be a hideous concoction of perilous, unstable snow cornices. But as Mark Wilford put it, there was an attractive alternative: 'What did look enticing was the south slope of the peak. It was relatively low-angled and led down to a mild-looking glacier system. This appeared to sweep around to the west and, we thought, would actually hook back up with our original approach route, the Arganglas valley. If all went well, we would be drinking beer in base camp the next day.' It looked so straightforward that they decided to leave one of their two ropes behind, keen to save weight. They descended quickly and efficiently, and that evening Mark Wilford was ecstatic. 'As the sun was setting, we stumbled into a high alpine meadow of grass and flowers and water. No signs of man or beast. I was so happy. I had clear skies, a warm sleeping bag and the prospect of a cold beer the next day.'

But there was no beer the next day. The meadows led down to a river, seducing the two climbers onward, down into an increasingly precipitous funnel.

> **'We had four carabiners, four pitons and a couple of wired nuts. We were thinking we were going to starve to death. I knew I had to climb the vein of mud and boulders.'**

For a while they were unperturbed: 'It was becoming harder to jump across the steam and stay dry. But it was still relaxing and beautiful.'

Until, that is, they had to start abseiling down vertical cliffs alongside the river. They had ditched much of their hardware, so it was hard to place anchors in the smooth, water-worn rock. And for abseiling you need a doubled rope, so that you can pull it down afterward; with only one 60-metre (196-ft) rope left, they could only abseil 30 metres (98 ft) at a time.

At one point they had to make an anchor by piling rocks on top of a tape sling. The canyon became ever steeper. Richey said, 'It was like being flushed down a giant toilet. That's when we came to the waterfall with the deep pool.' Wilford went first, detaching from the bottom of the doubled rope to swim across the pool, pushing his rucksack in front of him. Richey followed, they pulled the ropes down and continued, making endless abseils, until they found themselves on the lip of an immense waterfall at least 60 metres high. Even if their single rope reached the bottom, they would be unable to pull it back down. And below that? Wilford said to Richey, 'We could be trapped down there and no one would ever find us. We'd slowly starve to death if we couldn't get out.'

They couldn't go down, and they couldn't climb back up. The only other possibility was to climb sideways, out of the gorge. All around they were hemmed in by vertical walls of smooth, polished rock. But they noticed one weakness: a fault line, crammed full of a Karakoram specialty – a mass of huge boulders loosely cemented in a dried paste of alluvial mud.

Wilford eyed it up. 'It was getting late. We were totally soaked. We were out of food. We knew a rescue would be launched soon, and we didn't want others put at risk on our behalf. We had four carabiners, four pitons and a couple of wired nuts. We were thinking we were going to starve to death. I knew I had to climb the vein of mud and boulders.' He teetered nervously up horribly loose rock until the conglomerate wall began to overhang. Then he managed to wiggle an alloy nut between two rocks and took off his rucksack to hang on the nut. It held. He clipped the rope in, then took a deep breath. Richey watched from about 30 metres below: 'He started up over the blocks. The first one was about the size of a grand piano. And the only way up was right over it. I held my breath; it held. Next was a short roof followed by 4.5 metres [15 ft] of dead-vertical climbing on loose sandy flakes. … With the gun to the head, there are few climbers smoother than Wilford, and he pulled through the steep wall flawlessly. Shortly I joined him at the belay; amazingly, all the blocks had held. 'That's the scariest pitch I've ever led,' he said. And this coming from a climber who had made a career of bold solos and first ascents.'

Two less-frightening pitches led to the open mountainside. They had escaped the canyon, and it was now clear down to the Shyok valley. Back at base camp Kapadia and Bonington had grown increasingly worried. Kapadia had built a temple, which Bonington consecrated. He had also sent one of the porters, Bhakta, to run down to the road, just in case the two

men had descended on the south side of the mountain. He also had the military liaison officer standing by in case it was necessary ready to call a helicopter search.

But at that moment the two Marks emerged onto the road, just in time to send Bhakta running back up the Arganglas – three days' march in one day – to relay the good news to Kapadia. Hitching a ride up the valley to Tirgut, they met an American woman who was fascinated by their thrilling escape but who then asked whether they knew what had happened. It was 15 September, four days after the attack on the World Trade Center. Numbed by the horrific news, they made their way back to base camp, where, in view of the volatile international situation, they decided to end the expedition. At the suggestion of a local village elder, they named their mountain Yamandaka, after a fierce yet benevolent Buddhist deity.

Mark Wilford, buffeted by a fierce torrent, abseils down yet another waterfall, as the climbers descend irretrievably into the depths of the great gully. This unscheduled descent lay down the far side in the picture on page 164. The ascent route was up the right hand face, following the slanting spur, catching the sunlight at top and bottom.

Nanda Devi

Height
West Summit 7,816 metres
(25,644 ft)
East Summit 7,434 metres
(24,390 ft)

Location
Himalayas range, Garwhal,
India

Origin of name
The mountain is sacred to
Hindus and means Bliss
Giving Goddess

First ascent
West Summit 29 August
1936: Noel Odell/ Bill Tilman
by Southwest Ridge

East Summit 2 July 1939: J.
Bujak/J. Klarner by South Ridge

Other key routes
Northwest Face/North Ridge
of West Summit 1976: Lou
Reichardt/ John Roskelley/
Jim States

Northeast Face of West
Summit 1981: Horka/
Kadlcík/Karafa/Palecek/
Srovnal

Interesting facts
In the '60s a secret CIA-
sponsored expedition
placed a nuclear spying
device on the mountain,
which was later lost,
prompting fears of pollution
of a source of the Ganges

A member of the original
1936 expedition, H. Adams
Carter, returned 40 years
later to lead an American
expedition. During this
climb, a young woman
called Nanda Devi Unsoeld,
named after the mountain,
died on its North Ridge;
local porters believed that
she was a reincarnation of
the Hindu goddess.

Nanda Devi, rising from behind an apparently impenetrable circle of peaks, was an elusive object of desire for European climbers. In 1934 Bill Tilman and Eric Shipton finally found a route into 'The Sanctuary'. Two years later, Tilman returned to climb the 7,816-metre (25,644-ft) pinnacle, which remained the highest climbed summit for the next 16 years. His partner was Noel Odell – the last man to see Mallory and Irvine before they disappeared on Everest in 1924.

Mother Goddess of the Sanctuary
Noel Odell and Bill Tilman (1936)

The British-American Himalayan Expedition of 1936 planned to attempt the world's third-highest mountain, Kangchenjunga. But when its leader, Bill Tilman, arrived in Calcutta, he found a letter from the Indian government announcing that the expedition would not be given permission to enter the hill state of Sikkim. 'Like most oracular pronouncements', he wrote afterwards, 'no reasons were given.' But that bureaucratic intransigence was actually a gift: On Kangchenjunga, the team would probably have made little impression; on their alternative objective – Nanda Devi, 800 km (500 miles) to the northwest in the politically less restricted state of Garwhal – they were gloriously successful, making the first-ever ascent of a 7,620-metre (25,000-ft) peak, which would for sixteen years remain the highest summit attained by man.

Nanda Devi is one of the most striking mountains in the world. The snows of its twin summits are a source of the holy river Ganges, and the mountain itself – the Bliss Giving Goddess – is sacred to Hindus. To European explorers, trying to unravel the complexities of Himalayan geography in the early twentieth century, Nanda Devi presented a tempting puzzle, surrounded by an almost impenetrable ring of high peaks, pierced only at one point by the deep cleft of the Rishi Gorge.

It was Tilman himself who, in 1934, first penetrated this gorge. It was his first Himalayan expedition, and his only companions were three Nepalese Sherpas and one other Englishman, Eric Shipton. The two men had met in Kenya, where they both worked as coffee planters and climbed in their spare time, together pioneering some bold new routes on the remote mountains of East Africa. Immensely tough, resourceful and famously able to survive for months on spartan rations, they found a route up the precipitous flanks of the Rishi Gorge and became the first human beings to enter the Sanctuary of Nanda Devi, where they found abundant wild sheep grazing the high meadows. They had no plans – or supplies – to actually climb the mountain, but they had unlocked the secret of how to reach its foot. They then continued to explore other valleys nearby, at one point running out of food and surviving for several days on bamboo shoots. The following year, they both attempted Everest from Tibet, and in 1936 Shipton was invited on another Everest attempt. Tilman, deemed less reliable at altitude, was not included, but a team of Americans did invite him to lead a joint British-American expedition to the Himalayas, which now found itself, at the last minute, switching plans to make a full-scale attempt on Nanda Devi.

Eric Shipton (left) and Bill Tilman – the great Himalayan innovators. By travelling fast, light and bold, they discovered the route into the elusive Nanda Devi Sanctuary. Two years later Tilman returned to lead an expedition to the summit.

– the potential line that Tilman had spotted with Shipton just two years earlier.

This great ramp, slanting up the immense expanse of Nanda Devi's south face towards the higher west summit, was not desperately steep, but unlike modern expeditions, this team placed no 'fixed ropes' to safeguard progress up and down loose, shaly rock overlaid by snow. With help from their Nepalese Sherpa companions, the climbers placed five camps, one of them so precarious that the outer edge of the tent overhung by almost a foot. But the top camp, at about 7,300 metres (24,000 ft), was a spacious snow platform with room for two tents. From here it was decided that two men would attempt the final climb to the summit. The British climber selected by Tilman was Noel Odell. He was the geologist who in 1924 had been the last person to see George Mallory and Sandy Irvine alive, disappearing into the clouds near the top of Everest. The American was a young physician named Charles Houston. He would later lead two remarkable attempts on the world's second-highest peak, K2. But in 1936 he was unluckily gripped by agonizing stomach cramps just as he was poised for the summit – food poisoning from a tin of corned beef was the suspected cause – and the leader took his place at the top camp.

In his classic account, *The Ascent of Nanda Devi*, Tilman is gruffly humorous about the grim reality of setting off from the top camp at six o'clock on the morning of 29 August 1936. 'It was bitterly cold, for the sun had not yet risen over the shoulder of East Nanda Devi and there was a thin wind from the west. What mugs we were to be fooling about on this

It was an interesting exercise in international relations. Halfway up the Rishi Gorge, faced with a porter strike and having to reduce luggage, Tilman decided to leave all the food supplies that he deemed not strictly nutritious. In the words of one of the Americans, Adams Carter, this meant 'leaving behind the only edible food.' But gastronomic differences aside, this expedition was a harmonious, gentlemanly affair, the four Americans and four Brits working hard together once they reached the Sanctuary, to push a route up the south ridge

'What mugs we were to be fooling about on this infernal ridge at that hour of the morning! And what was the use of this ridiculous coil of rope, as stiff as a wire hawser, tying me for better or for worse to that dirty-looking ruffian in front!'

infernal ridge at that hour of the morning! And what was the use of this ridiculous coil of rope, as stiff as a wire hawser, tying me for better or for worse to that dirty-looking ruffian in front! Such, in truth, were the

reflections of at least one of us as we topped a snow boss behind the tent, and the tenuous nature of the ridge in front became glaringly obvious in the chill light of dawn. It was comforting to reflect that my companion in misery had already passed this way, and presently as the demands of the climbing became more insistent, grievances seemed less real, and that life was still worth living was a proposition that might conceivably be entertained.'

This narrow ridge, which Odell had previously reconnoitred with Houston, was like a causeway flanked by immense drops on either side, linking the lower south ridge to the final slopes of the mountain. Tilman was thrilled at last to discover solid rock: 'The soft crumbly rock had at last yielded to a hard rough shistose-quartzite which was a joy to handle; a change which could not fail to please us as mountaineers and, no doubt, to interest my companion as a geologist.' But above the causeway they found deep snow – 'like trying to climb cotton wool' – where every step 'cost six to eight deep breaths' and 'on top of the hard work and the effect of altitude was the languor induced by a sun which beat down relentlessly on the dazzling snow, searing our lips and sapping the energy of mind and body.'

But they persevered and at one o'clock were pleased to see that East Nanda Devi was now below them. About an hour later they stood on top of the higher west summit. Still poking gentle fun at his scientist companion, Tilman remarks, 'Odell had brought a thermometer and no doubt sighed for the hypsometer. From it we found that the air temperature was 20°F [-7°C], but in the absence of wind we could bask gratefully in the friendly rays of our late enemy the sun. After three-quarters of an hour on that superb summit, a brief forty-five minutes into which was crowded the worth of many hours of glorious life, we dragged ourselves reluctantly away, taking with us a memory that can never fade and leaving behind "thoughts beyond the reaches of our souls."'

Tilman, the man who was not supposed to be very good at altitude, had reached the highest summit yet attained by human beings. It was a glorious achievement but, ever sensitive, he noted that with victory 'came a feeling of sadness that the mountain had succumbed, that the proud head of the goddess was bowed.' With that sensitivity came also an acknowledgement that the climb had been a team effort, so that when he sent his telegram home a few days later, he stated simply that 'two reached the summit.'

A modern Anglo-American expedition repeats the original Anglo-American route of 1936, following the long sloping ramp of the South Ridge.

Changabang

Height
6,846 metres (22,461 ft)

Location
Himalayas range, Garhwal,
India

Origin of name
In the Garhwali language,
Changa means 'steep' and
bang means 'rock'.

First ascent
4 June 1974: Chris Bonington/
Martin Boysen/Tashi
Chewang/Dougal Haston/
Balwant Sandhu/Doug Scott,
by Southeast Face/East
Ridge.

Other key routes
West Face 1976: Peter
Boardman/Joe Tasker

South Buttress 1978: Voytek
Kurtyka/Alex MacIntyre/
John Porter/Krystof Zurek

North Face 1997: Andy
Cave/Mick Fowler/Brendan
Murphy/Stephen Sustad

Interesting facts
One of the earliest British
pioneers WW Graham

but that claim is widely
discredited. The first person
known to set foot on the
mountain was Eric Shipton,
during his 1934 exploration
of the Nanda Devi
Sanctuary, and the notch
he visited on the Southwest
Ridge of Changabang is
still called the Shipton Col.

First admired by Edwardian explorers, Changabang became a symbol of unassailable beauty. It was first climbed in 1974 and each successive new route became a yardstick of Himalayan difficulty. Cave and Fowler were in the six-person team which finally scaled the fearsome North Face. Near misses from falling rocks, a fall resulting in broken ribs, frostbite, near starvation and avalanches turned their descent into an epic fight for survival.

The Shining Mountain

Andy Cave, Mick Fowler, Brendan Murphy and Stephen Sustad (1997)

Changabang has entranced mountaineers for more than a century. The famous Scottish climber, Bill Murray, described it as 'a vast eyetooth fang, both in shape and colour, for its rock was a milk-white granite … a product of earth and sky rare and fantastic, and of liveliness unparalleled so that unaware one's pulse leaped and heart gave thanks – that this mountain should be as it is.'

Murray wrote those words in 1950, content just to look and admire, but sooner or later someone was bound to rise to the challenge of climbing this great pale tooth. That finally happened in 1974. Because of the team's mixed abilities, it followed an oblique approach, seeking out the snowy line of least resistance, but even this route finished with a spectacular knife-edge ascent of the east ridge. After that, Changabang became a forcing ground – a laboratory of climbing standards, where some of the world's finest mountaineers came to experiment. In 1976 Peter Boardman and Joe Tasker stunned the world with their two-man ascent of the bitterly cold, relentlessly steep west face. Two years later an Anglo-Polish team climbed an equally steep route up the south face. Then for two decades Changabang lay deserted, forbidden to foreign visitors because the approach, via the Nanda Devi Sanctuary, had been closed because of both political and environmental reasons.

But there was another approach, outside the Sanctuary, from the north. In 1996 four British climbers received permission to enter the area, set up base camp beside the Bagini Glacier, and took the first steps onto Changabang's most impressive wall of all – the north face. They got quite high but had to retreat when one member had a sudden attack of salmonella. In 1997 three of the team – Roger Payne, Julie-Ann Clyma and Brendan Murphy – decided to return.

By now several of the world's best mountaineers were eyeing up Changabang's north face, entranced by photos of its smooth granite walls, smeared with fantastically steep seams of ice. Among the aspirants was a British tax inspector renowned for bold first ascents, Mick Fowler, who climbed regularly with a furniture maker from Seattle named Stephen Sustad. After some negotiation these two joined the existing expedition, led by Roger Payne. Fiercely resistant to any unit larger than two, Fowler wanted to operate as an independent pair with Sustad. Roger Payne would climb with his wife, Julie. Brendan Murphy invited Andy Cave, an ex-coalminer from Yorkshire who had become an academic language researcher, and who also happened to be a phenomenally talented climber.

So in May 1997 the three pairs of climbers set up base camp beside the Bagini Glacier. The previous year's grassy meadow was still smothered in winter

The line up Changabang's North Face (the right-hand summit on page 172) traced a series of tenuous icy smears plastered to horribly steep smooth granite. Cave's photo of Brendan Murphy in action shows just how difficult this climb was.

snow. Temperatures were very low, and snowstorms arrived every afternoon with tedious regularity. On the 1,700-metre (5,580-ft)-high wall above them, cataracts of spindrift poured down the line of rivulets they hoped to follow. The wall was so steep – steeper even than the legendary west face – that there were no obvious ledges to bivouac on, so to avoid overcrowding, they staggered their ascent, Cave and Murphy starting one day ahead of Fowler and Sustad, Clyma and Payne following on the third day, taking a different line to the left.

On 21 May Andy Cave wrote to his girlfriend: 'Dear Love, I won't be able to write for a week or so as we are setting off towards Changabang in a few hours. We will hopefully spend 6–8 days climbing and descending it. I will think of you every day and miss you every night as I sit on some ledge.'

At dawn the next day, following Murphy up steepening snow slopes, that cheerful confidence was temporarily dented. 'Seeing the mountain again brought a tightness in my stomach, a fear of what we were hoping to achieve. The sheer enormity of the wall, the commitment, all the things that could go wrong.'

As the snow slope steepened into the first uprearing of the wall, they began to strike ice, so hard that two of their six ice screws, vital for making anchors, broke. It snowed in the afternoon, and that night they slept on pathetically meagre ledges, hanging in their sleeping bags, unable to pitch the bivouac tent. But the sun was shining on Day 2 and they enjoyed the total focus on intricate, strenuous, very steep climbing, until the afternoon snowstorm forced them to hack out a ledge and pitch their tent on the first of the tilted, glassy icefields. Late that evening, unzipping the tent door to collect more snow to melt for drinks, Cave was transfixed as 'a sea of snow danced down the vast, steep sheet of ice, collecting and breaking like surf on either side of our tent before cascading down towards the glacier.'

Day 4 almost ended in disaster when the two climbers were caught in the worst storm so far, four rope lengths short of the only possible bivouac site. At one point Cave, who was in the lead far above Murphy, battered by wind and torrents of spindrift and trying desperately to place an ice screw, had to clip his entire body weight onto one of his ice axes to free his numb hands. Suddenly the axe ripped and both of his cramponed feet skidded off the ice, leaving him hanging from his remaining ice axe. Frantic to survive, he somehow regained contact, got the ice screw in, tied himself to it and shouted to Murphy to come up. 'When Brendan arrived, he was retching with pain. I had never seen him show his suffering so openly. Seeing this hard little bastard wince and groan only served to underline the seriousness of our predicament.' Following the next pitch, a traverse in the dark, Murphy fell off and pendulumed 18 metres (60 ft) diagonally leftward in a huge swing. 'That was lucky,' he commented when he arrived. 'I could have lost my headtorch.'

At 11:00 P.M. they finally crawled into their tent. Cave admired Murphy's cheerful stoicism but was himself profoundly shaken and asked for a rest day. 'He could see that I was struggling, and I appreciated his relaxed, gentle manner; had he coerced me into going up that day, I would almost certainly have rebelled.' So they rested, took stock, wondered about retreating, but decided that they had failed on too many mountains in the past. They had invested too much in this Changabang climb to give up so easily. And on Day 6 they continued upward.

Meanwhile, Fowler and Sustad had been following the same tenuous line of ridiculously steep cracks and corners and were slightly displeased when they reached the third of the big, less steep icefields to find Cave and Murphy still camped there. They too were forced to take a rest day while the first pair led the way up the next huge, vertical corner system. At 1:00 that afternoon they were sitting in their tent, perched precariously on the 50° slope, when a lump of rock ripped through the fabric, missing Sustad's head by inches. They hurled abuse up at the other pair, who shouted back an apology. Fowler and Sustad sewed up the rip in the tent and the next morning continued climbing behind the other two.

And so it went on, day after day, living in this extraordinary vertical environment. Despite the hardship, Cave began to enjoy the climbing, marvelled at his partner's skill, and was again seduced by Changabang's 'splendid, opulent architecture'. This great sheet of pale leucogranite was truly beautiful. Fowler, too, revelled in the technical intricacy of the upper corner system, despite one unspeakably awful night hanging from a ledge with just a single ice screw from which to hang on. 'Still enjoying your holiday, Michael?' asked his phlegmatic American companion. 'Most rewarding,' replied the tax inspector.

After nine days on the wall, Cave and Murphy finally emerged onto the crest of the east ridge. The following day, when their six days' worth of stretched food rations ran out, they climbed that final ridge to the summit of Changabang. 'We stood there for a few slow minutes trying to digest the raw beauty of the scene, both of us silently acknowledging that in those precious moments we were somewhere very close to the inexplicable kernel of all our desires and ambitions.' Then they started back down the ridge towards their tent.

As they descended, they saw Sustad and Fowler, who had just exited from the north face. They shouted down, eager to join them, knowing that they still had some dried potato powder left. Cloud obscured their view, and when they next saw the same spot, Sustad and Fowler had vanished. Then they heard a shout from 60 metres (200 ft) down the south face. It was Fowler, and he sounded very distressed.

'Steve had been having trouble with his crampons balling up with snow. Suddenly one foot slipped away from beneath him. … I watched with horror as he started to slide down the south side of the ridge.' Fowler braced himself to take the strain on the rope, but he could feel his ice axe being pulled out of the

> **'He could see that I was struggling, and I appreciated his relaxed, gentle manner; had he coerced me into going up that day, I would almost certainly have rebelled.'**

snow. As he began to slide towards the 1,000-metre (3,300-ft) drop, he remembered his promises to wife and children. 'I swear I saw their faces as I fell. More than fear was a tremendous feeling that I'd let them down.'

He accelerated, then flew through the air, then felt a violent thump, then found that he had stopped, bleeding from the face and wrapped in a tangle of rope close to Sustad. Both men had come to rest on a snow ledge, just 60 metres down the face. Apart from facial cuts, Fowler was fine. But Sustad was in serious pain, with two cracked ribs. Continuing to the summit was now out of the question for this pair, and when Cave and Murphy joined them, it was clear that all four should now join forces and concentrate on getting off this mountain alive. The first pair had already been on the mountain for eleven days, food and fuel were virtually finished, Sustad was seriously

The murky dawn of Day 11 for Cave and Murphy, Day 9 for Fowler and Sustad, who has broken ribs. Behind them, shrouded in storm clouds, is Changabang's summit. To the right is the North Face they have been the first to climb. To the left is the South Face – the unknown route they are about to descend. By the evening, only three of them will still be alive.

injured, and Cave had a badly frostbitten thumb. As Fowler put it with typical understatement, 'Things were getting rather out of hand.'

They had two choices. The first was to make an epic series of abseils all the way back down the 1,700 metres (5,600 ft) of the north face. The second was to descend the much easier southeast face into the Nanda Devi Sanctuary, then climb back out of the Sanctuary onto the Ramani Glacier, then cross yet another pass back to the Bagini Glacier – in effect, a complete circumnavigation of the mountain. Sustad favoured the first, quicker, option. The others were not sure his broken ribs could stand all that abseiling; they also thought that the marathon southern option would be safer.

So the next morning they started down the southeast face, hoping to follow the line through glacier slopes that Chris Bonington's expedition had taken on the first ascent, twenty-three years earlier. But first they had to climb down the remaining knife edge of the east ridge, so it was not until the following day that they reached the glacial steps leading beneath the neighbouring peak of Kalanka.

Day 12 for Cave and Murphy. Day 11 for Sustad, coping well despite the pain, and Fowler, who noted: 'By the time we had been going for two hours it was snowing heavily and impossible to see the way ahead. I was uncomfortably aware of the avalanche risk inherent in the vast 40° snow slopes stretching up above us towards the summit of Kalanka.' They traversed diagonally left until it was necessary to abseil down though an ice cliff.

'Brendan saw it but had nothing with which to clip into the ice screw. No rope. No sling or carabiner. No second ice tool. Absolutely nothing. I turned away, terrified. Eventually it came. So quietly and so softly, it took Brendan away first, like a waterfall.'

Fowler went first and found himself hanging free, rotating in the air beneath a huge overhang of crumbling ice. Once down on firm rock, he looked up and saw that it would be much safer for the others to abseil further to the left, so he shouted up to move the anchor further left. Out of sight above him, Murphy volunteered to reset the anchor. Sustad and Cave watched admiringly as he moved across the slope.

'He declined our offer of a rope, preferring to solo, as the angle was modest enough. We were utterly exhausted by now. Brendan spent at least twenty minutes trying to get a screw in. "I've got a solid one in now," he eventually shouted across to us.

Seconds later a quiet noise came from above. Way up, an avalanche was released, and then another and another. Three or four silent slides joining forces and rushing towards us. In panic I began screaming, "Brendan, Brendan, Brendan!" … The whiteness took an eternity. Brendan saw it but had nothing with which to clip into the ice screw. No rope. No sling or carabiner. No second ice tool. Absolutely nothing. I turned away, terrified. Eventually it came. So quietly and so softly, it took Brendan away first, like a waterfall.'

Amazingly, the avalanche stopped just short of Cave and Sustad, who were off to the side, but Brendan Murphy had been right in the path of its main flow. Down below, Fowler cowered as the sky darkened and heavy wet snow battered around him.

Eventually, after the avalanche had passed, Cave shouted down to Fowler, who was completely unaware of what had happened, 'Is Brendan with you?' The only reply was a resounding 'No!'

Cave and Sustad made their way down the overhanging ice cliff to Fowler, and then the three men continued abseiling until they found a safe spot to pitch the tents. And while they organized their camp, they shouted Brendan's name over and over again into the night. But they knew he was dead.

In the morning, staring down a 600-metre (2,000-ft) slope of rock cliffs and snow gullies, funneling down into mounds of avalanche debris, they knew that any search would be pointless and dangerous. All they could do was try to get themselves back alive. Cave removed five rolls of exposed film, the remaining tea bags and a gas canister from his friend's rucksack, which he left on the mountain. His frostbitten thumb was black, blistered and painful, so Fowler taped it up in a protective cardboard wrapping and handed him a spare pair of thick, warm mittens. Then they set off on the long march home.

As they descended steep slopes, they kept glancing across at the huge gully filled with avalanche debris, but there was no sign of Murphy. That night they camped on the Changabang Glacier beneath the mountain's south face. The next day, Cave's fourteenth day out, they continued across hideous, breakable snowcrust. It is the most exhausting terrain, and for Sustad, every time his foot shot down through the surface, his ribs were racked with pain. They still had to face a hot, gruelling climb up to the Shipton Col, and then more abseiling, down the steep far side, putting more strain on Sustad's cracked ribs. That night they camped on the Ramani Glacier beneath Changabang's west face.

Breakfast on Day 15 was very simple: one teabag shared between three. They still had to cross the Bagini Col, and Sustad pleaded to be left where he was, but the other two insisted that he come with them. Fowler led the way but frequently dozed, slumped over his ice axe, thinking, 'This is how it could all end … just falling asleep and not waking up again.' Heat, not cold, was now the enemy, as the sun burned them mercilessly and melted the snow to a heavy mush. But they forced themselves over the col and down the far side, back to the Bagini Glacier.

Payne and Clyma's tent was gone from advance base: they had obviously failed on the north face and retreated back to base camp. Unable to face more that day, Fowler and Sustad decided to stop at advance base, but Cave was desperate to get back to base camp: 'The rotting-fish smell of the festering frostbite forced me on; I had to get some medicine. I had to get there before they abandoned camp. I had to tell them what had happened.'

So he staggered on alone. But he was so slow that he had to stop and sleep out on the glacier moraine, and it was only the next morning, Day 16, that he finally stumbled into base camp. Payne and Clyma were asleep in their tent, having only returned the previous day after an epic storm-lashed retreat back down the north face. Their faces were still sunken and windburned, and their eyes filled with sorrow as Cave announced that Brendan had died. Fowler and Sustad returned later that morning. Before they arrived, Cave went and laid down in the tent he had shared with Murphy. 'On top of Brendan's clothes was his Walkman. I reached for the headphones and flicked the PLAY button. Oasis. I should have guessed; he seemed so obsessed with this album. I turned onto my side and began to sob uncontrollably.'

Kangchenjunga

Height
8,595 metres (28,200 ft)

Location
Himalaya Range, Nepal-Sikkim border

Origin of name
Scholars are divided. It could refer to a local Sikkimese god who rides a white horse, waving a banner from the mountain's summit; or may derive from the Tibetan Kang-chen-dzo-nga, meaning snow-big-treasury-five – the Great Treasury of the Five Snows

First ascent
25 May 1955: George Band/Joe Brown (main summit), by Southwest Face

19 May 1978: Eugeniusz Chrobak/Wojciech Wröz – first ascent of Kangchenjunga South

Other key routes
Northeast Spur/North Ridge 1977: Prem Chand/Nima Dorjee

North Face/North Col/North Ridge 1979: Peter Boardman/Doug Scott/Joe Tasker

North Face Direct 1980: Dawa Norbu/Motumo Ohmiya/Toshitaka Sakano/Pemba Tsering

South Ridge of South Peak 1991: Marko Prezelj/Andrej Stremfelj

Interesting facts
Kangchenjunga is the third highest mountain, and the most easterly of the 8,000-metre (26,250-ft) peaks.

The rich history of the exploration of this holy mountain starts with the botanist Joseph Hooker in 1841 and culminates here with Slovenians Marko Prezelj and Andrej Stremfelj climbing 'alpine style' up the immense South Ridge – two men, unsupported, utterly committed on the world's third highest mountain.

The Treasury of the Five Snows

Marko Prezelj and Andrej Stremfelj (1991)

Of all the fourteen 8,000-metre (26,250-ft) peaks, Kangchenjunga is the most visible and most celebrated. Ever since the British rulers of India established their hill station at Darjeeling in the nineteenth century, visitors have gazed in awe at the immense mountain that dominates the northern horizon, its summit rising 7,924 metres (26,000 ft) above the surrounding jungle. It seems to hang in the sky, gleaming and ethereal, but the reality, close up, is a complex sprawling massif with five distinct summits.

In that famous view from Darjeeling, the subject of countless oil paintings, watercolours and photographs, you can see clearly Kangchenjunga's Great Shelf. It was this gigantic ice terrace, high on the southwest face, that proved the key to the mountain's first ascent in 1955. That ascent went to the highest summit on the left. Or to be precise, it stopped about 3 metres (10 ft) short of the highest snowy mound, out of deference to the people of Sikkim, who regard the mountain as a deity.

Twenty-three years later a team of Polish climbers revisited the Great Shelf and from there made first ascents of Kangchenjunga's central and south summits. But the real challenge – the most stunningly obvious line, seen with brilliant clarity from Darjeeling – was the south ridge, running arrow straight, directly to the south summit.

I myself pondered this line in the early '80s; then I became nervous about the difficult approach, threatened by those gigantic ice cliffs poised on the edge of the Great Shelf. And in any case, other climbs took over, and I never went to Kangchenjunga. In the end, it was two other climbers – much better and bolder – who eventually took up the challenge in 1991.

The Slovenian climber Andrej Stremfelj made his name in 1979 with the first ascent of Everest's 5-km (3-mile)-long West Ridge Direct – possibly the hardest route ever climbed up the mountain. That led to a succession of other Himalayan climbs, including, in 1989, a new route on the world's thirteenth-highest mountain, Shishapangma. The Shishapangma route was climbed 'alpine style', in a single, unsupported push for the top. Stremfelj's companion – and protégé – on that climb was the young Marko Prezelj. Impressed by Prezelj, he invited him two years later to come to Kangchenjunga.

The expedition was a large, carefully organized affair under the leadership of Tone Skarja, with multiple objectives on Kangchenjunga and several surrounding peaks. Benefiting from this infrastructure, Stremfelj and Prezelj operated as a highly mobile raiding party, snatching two summits – one of them over 7,000 metres (22,960 ft) – in preparation for their main objective: the South Ridge of Kangchenjunga.

Slovenian master climber Andrej Stremfelj (top), veteran of Everest's West Ridge Direct, and his young protégé, Marko Prezelj.

It was a huge objective – with a height rise of over 3,000 metres (9,800 ft) along some very hard terrain, virtually none of it explored before. And there was that very dangerous approach. But now they were so fit and acclimatized, they knew that they could move fast, minimizing their time in the danger area. Stremfelj, age 36, was at the peak of his powers. The previous year, he had climbed Everest a second time, on this occasion with his wife, Marija. This route on Kangchenjunga would present a new order of commitment, but he was confident in his young protégé, Prezelj. Beside Stremfelj

the younger man seemed lean, slight, almost flimsy, but he was actually a brilliant and very strong climber.

Early on 26 April helped by Tony Skarja and another expedition member, they hurried across the glacier, beneath those threatening ice cliffs, to the start of the climb. Then their friends left them on their own, shouldering heavy packs for one of the most ambitious Himalayan climbs ever attempted.

That day they climbed 650 metres (2,150 ft) up a huge rock buttress. One pitch, or rope length, was so technically difficult that it took Prezelj three hours to lead it. They hoped to continue climbing through the night, but a thunderstorm forced them to stop late that afternoon and pitch their tiny tent.

> **'Only in the dark, after eleven hours of climbing, do we find a sufficiently safe place at 7,250 metres [23,800 ft] in the bottom of a crevasse for our bivouac. The furious winds the next morning nearly blow away my enthusiasm for going on.'**

In his idiosyncratic English, Prezelj takes up the story on Day 2.

'In the morning only the sun could invite us out of the tent. New snow had made the climbing more difficult, covering steep, smooth rock slabs. ... Only in the dark, after eleven hours of climbing, do we find a sufficiently safe place at 7,250 metres [23,787 ft] in the bottom of a crevasse for our bivouac. The furious winds the next morning nearly blow away my enthusiasm for going on.'

Exposed to the full fury of Kangchenjunga's notorious winds, they found it impossible to stick to the precarious crest of the ridge. The ideal aesthetic line might look beautiful in those photos, but the reality was impossible for a team of two with no fixed ropes to clip into. So, canny survivors that they were, they sidled leftward onto the Great Shelf, then found a more sheltered gully, weaving its way back to the ridge crest at 7,600 metres (24,935 ft), where they made their third bivouac.

The following day they climbed another 300 metres (1,000 ft), finding a ramp that led through some over-hangs, and bivouacked. At that altitude, almost 7,924 metres (26,000 ft) above sea level, you are effectively dying. The human body simply cannot survive here for long. Speed is everything, and yet the body's muscles have to operate with only a third of the normal oxygen intake. So to give themselves a chance of getting to the summit and back the next day, 30 April, the two men left tent, stove, sleeping bags – virtually everything – to collect on their way down.

Stremfelj led the way up the final ridge, helped by remains of fixed ropes – they had now joined the final section of a Russian route climbed in 1989. The climbing was so hard that they wondered whether they would be able to reverse it. But dangerously late in the afternoon, at 4:45, they reached the summit.

'The top! The top of what? Dead, cold rocks, chained together by ice. The only joy is the end of a tiresome climb. For a moment I have a feeling of relaxation, and then emptiness. We take pictures. We talk, but I don't know about what. Slowly, we set out for a descent of the Polish route. Andrej cuts some of the old fixed rope to take along for rappels. I am in no particular hurry and enjoy the solitude around me. The sunset is magnificent.'

Eventually he managed to rouse himself from that dangerous dreamlike state and set off down after Stremfelj. Convinced that it was impossible to reverse their route to the tent, they had committed themselves to descending the old Polish route to the Great Shelf, where their fellow Slovenians, attempting the main summit, had a camp.

Prezelj found himself struggling. 'Soon it is black night. By chance or by luck, we find old fixed ropes. These and not being able to see where we are going speed us on our way.' But then the ropes ran out, and they had to down-climb precariously in the darkness. Prezelj dropped his ice axe. The remaining headlamp battery faded. They stopped ever more frequently to slump in the snow.

'There I see Andrej, who is resting often too. I stumble after him. I lost the trail long ago as well as any feeling of danger or fear. Then I'm sure I see Tone and Damijan waiting for us with tea and beer. I can

even smell those drinks. I decide which I prefer. Then I realize it is again a hallucination. I shake my head and spot a tent. But this time it is for real. I climb in and fall fast asleep. After twenty hours of continuous exertion, my fondest dream was for that warm sleeping bag.'

Stremfelj made it to base camp the next day. Prezelj took a day longer, arriving on the same day that two members of the expedition died, falling due to total exhaustion near the main summit. It was a cruel end to what was otherwise a hugely successful expedition. But it was hardly surprising. The south ridge team had come close to disaster in the final stages of their daring raid. It was a dangerous game, not easy to justify. Prezelj concluded afterwards: 'What did Andrej and I achieve in those six days? Only a line on a photograph of the mountain. But all this I experienced so intensely that I will never be able to forget or repeat.'

The two men spent five days climbing in a single totally committing push up Kangchenjunga's south ridge, which appears in profile on the extreme right on the picture on page 178. Here, on the fifth day, leaving behind rucksacks and bivouac equipment, Stremfelj is seen leading the climb up extreme rock, over 8,000 metres (1,800 ft) high.

Mt Huiten

Height
4,374 metres (14,351 ft)

Location
Tavan Bogd Range, Altai
Mountains, Mongolian/
Russian/Chinese border

Origin of name
Huiten, pronounced
Who-eeten, means
'cold mountain'.

First ascent
1956: Pieskariow and party
by Northeast Ridge

Other key routes
East Ridge date unknown:
Mongolian party, names
unknown

South Ridge 1992: Julian
Freeman-Attwood/Lindsay
Griffin/Ed Webster

Interesting facts
Huiten is the highest
mountain in Mongolia. The
summit of Triple Border
Peak (Tavan Bogdo Ola),
10 km (6 miles) to the
north of Huiten, is where
the borders of Mongolia,
China and Russia converge.
These mountains, the
furthest on earth from any
ocean, are home to the wild
Altai Argali sheep, which
has immense curled horns
up to 1.5 metres (5 ft) long.
This sheep is one of several
wild species on which the
rare snow leopard depends
for food. Western tourists
pay up to US$50,000
(excluding trophy fees) for
holidays to shoot Argali
sheep and other rare wild
animals in the region.

This is a tale of adventure at the heart of Asia, where the frontiers of Russia, China and Mongolia converge near a mountain called Huiten. It is a tale of serendipitous meetings and an incredibly lucky escape from an incredibly unlucky accident. It is also a tale of larger-than-life characters, starting with a man named John Blashford-Snell.

The Great Mongolian Escape

Lindsay Griffin, Julian Freeman-Attwood and Ed Webster (1992)

Blashford-Snell is the last surviving relic of the imperial age of exploration. It was he, in his tropical pith helmet, who in 1968 led a quasi-military expedition to descend the Blue Nile, warding off hostile natives with his pistol. An affable, generous-spirited man with a brilliant gift for storytelling, he met Julian Freeman-Attwood and Lindsay Griffin in 1987 on a mountain in Tibet. They became friends and in 1992 he asked them if they would like to join one of his Operation Raleigh expeditions to explore the Tavan Bogd mountains, where the 2,413-km (1,500-mile)-long Altai range forms the northwest frontier of Mongolia.

Griffin was delighted: 'We would spend the greater part of our time acting as guides and instructors to a small group of aspirant mountaineers. Almost as an afterthought, John added that most of the "students" would be unattached girls in their early twenties.' Griffin was also enticed by the actual mountains. After twenty years' tireless exploration of remote ranges on every continent, here was a whole range about which virtually nothing was known, apart from a single magazine article he had managed to track down, written in Polish.

Freeman-Attwood, a forestry consultant in his late thirties who had only recently become interested in mountaineering, was also thrilled by the prospect

of visiting Mongolia – a country almost the size of Western Europe, with just 2.5 million inhabitants. The third mountain instructor would be Ed Webster, an American climber famous for his pioneering rock climbs in Colorado and for having climbed a new route up the east face of Everest, getting to within 100 metres (328 ft) of the summit without oxygen and getting badly frostbitten in the process. This would be his first big expedition since losing his fingertips four years earlier.

So with logistical support from Blashers, the threesome made its way to Mongolia's capital, Ulan Bator, and continued west by train to Hovd – a remote, dusty town consisting mainly of nomadic felt tents called gers. Griffin was still clutching his untranslated Polish article, desperate for some more comprehensible information about the mountains they were about to visit, when one of the Operation Raleigh students bumped into a Polish man in the street. She brought him back to meet Griffin. 'When Ryszard Palczewski stepped inside the ger an hour later and announced in perfect English that he ought to make a reasonable translation, as it was he who had written the article nearly twenty-five years ago, we were, well, simply lost for words. More so when he told us that he lived in Brighton but made regular trips to Mongolia to visit a farming project.'

Lindsay Griffin passing the time of day with a Bactrian camel.

Alexandrov Glacier, then over Yeti Col and down into China, onto the Przjevalski Glacier, named after the Russian colonel who had in 1878 discovered the world's only surviving species of wild horse, Equus Przjevalski.

The weather turned bad, so they waited a day. Then the clouds lifted and, keen to take advantage of safely frozen snow, they set off on the evening of 11 July 1992, climbing though the night, to emerge on the summit the next morning.

'The weather was perfect and the summit views were intriguing. To the north lay the vast uninhabited nothingness of the Siberian Steppe, to the south and west a myriad of unclimbed and mostly unnamed peaks ran away into China. East, the long gentle glaciers on the Mongolian side of the range flowed towards wide, grassy glens and barren, rounded tops that were strangely reminiscent of the Scottish Highlands. It was a mountaineer's dream, but a dream that was, unfortunately, soon to be shattered.'

They stayed roped up for the first part of the descent, reversing their route on the south ridge. Once they reached easy ground, they unroped to take their own separate routes back to the tent. Lindsay Griffin's approach to mountaineering was ruminative: he liked to savour his mountains, not rush up and down them. So he let the other two go ahead. At about 2:00 P.M. he began to make his way down a big boulder field. 'It was a slope typical of those found all over the lower reaches of Asian mountains – large, angular blocks that, now and again, wobbled underfoot. Only this one triggered something above!' He was suddenly hurled forward into a hollow, and as he fell, a huge granite boulder crashed down on top of his leg.

'I must have passed out for a while, because when I came to, the lower part of the leg had lost all sensation. Miraculously the boulder had trapped it in a slot just wide enough to stop the full crushing power, but alas, not wide enough to avoid a serious double compound fracture.'

He was alone, illegally in China, on a remote mountainside at the heart of Asia, and not even his two companions, now probably back at the tent, knew where he was. Some people faced with that situation might just have given up. Griffin was more resourceful. First he took a couple of strong oral

Armed now with expert knowledge, Freeman-Attwood, Griffin and Webster spent five weeks roaming the Tavan Bogd mountains with their 'students', climbing several new routes up a series of snowy peaks reminiscent of the Swiss Alps, but rising above the huge open spaces of the Mongolian steppe. Camping on one glacier, they woke in the morning to find a line of bare footprints running across the snow past their tent. 'They were large, showed a definite toe-shaped formation and, inexplicably, were in sets of three. We decided they could only be those of a Yeti carrying a snow leopard under one paw.' There certainly were snow leopards in the area. As for yetis, Blashford-Snell – a man enthralled by all things zoologically enigmatic – did some research and discovered that Mongolia was considered a popular refuge for the mystery snowman more usually associated with the Himalayas.

After five weeks the young students had to move on to another project. This left the three veterans with just enough time for one final climb: Huiten, the highest peak in the range. Determined to tackle a new route to its summit, they settled on the untrodden south ridge. Just getting to the foot of the ridge was a two-day journey, first up the badly crevassed

painkillers. Then he set to work, trying desperately to relieve some of the pressure to restore circulation to his mangled leg. 'Pushing, heaving or even cursing the block proved useless. I tried to reduce the size of the leg by cutting away at the various layers of clothing with an annoyingly blunt penknife. But as fast as the material came away, the uncooperative leg would swell to fill the gap. Using my axe and hammer, I tried to chisel away at the granite constriction below. Whatever I did appeared to be futile.'

He was now getting desperate; if he could not restore circulation soon, he risked losing his leg. Then he remembered the climbing rope. Fighting the pain and nausea, he forced himself to make a lasso, which he flung up behind his head, around another large boulder. Then he leaned forward to thread another loop around the block crushing his leg, setting up a pulley system with carabiners.

'Although unsuccessful at first, by increasing to a six-to-one mechanical advantage, I just succeeded in shifting it – not enough to withdraw the leg, but enough that a minute or so later a tingling sensation moved down towards my toes.'

Meanwhile, Freeman-Attwood and Webster had reached the tent at 3:30. When Griffin still had not appeared at 6:00 P.M., they set off back up the mountain, wondering exactly where to search on the huge rocky shoulder above.

Hidden 610 metres (2,000 ft) higher in a sea of boulders, Griffin was keeping up his lonely battle, 'pausing occasionally to yell, "Ed! Julian!" as though

> **'I tried to reduce the size of the leg by cutting away at the various layers of clothing with an annoyingly blunt penknife. But as fast as the material came away, the uncooperative leg would swell to fill the gap.'**

Huiten's east ridge rises above the great sweep of the Przjevalski Glacier, which flows down into China. It was down this valley that the helicopter pilot made his unauthorized landing to offload the heavy batteries.

Julian Freeman-Attwood (left) and Lindsay Griffin, photographed on Huiten's summit a few hours before the accident.

a "comfortable" position. When I slipped on loose stones and twisted the leg, Lindsay screamed in bloodcurdling agony. Blood slowly dripped from the top of his left boot.' They crawled all night and continued through the next day, eventually reaching the new tent site at 4:00 in the afternoon. There the two rescuers left Griffin lying in his sleeping bag while they set off on the long journey back to base camp, which they reached at 2:30 A.M. on 14 July completing a fifty-hour, nonstop marathon.

Griffin lay in his tent, reaching out periodically to scoop fresh water from a stream. 'The first day was spent brushing up on my tourniquet technique. It had to be Ed's suggestion – Americans know all about snake bites. … Occasionally, odd statistics, read somewhere in the dim and distant past, would enter my mind, like "70 percent of all victims with untreated compound fractures die after ten days".'

His worst fear was that some accident would have stopped the others from getting back to base. During the long crawl his leg had been splinted with ice axes, but the others had had to remove them to get themselves safely back across the mountains. Now, with his leg unsplinted, there was no chance of Griffin moving anywhere unaided. In any case, where could he crawl *to*? But the others *were* safely back *and* there was a radio at base camp to contact Hovd, where Blashford-Snell applied his legendary energy towards organizing a major international rescue, including a Learjet chartered specially to fly to Hovd. First, though, Griffin had to be lifted from Huiten to the Hovd airstrip, and only a helicopter could do that. Working all his contacts, Blashford-Snell managed to persuade the Mongolian authorities to release an ancient Soviet cargo helicopter to fly 1,600 km (1,000 miles) from the capital to Hovd, where the last remains of emergency aviation fuel were released. After refuelling, the helicopter continued to base camp.

Webster couldn't believe his eyes when the helicopter appeared at 5:40 P.M. on 15 July: 'This thing looked like the *school bus*!' But it was all he was getting, so he jumped aboard to join two of the Operation Raleigh staff, Jan and George, and directed the pilot over the range to the far side, where they located Griffin in his tiny tent.

The pilot, with no previous mountain-rescue experience, was operating dangerously close to his

there were a dozen or so people to choose from. Then I tried "Help!" but it sounded so ridiculous that I reverted to a high-pitched wail.' The other two heard the wail and raced up the mountainside, shouting Griffin's name and homing in on his pained cries, eventually reaching him at 7:00 P.M.

He had now been trapped for about five hours, and it took another three hours for the two fit men to shift the ton of granite sufficiently to withdraw Griffin's mangled leg. Then, while Freeman-Attwood went to collect the tent, Webster began the long, grinding task of helping his injured friend down the boulder slope to a reasonably flat spot where they could re-pitch the tent and pray that a helicopter might be able to land. 'While Lindsay slid forward on his buttocks, propped up by his arms and hands, I crept backward blindly, holding his splinted leg in altitude ceiling, in an ancient and unsuitable helicopter, with rapidly dwindling fuel reserves. He put the three rescuers down some distance from Griffin, then took off and vanished. Soon Griffin was strapped into a stretcher and his three rescuers waited eagerly for the helicopter to return. But nothing happened. Griffin was ecstatic just to know that help was at hand, but the others were disconsolate: 'Ed, Jan and George huddled miserably around the stretcher, shivering, realizing that one or more nights out with no food were becoming increasingly likely. They cursed their folly in being off-loaded from the helicopter without any equipment.'

They waited for nearly three hours. Unknown to them, Jamaldorf, the pilot, had made a daring decision to fly down into China to an altitude low enough to make a comfortable landing. There he cut off the engines to save fuel, allowing plenty of time for the others to prepare the stretcher. Then, once he had restarted the engines, he off-loaded all inessential equipment, including the medical kit and the helicopter's heavy batteries! Now, with the helicopter light enough to have a chance of executing a highly risky pickup at high altitude, he took off again, praying that the engine would not stall.

A few minutes later Jamaldorf was signalling frantically to the ground party, pointing out a snow patch some distance from Griffin. The moment he put down, they started to run. 'I just yelled with pain, bumping and crashing across giant blocks. Bits of bone were moving in all directions. I saw the co-pilot jump and moments later struggle across the snow patch to help, flip-flops clenched tightly between his teeth.'

On the first attempt to get Griffin aboard they tripped and dropped him in a howl of agonized screaming. But then they succeeded and were away,

'the co-pilot fighting with the door as the helicopter lurched forward over the moraine and skimmed across the glacier, struggling to gain height. I lay back, propped on one arm, gasping with relief. Jan had his head buried in my shoulders, crying. Ed … was still gripping my legs firmly, also crying. George… collapsed in a seat, wetting both cheeks. In a sudden release of emotion, I joined them, and there we were, four grown men all crying our eyes out. Then

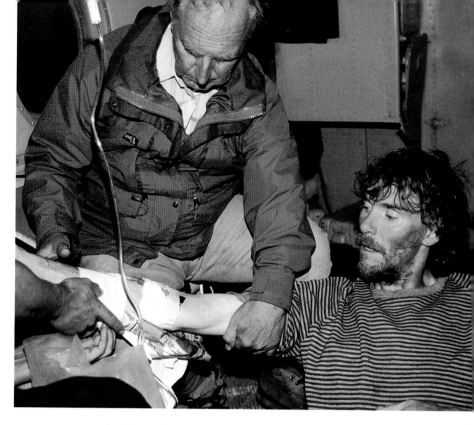

someone realized the chopper was flying in completely the wrong direction. It was only on landing to collect the batteries that the reason became clear.'

There was just enough fuel left to fly Griffin to a remote Mongolian aerodrome, but not enough to get back to Hovd. However, Blashford-Snell had been hard at work, negotiating with the pilot of a Kazakh aircraft that had landed unofficially that day, persuading him to siphon off some fuel with an old hosepipe in return for five bottles of vodka. That gave the chopper just enough flying time to reach Hovd, where Griffin had his first meal in five days.

The following day the Learjet arrived from Singapore, the first foreign aircraft ever to land legally, after obtaining special clearance, in western Mongolia. Griffin was loaded aboard and flown straight to Hong Kong, where the Swiss pilot managed to make an emergency landing just one hour before a typhoon struck the airport. Within hours Griffin was in the hospital starting a long series of operations to reconstruct his damaged leg. As he concluded, in his account of this epic escape for the *Himalayan Journal*, 'The success of this rescue was due to the immense cooperation and strong bonding between all those concerned; but their efforts would have been doomed had it not been for that spirited helicopter pilot, Jamaldorf, who, against all odds, was prepared to have a go.'

Safe at last, Griffin is attached to a drip, aboard the Learjet bound for Hong Kong.

Glossary

a cheval Literally 'on horseback' – negotiating a knife-edge ridge by straddling with one leg each side.

abseil See rappel

arm bar An extreme move where you lock your forearm horizontally, hand to elbow, between two walls.

belay *noun* A secure anchor where leader pauses at the end of a **pitch** (ropelength) to bring up second person; *verb* To safeguard climbing partner with the rope.

bivvy boots Insulated soft boots, usually down-filled, for keeping toes warm during miserable bivouacs.

cam Generic term for a variety of devices which use sprung curved metal plates on a central axle that expand to fit a rock crack and jam tight when weighted. Useful in awkward cracks where a traditional nut may not hold.

crampons A set of steel spikes on a frame, clamped to the bootsole for snow and ice climbing.

dry tooling Using ice-axes and crampons to climb dry ice-less rock.

etriers Stirrups, usually with three or four steps, like a miniature rope ladder, used in artificial or 'aid' climbing, suspended from a piton, nut, cam or skyhook.

free climbing Climbing rock without any artificial aids – making progress purely with hands and feet, using what holds the rock offers. The rope is used only to safeguard, not aid, progress.

grades (e.g. 5.12a, 5.10d) Grades denote the difficulty of a particular climb or pitch. There are many different grading systems around the world and this arcane topic is best left to the serious rock climbing geek.

jumar Generic term for devices used to climb fixed ropes. Sprung metal cams slide up the rope but jam tight when weighted.

karabiner/carabiner Metal snaplink used to clip the rope into an anchor.

layback To climb a crack by pulling horizontally on the arms, and pushing on the feet. Works particularly well in a right-angle corner.

nut Generic term for alloy wedges, jammed into rock cracks to make anchors.

palming Another desperate move, where you push down with what you hope are unsweaty palms, trying to gain some friction on blank rock.

pinch To pinch a small projection of rock between your fingers and thumb.

piton Otherwise known as a **peg** or a **nail**, a piton is a steel blade with an eye at one end. The blade is hammered into a natural crack in the rock and, when secure, the rope can be clipped into the eye with a karabiner. Pitons come in all shapes and sizes, from thumbnail- to U-shaped cowbell-sized.

rappel To abseil – to descend a rope, usually with a friction device attached to the one's waist harness.

skyhook A curved steel hook which can be hooked into a tiny pocket or over a miniscule ledge, to provide a tenuous safeguard or to aid progress in artificial climbing.

smear To maximise the friction of a rock shoe's rubber sole by pressing it flat against smooth rock.

stance Secure ledge or foothold where climbers make an anchor between pitches. See also belay.

stem The American climbing term for **bridge** – to stretch legs wide, often across a rock chimney or crack, maximising balance and stability.

tension Using tension from the rope to lean sideways and traverse across holdless rock.

Sources

AORAKI
Personal interviews; *New Zealand Alpine Journal* 1983; Mark Inglis *No Mean Feat* Random House 2002

BALL'S PYRAMID
Mountain magazine; *Sydney Morning Herald*; Personal interviews

BLOUBERG
Personal interviews

MT CARSE
Personal interviews; Stephen Venables *Island at the Edge of the World* Hodder & Stoughton 1991

CARSTENSZ PYRAMID
Heinrich Harrer *I Come from the Stone Age* London 1964 (Hart Davis); Dr Kal Muller *Indonesian New Guinea* Singapore 1990 (Periplus Editions); *American Alpine Journal* 1981

CERRO TORRE
Mountain magazine No.23, September 1972; *American Alpine Journal* 2004 (including translated excerpts from Maestri's accounts); personal interviews with Rolando Garibotti

CHANGABANG
Andy Cave *Learning to Breathe* Hutchinson 2005; Mick Fowler *On Thin Ice* Batôn Wicks 2005

MT DEBORAH
David Roberts *Deborah – A Wilderness Narrative*; *Mountain* magazine No.96; *American Alpine Journal* 1984

EIGER
Personal interviews; Heinrich Harrer *The White Spider* Harper Perennial 2005

EL CAPITAN
Personal interviews; Lynn Hill & Greg Child *Climbing Free* W. W. Norton 2003

MT EREBUS
Biography of Ernest Shackleton; Douglas Mawson *The Life of an Explorer* Lincoln Hall Australia 2000

MT EVEREST
Personal interviews; John Hunt *The Ascent of Everest* Hodder & Stoughton 1953; Sir Edmund Hillary *View from the Summit* Doubleday 1999; Ed Douglas *Tenzing – Hero of Everest* National Geographic 2003; Stephen Venables *Everest – Alone at the Summit* Adrenaline Classics 2000; Ed Webster *Snow in the Kingdom* Mountain Imagery 2000

FINSTERAARHORN
Alpine Journal 1923; *Selected Letters of Gertrude Bell* Penguin 1953; Miriam O'Brien (Underhill) *Give me the Hills* Dodd Mead 1971

GASHERBRUM IV
American Alpine Journal 1986

MT HUITEN
Personal interviews; *Himalayan Journal* 1993; *American Alpine Journal* 1993

KANGCHENJUNGA
Personal interviews; *American Alpine Journal* 1991

MT KENYA
Personal interviews; *Mountain Club of Kenya Bulletin* November 1971; Gordon Boy, Iain Allen & Clive Ward *Snow on the Equator* The Bodley Head 1988

KUBBESTOLEN
Personal interviews; *Live Your Dreams* Cestmír Lukes

MT LUCANIA
Personal interviews; *Great Climbs*, ed Chris Bonington Mitchell Beazley 1994

MARGHERITA
Il Ruwenzori Filippo de Filippi 1908 Milan; Mirella Tenderini & Michael Sahdrick *The Duke of Abruzzi – An Explorer's Life* The Mountaineers Seattle 1997; Henry Osmaston & D Pasteur *Guide to the Ruwenzori* West Col 1972/2006

MONT BLANC
Walter Bonatti *The Mountains of my Life* Random House Modern Library 2001

NANGA PARBAT
Personal interviews; Reinhold Messner *The Naked Mountain* The Crowood Press 2003

NORTH TWIN
Ascent 1975; *American Alpine Journal* 1986 & 2004; *Rock & Ice* magazine July 2004

OGRE
Mountain Magazine 57; *American Alpine Journal 1978*, Chris Bonington *The Everest Years* Hodder & Stoughton 1986; Doug Scott *Himalayan Climber* Diadem 1991

MT WADDINGTON
Don Munday *The Unknown Mountain* Hoddder & Stoughton 1948; Chris Jones *Climbing in North America* London: University of California Press 1976

YAMANDAKA
Himalayan Journal 2002; *Alpine Journal* 2002

PEAK 4111
Personal interviews; *American Alpine Journal* 1996

Index

Note: Entries in italics are book titles: page references in boldface denote illustrations.

Continental Range Photographs

EUROPE, pages 10–11
Snow lies down to the resort of Megeve, in this winter shot of Mont Blanc, the highest mountain in the Alps. On the left is the Aiguille du Gouter; on the right the Aiguille Bionassay.

NORTH AMERICA, pages 32–33
The Merced river flows through California's incomparable Yosemite Valley, whose pristine beauty inspired the environmentalist John Muir to campaign for the establishment of America's first national park. On the left the mighty Nose of El Capitan is profiled in the glow of the evening sun.

SOUTH AMERICA, pages 60–61
Dawn light on Patagonia's most spectacular granite towers. On the left, wreathed in mist, is Cerro Torre, with the deep gash of the 'Col of Conquest' between it and Torre Egger to the right. Next right is Cerro Stanhardt, with the isolated spike of Aguja Bifida on the extreme right.

AUSTRALIA, pages 80–81
Evening light on New Zealand's highest summit, Aoraki/Mt Cook (right) and its fine neighbour, Mt Tasman, photographed from the Fox Glacier rain forest on the West Coast.

AFRICA, pages 96–97
Giant groundsel and lobelia growing amongst the outlying pinnacles of Mt Kenya – eroded volcanic remnants of a mountain which was once as high as Everest.

ANTARTICA, pages 112–113
Looking northwest from near the summit of Mt Carse, along the mountain chain of South Georgia to the distant summit of Mt Paget. Beyond Paget lie the glaciers first crossed by Sir Ernest Shackleton in 1916.

ASIA, pages 130–131
Evening alpenglow on Everest, Lhotse and Makalu (left to right) the world's first, fourth and fifth highest mountains.

Acknowledgements

It would have been impossible to prepare this book without the generous help of friends, colleagues and fellow mountain writers and photographers. I fear that this list may be incomplete, but I would like in particular to thank Daniel Anker, Anne & John Arran, Phil Bartlett, John Barry, Barry Blanchard, Walter Bonatti, Chris Bonington, Willi Burkhardt, the late Duncan Carse, John Cleare, Frances Daltrey, John Davis, Erik Decamp, Catherine Destivelle, Russ Dodding, Thorbjørn Evenold, Paul Fatti, Julian Freeman-Attwood, Rolando Gabirotti, Lindsay Griffin, John Harlin III, Lynn Hill, Ian Howell, Luke Hughes, Mark Inglis, Chris Jones, Harish Kapadia, George Lowe, Cestmír Lukes, George Mallory II, Roger Mear, Colin Monteath, Greg Mortimer, Divyesh & Vineeta Muni, Irene Oehninger, Marko Prezelj, Mark Richey, Ann Roberts, John Roskelley, Robert Schauer, George Spenceley, Andrej Stremjelj, Mirella Tenderini, Louise Thomas, Bradford Washburn, Ed Webster, Jim Wickwire, Odd-Roar Wiik and Heinz Zak.

I would also like to thank my wonderful editorial team at Cassell – Anna Cheifetz, Karen Dolan and Robin Douglas-Withers, picture researcher Vickie Walters and designer Anthony Cohen.

The principal sources for all the mountain stories are listed on page 188. I am extremely grateful for the author's permission to quote from their various books and articles. Particularly useful were the now sadly defunct Mountain Magazine, as well as the still flourishing Alpine Journal, American Alpine Journal and Himalayan Journal. I acknowledge gratefully permission from their respective honorary editors to quote from these invaluable publications.

Stephen Venables
Bath, England June 2006

Photo credits

The publishers would like to thank the following individuals and organisations for supplying images for this book. Every effort has been made to contact the copyright holders. Please contact the publishers if any credits have inadvertently been omitted.

Alamy/John Cleare/Worldwide Picture Library 22.
The Alpine Club 18 top left, 20 top left, 36, 170.
Anne & John Arran 64, 65.
Julian Freeman-Attwood 184, 185, 186, 187.
John Barry 34.
George Bell 52, 68.
Barry Blanchard 55.
Arlene Blum 49.
Walter Bonatti 16, 17.
Chris Bonington Picture Library 7, 142, 144, 145, 147.
British Columbia Archives 50 (1-61552), 51 (1-51587).
Nick Bullock 66.
Willi Burkhardt 18. Andy Cave 174, 176.
John Cleare/Mountain Camera 15, 25, 26, 56, 100, 101, 102, 105, 107, 154, 160, 168; /Ray Brooks 37; /Joe Josephson 46; /Tadashi Kajiyama 152; /Colin Monteath 92, 118, 126; /Pat Morrow 44, 70; /Doug Scott 148.
Corbis U.K. Ltd. 120; /Barnabas Bosshart 94; /Owen Franken 10-11; /Marc Garanger 12; /Reuters 134 bottom; /Galen Rowell 6, 132.
Erik Decamp 128.
Empics 69.
Paul Fatti 108.
Ralf Gantzhorn 77.
Rolando Garibotti 73, 74, 75.
Getty Images 14, 150; /Philip Schermeister 32-33; /Juan Silva 62.
Anderl Heckmair Collection 24.
Hedgehog House 84, 95, 178; /Jean-Paul Ferrero 82; /Colin

Monteath 1, 2-3, 80-81, 86, 130-131.
Mark Inglis 88, 89, 91.
Mark Jenkins courtesy of John Harlin 26 right.
Stephen Koch 180 bottom.
Giulio Malfer 72.
George Mallory 110, 111.
Roger Mear 38, 39, 121, 153.
Reinhold Messner 151.
Divyesh Muni 164.
Museo della Montagna, Torino, Italia 78 left, 78 right.
North Shore Rescue 47.
Irene Oehninger courtesy of Walter Theil 124; /Mirek 122, 125.
Roger Payne 172.
Panopticon Gallery/Bradford Washburn, Courtesy Panopticon Gallery, Waltham M.A., U.S.A. 42, 43.
Marko Prezelj 60-61, 180 top, 181.
Mark Richey 167.
Gerry Roach 40.
Eric Roberts courtesy of Ann Roberts 171.
John Roskelley 157, 159.
Royal Geographic Society 134 top, 135.
Robert Schauer/Mountain Film 162 left, 162 right, 163.
George Spenceley 116.
Gary Steer courtesy of John Davis 85.
Louise Thomas/Twid Turner 30.
TopFoto 104.
Stephen Venables 20 right, 21, 27, 79, 96-97, 106, 112-113, 114, 117.
Ed Webster/Mountain Imagery 9, 28, 31, 98, 136, 138, 139, 140, 182.
Jim Wickwire 156.
Heinz Zak 58, 59.